Rural Project
MANAGEMENT

Rural Project MANAGEMENT

Devendra Prasad Pandey
Department of Rural Management
Mahatma Gandhi Chitrakoot Gramoday Vishwavidyalaya
Chitrakoot, MP

PUBLISHING FOR ONE WORLD
NEW AGE INTERNATIONAL (P) LIMITED, PUBLISHERS
New Delhi • Bangalore • Chennai • Cochin • Guwahati
Hyderabad • Kolkata • Lucknow • Mumbai
Visit us at **www.newagepublishers.com**

Published by New Age International (P) Ltd., Publishers
First Edition: 2008
Reprint: 2025

GLOBAL OFFICES

- **New Delhi** **NEW AGE INTERNATIONAL (P) LIMITED, PUBLISHERS**
7/30 A, Daryaganj, New Delhi-110002, (INDIA)
Tel.: (011) 23253771, 23253472, **Telefax:** 23267437, 43551305
E-mail: contactus@newagepublishers.com • Visit us at www.newagepublishers.com
- **London** **NEW AGE INTERNATIONAL (UK) LTD.**
27 Old Gloucester Street, London, WC1N 3AX, UK
E-mail: info@newacademicscience.co.uk • Visit us at www.newacademicscience.co.uk
- **Nairobi** **NEW AGE GOLDEN (EAST AFRICA) LTD.**
Ground Floor, Westlands Arcade, Chiromo Road (Next to Naivas Supermarket), Westlands, Nairobi, KENYA
Tel.: 00-254-713848772, 00-254-725700286
E-mail: kenya@newagepublishers.com

BRANCHES

- **Bangalore** 37/10, 8th Cross (Near Hanuman Temple), Azad Nagar, Chamarajpet, Bangalore- 560 018
Tel.: (080) 26756823, **Telefax:** 26756820, **E-mail: bangalore@newagepublishers.com**
- **Chennai** 26, Damodaran Street, T. Nagar, Chennai-600 017, **Tel.:** (044) 24353401, **Telefax:** 24351463
E-mail: chennai@newagepublishers.com
- **Cochin** CC-39/1016, Carrier Station Road, Ernakulam South, Cochin-682 016, **Tel.:** (0484) 2377303, **Telefax:** 4051304
E-mail: cochin@newagepublishers.com
- **Guwahati** Hemsen Complex, Mohd. Shah Road, Paltan Bazar, Near Starline Hotel, Guwahati-781 008,
Tel.: (0361) 2513881, **Telefax:** 2543669, **E-mail: guwahati@newagepublishers.com**
- **Hyderabad** 105, 1st Floor, Madhiray Kaveri Tower, 3-2-19, Azam Jahi Road, Near Kumar Theater, Nimboliadda Kachiguda, Hyderabad-500 027, **Tel.:** (040) 24652456, **Telefax:** 24652457
E-mail: hyderabad@newagepublishers.com
- **Kolkata** RDB Chambers (Formerly Lotus Cinema) 106A, 1st Floor, S N Banerjee Road, Kolkata-700 014
Tel.: (033) 22273773, **Telefax:** 22275247, **E-mail: kolkata@newagepublishers.com**
- **Lucknow** 16-A, Jopling Road, Lucknow-226 001, **Tel.:** (0522) 2209578, 4045297, **Telefax:** 2204098
E-mail: lucknow@newagepublishers.com
- **Mumbai** 142C, Victor House, Ground Floor, N.M. Joshi Marg, Lower Parel, Mumbai-400 013
Tel.: (022) 24927869, **Telefax:** 24915415, **E-mail: mumbai@newagepublishers.com**
- **New Delhi** 22, Golden House, Daryaganj, New Delhi-110 002, **Tel.:** (011) 23262368, 23262370, **Telefax:** 43551305
E-mail: sales@newagepublishers.com

ISBN: 978-81-224-2149-1

C-25-02-1643

Printed in India at Inkfinity Prints (P) Ltd., Noida.
Typeset at Aakriti Graphics, Delhi.

NEW AGE INTERNATIONAL (P) LIMITED, PUBLISHERS
7/30 A, Daryaganj, New Delhi-110002
Visit us at **www.newagepublishers.com**
(CIN: U74899DL1966PTC004618)

Foreword

India can boast of becoming a developed nation only when rural India gets a respectable face-lift and the rural folk are provided all the amenities of a developed nation. It is possible only through sustained systematic planning and its implementation. The book 'Rural Project Management' is a good attempt to suggest ways and means for undertaking projects for rural development. Dr. Pandey who is deeply grounded in the area of rural management has dwelt upon various rural projects and their management in this book. It speaks for the knowledge which the writer possesses about management of rural projects. In fact, the subject needs to be included as an option in MBA curriculum all over the country in view of its importance. The book is also useful for administrators, professionals and national planners engaged in the onerous task of rural development.

Anil Chopra
St. Soldier Educational Society
H.O. : J-34, Vikas puri, New Delhi

A Word of Appreciation

The book entitled "Rural Project Management" is a very comprehensive book and bears testimony to the author's knowledge of the subject. Writing a book on a subject like this is not everybody's cup of tea. Dr. Devendra Pandey, because of his rich experience and scholarship has made a useful compilation, which would go a long way to help the students. The rural India certainly needs a well-planned programme for development and this book will be a handmaid for all those who are engaged in rural development. The author has more potential to produce books in this field.

K.K. Dhir

Managing Director

St. Soldier Educational Society

H.O. : J-34, Vikas puri, New Delhi

Preface

During a training programme of representatives of voluntary organizations organized by me, when trainees were asked to demonstrate their capacity and response on different dimensions of project management, their response very well needed in-depth information on different aspects of project management. They requested for the literature on project management, specifically for rural development projects.

If we promise something, learn to deliver. NGOs working in the rural sector found this out the hard way when 295 of them got blacklisted in 2004-05. This was after they took funds from the government and failed to deliver on projects proposed by them. A majority of these NGOs were from U.P., Haryana, West Bengal, Bihar and Andhra Pradesh. This action was meted out by the Council for Advancement of People's Action and Rural Technology (CAPART), the nodal agency coordinating partnerships between NGOs and the government for sustainable development in rural areas. The CAPART banks on NGOs to carry forward its development agenda by disbursing funds in the right direction. Monitoring of the projects is carried out in phases once after getting satisfactory report of NGO and the project need etc., then mid-term evaluation after which the rest of funds are released. Despite the black-listed NGOs, there are good ones which have done commendable work in rural areas and have made a difference to the lives of people.

It has been revealed by various reports that functionaries of NGOs need capacity building on various aspects of rural project management. The book will help in the enhancement of knowledge and will equip them with literature on different aspects of rural project management viz. project design, implementation, evaluation etc.

Rural project management is being taught to postgraduate students of Rural Management, Social Work, Sociology, Economics and other disciplines. Students and academicians will find this book informative on different aspects.

Corporates are doing rural development work as a part of corporate social responsibility, and officials of such corporates will find this book useful in the effective management of rural projects.

I am thankful to all my colleagues, students and publisher who helped me in writing this book. I am highly indebted to my family members for their encouragement and cooperation.

I earnestly look forward to suggestions from readers for improvement of the subject content and material of this book.

I gratefully acknowledge the references like CRS PROPACK, ILO's manual, study materials of international agencies like IFAD, UNDP and other sources, which helped me in writing the book.

Dr. Devendra Prasad Pandey
Principal
St. Soldier Management & Technical Institute,
Mithu Basti, Kapurthala Road, Jalandhar (Punjab).

Contents

Rural Project Management

Chapter 1

Management has been called "the art of getting things done through people". This definition, by Mary Parker Follet, calls attention to the fact that managers achieve organizational goals by arranging for others to perform whatever tasks may be necessary – not by performing the tasks themselves.

Management has been viewed as a process of planing, organizing and controlling the organizational members and of using all other organizational resources to achieve organizational goals. Process is a systematic way of doing things. We define management, as a process because all employees, regardless of their attitude or skills engage in certain interrelated activities in order to achieve desired goals.

The classical, behavioural and quantitative schools of management focused on aspects of the organization the functionaries could influence directly. External environment continuously undergoes rapid changes having far-reaching effects on organizations and their management strategies. At the same time, the standards by which managers are judged have changed. Now, organization must consider the effects of their actions on the quality of life, holding themselves responsible to their stakeholder's community those groups or individuals who are affected directly or indirectly by the organization's pursuit of goals.

A project is accomplished by performing a set of activities like manufacturing a product, organizing health programmes or managing relief work. Manufacturing a product consists of many activities like sourcing raw material, staffing etc. Every project requires resources; these may be money, material and others.

According to Project Management Institute, USA, "Project is a system involving the co-ordination of a number of separate department entities throughout the organization and which must be completed within prescribed schedules and time constraints. Managing a project involves application of scientific tools like operation research, quantitative techniques, planning, implementing, monitoring and coordinating all the activities or tasks to produce desirable outputs in accordance with the pre-determined objectives.

Coordination among the diverse areas requires teamwork. Considering the challenges, a project has complexity in choosing methodology or technology, staffing right kind of people, arrangement of financial and other resources. A sound and need based project seems to be risk free. The risk factor will come up when conditions become conducive to it. Project management helps in foreseeing some of the risk elements to strengthen the project and encounter the risk.

PRE-FEASIBILITY STUDY

A well-planned rural project requires pre-feasibility study to explore the opportunities, find-out problems, avenues of coordination etc. Government, being a regulator, spells out priorities for the national and regional economy and lays the framework for development and resource allocation. Government asks for cooperation from entrepreneurs, NGOs, business and others to contribute in socio-economic development of the region as well country. Rural projects can be undertaken as per the policy framework for development laid down by the government. A survey is required to assess the need of the community and area and prioritization of needs and problems. Survey also ensures the availability of raw material, skilled manpower and the environment. Various publications of government, financial institutions, consultancy organizations, research institutions, NGOs have data and statistics, which may be helpful in getting desired information. An analysis of the economic and social trends of the society will be very helpful in identifying and projecting the needs of various services, interventions and project. Pre-feasibility study is required to:

(*i*) To determine whether the project offers a promising investment opportunity.

(*ii*) To determine whether the project will be able to reap social benefits.

(*iii*) To determine whether any aspects of the project are critical requiring in-depth investigation by way of survey, study, PRA or any other methods.

(*iv*) To study the projects of other line agencies; viz. Government, NGOs; about the activities, operational areas, modus operandi of project management.

(*v*) To study the requirement and availability of manpower, resources and project cost.

If the pre-feasibility study indicates that the project is a worthwhile proposition, a detailed feasibility study is taken up. Support or functional studies are required to be conducted if the pre-feasibility study indicates certain areas of project that need a detailed study.

Project Cycle

Chapter 2

A project is a set of planned, interrelated activities that achieve defined objectives within a given budget and a specified period of time. The project cycle illustrates the set of actions: design, planning, implementation, monitoring, evaluation, reporting and learning.

PROJECT DESIGN

The project cycle is shown as circle because insights and learning from project evaluations inform the design of new projects "learning after" and "learning before". Within individual project cycle actions there are loops that illustrate how learning and insights change and improve ongoing projects "learning during". International agencies develop their own project cycle, but they are broadly similar. UNICEF uses a simplified "Triple A" circle: Assessment, Analysis and Action.

The quality of design is important because it affects every other step in the project cycle. While design is an important starting point, it is also an ongoing process throughout the project cycle. Depending upon the situation, new understanding that emerge during project implementation should lead project officers to adjust the project design.

ADJUSTING A PROJECT DESIGN IN LIGHT OF POSITIVE IMPACTS

A women's health project in one area was so successful that health monitors were overwhelmed with requests to join the programme. A slight change to the project design allowed the project managers to hire and train more health monitors and increase the number of targeted beneficiaries.

A small-scale water harvesting under the watershed project unexpectedly led to an increased risk of children's exposure to uncleaned water. Although the project was successful in trapping water, the original design had not foreseen that children and animals might use the same water. Project managers decided to revise the project's design and included fencing and other measures once they realized the problem.

Project is a bundle of activities designed to get the desired results. Terminology of project word itself make clear the concept: P– Problem, R – Rhythm, O – Objectivity, J – Justified, E – Effort, C – Creativity and T – Time bound.

Project has a cycle of activities known as stages. These 6 stages are as follows:

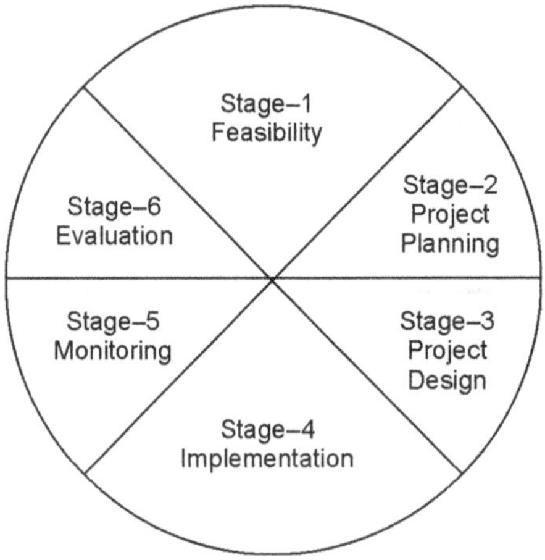

Project management is the planning, organization, directing and controlling of organizational resources for a relatively short/long term objective that have been established to achieve specific goals and objectives.

Successful project management can be defined as having achieved the project objective:

- Within time-frame.
- Within cost.
- At the desired performance
- While utilizing the assigned resources effectively and efficiently.

The management of social development project involves application of different managerial skill in all the stages of project cycle. These skills are applied in decision making, supervision, budgeting and reporting.

FEASIBILITY

Feasibility is the first step in the project management. It is a device to test the viability of the proposed project from all the actors involved towards sustainability of the project. A project should only be planned when it has feasibility. Few feasibility tests are prescribed as follows:

1. Economic Feasibility

The economic feasibility test of a project aims to show the economic viability of the project. Whether it is in the interest of the economy of the people, community and area. At local level many projects have shown poor performances viz. A training programme in income generation activity which in the beginning assured trainees about raw material and later they are asked to come with raw material which they couldn't and lastly the project found it difficult to survive, the trainees left the training because their economy did not allow to participate in the training with raw material. Many projects have become a burden because either operational schemes are closed or the allocation to the particular schemes has dwindled off.

2. Technical Feasibility

Technical feasibility denotes the technical know-how, technology and its advances. There are NGOs who have installed devices but they lack knowledge of operation and maintenance. The training was imparted but it was inductive. Many projects yet require technical know-how or the technology could be developed for some areas, it will be helpful in all-round development. At the grass-root, in a study we found that the solar cooker purchased in different villages are not operational, when explored, minor repairing and maintenance was required, which would have been done by training, skill upgrading and studying technical viability.

3. Managerial Feasibility

The success or failure of a project largely depends upon the ability of the functionaries of the organization. The demand of professionally managed NGOs is growing tremendously and representatives of NGOs are attending training courses for their capacity building and empowerment to increase their managerial capability. Managerial skill is not only required in technology, finance, production etc. but also in organization development, decision making etc. The concept of general management specialist is converting into specialized management disciplines because of effective management is required at all levels.

4. Organizational Feasibility

Many NGOs have been denied funding due to reason that their organization didn't meet the criteria to be eligible for support, and many credible NGOs don't apply for funds to many funding agencies for fund, the reason seems to be organizational feasibility. A teamwork concept is required to be developed, second line leadership should be developed and authority should be delegated for the effective organizational development.

5. Commercial Feasibility

The end of the production process is not only to produce goods and services but is also required to satisfy with the taste temperament and need of the consumer, hence the goods produced should have all the commercial qualities so that it can be transacted in the market because the ultimate aim of the production process is to convert the produced goods in the form of cash. Many NGOs are involved in the production of products but their identity is doubtful because of the reason of lack of commercial feasibility. Many appropriate technologies couldn't be sustained because the marketing or after sale service was poor. In this context, effort of Social Work & Research Centre (SWRC), under the stewardship of Shri Sanjit 'Bunker' Ray, is tremendous in the commercialization of solar devices. The organization has appointed field based "Barefoot technicians" who not only provide technical assistance in operation and maintenance but work for marketing of solar devices like solar lantern, etc.

6. Social Acceptability

Government and international agencies have allocated huge amount for bio-mass energy, solar energy but due to lack of people's acceptability, the programme couldn't get success. Many programmes have failed due to lack of social acceptability. In Bhadohi district of U.P., carpet weaving is usually performed by members of backward caste, S.C. and others, few youths of forward caste were imparted training in the carpet weaving, they took loan from a regional rural bank and started their carpet weaving enterprise, they felt humiliation in the community and few of them closed their enterprises. This was the result of effect of social acceptability. To start any project NGOs must ensure the feasibility of social acceptability.

Feasibility is most important phase in the project management, once the project is planned on feasibility studies, possibility of success increases. Feasibility test is a parameter to improve the quality in implementation strategy. It analyses the organizational strength and weaknesses.

Logical Framework Approach (LFA)

Chapter 3

LFA is a tool for improving the quality of projects. It is an analytical tool for objective oriented project planning and management. LFA enhances planning, analysis and communication. Using LFA helps:

- Clarify the purpose of, and the justification for, a project
- Identify information requirements.
- Clearly define the key elements of a project.
- Analyse the project's setting at an early stage.
- Facilitate communications between all parties involved.
- Identify how the success or failure of the project should be measured.

LFA is a management tool which facilitates planning, execution and evaluation of a project. In this case LFA also means:

- A format for presentation to donor and partner authorities: project ideas, pre-appraisal reports, project documents, progress reports, etc.
- A summary of the project in the form of a matrix that remains valid during project implementation but can be modified.
- A sequence of analytical tools which is used in an external/internal workshop situation.

GOAL

The goal describes the wider and longer term development aim of the project. The project is only among many factors contributing to success at this level. Example- rural households in the most vulnerable region have reduced food insecurity. Project is a set of planned, interrelated activities that achieve defined objectives within a given budget and a specified period of time.

STRATEGIC OBJECTIVES

Strategic objectives describe the beneficial effects of the behavioural changes observed in the intermediate results. It ensure focus on the central reasons why the project was proposed. Strategic objectives can realistically be achieved by the end of the project. 'Women farmers in the 4 villages have increased their rice production.'

LOGICAL FRAMEWORK

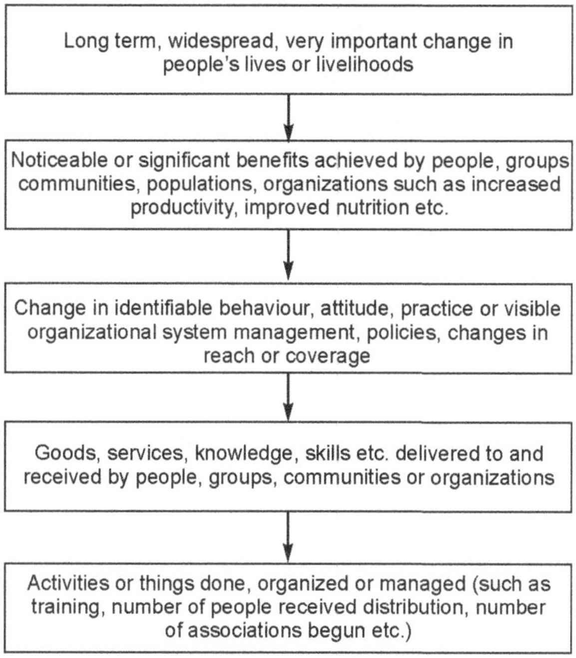

INTERMEDIATE RESULTS (IRs)

IRs indicate the behavioural or system change anticipated from successful delivery of outputs to end-users. IRs focuses on end-user's actual use of the goods, services and knowledge provided by the project. Adoption uptake, use, reach, coverage of project outputs. Behaviour change can occur among people, systems or organizations." Women farmers use the new farming techniques they have learned."

OUTPUTS

Outputs are- what the project delivers goods, services, knowledge, skills, attitudes, enabling environment. Outputs arise directly from successful implementation of activities. Example- 'women farmers have increased their knowledge of good techniques of rice cultivation.'

ACTIVITIES

Project activities describe the functions that need to be undertaken and managed in delivering the outputs.

CRITICAL ASSUMPTIONS

Critical assumptions are factors that project designers cannot (or choose no to) control, but that could imperil success if the assumptions are incorrect. Critical assumptions include expectations that are fundamental to the working of the objectives hierarchy. Think of them as possible risks, but not probable ones like "There will be no drought or earthquake" in specific regions where such natural events are historically known to occur, longtime project experience suggests a few common categories of assumptions that almost always have to be examined during design.

- Government plans, policies, and actions-whether historical, actual, or anticipated.
- The plans, policies and actions of other relief and development organizations operating in the area.
- Trends in national and international markets (supply, demand, prices, credit, etc.), and also plans and policies of pan-regional or international trade bodies.
- The possibility (but again, not the probability) of human made or natural difficulties.

The key point to remember is- "If any external factor (critical assumption) is important and unlikely to be realized in the project, the project might need to be redesigned with additional activities or the strategic objective needs to be reformulated."

SPECIFIC, MEASURABLE, ACHIEVABLE, RELEVANT, TIME-BOUND (SMART) INDICATORS

Project Planning Matrix (PPM)

Project	Project Planning Matrix (PPM)	Country/State/Region: Project No.: Duration of PPM:	PPM prepared on (Date): Remark:

Descriptive Summary	*Objectively Verifiable Indicators*	*Means/Sources of Verification*	*Important Assumptions*
Overall goal to which the project contributes	For goal achievement		For sustaining objectives in the long term
Project purpose	For purpose achievement		For achieving the overall goal
Results/outputs	For results achievements		For achieving the project purpose
Activities	Specification of inputs/costs of each activity		For achieving the results/ outputs.
			Preconditions

Project Planning Matrix
Project Title:
Project No.:
Country/State/Region:

PPM prepared on:
Estimated project duration:
Implementing Agency:
Funding Agency:

Summary of Objectives/activities (1)	***Objectively Verifiable Indicators*** (2)	***Means/Sources of Verification (MOV)*** (3)	***Important Assumptions*** (4)
Overall goal (OG) to which the project contributes: How do we word the OG taking into account the results of the analysis of objectives?	**Indicators** that overall goal has been achieved. How do we define the contents of OG (in various phases) *i.e.* the contribution to the achievement of the OG. **Note:** Quality, quantity, time and possibly location and target group.	MOV; which database is available or which documents have been drawn up or can be obtained elsewhere to prove that the OG has been achieved.	**Assumptions** for sustaining objectives in the longer term.
Project purpose: With which PP (independent factors managed by the project) will we make a considerable impact to the achievement of the OG.	**Indicators:** Proving purpose has been achieved (end of project status).	Which database is available or which have been drawn up or can be obtained elsewhere to prove that the project purpose has been achieved?	For achieving the overall goal. Which external factors will have to occur for the anticipated contribution to the overall goal to actually take place?
Results/Outputs: Which results/ outputs (as a whole and in effective contribution) will have to be obtained in order to achieve anticipated impact (the project purpose).	**Indicators:** Proving that the results/ outputs have been achieved. How do we define the contents of each individual result/output (in various phases) so that they become measurable? **Note:** Quality, quantity, time and possibly location and target group.	Which database is available or which have been drawn up or can be obtained elsewhere to prove that the results/outputs have been achieved?	For achieving the project purpose: Which important assumptions in relation to the results/outputs to that can not be influenced by the project have been consciously defined as external factors must occur in order for the project purpose to be achieved.

Summary of Objectives/activities	*Objectively Verifiable Indicators*	*Means/Sources of Verification (MOV)*	*Important Assumptions*
(1)	(2)	(3)	(4)
Activities: Which activities (also as complex packages of measures will the project have to tackle and implement in order for the results/ outputs to be obtained.	**Specifications** of inputs/costs of each activity: What does it cost and what inputs are needed (including personnel, inputs in person-months) in order to implement each individual activity.	What records voucher for the costs entailed. Consumption of materials. Use of equipment, inputs of personnel, etc.	For achieving the results/ outputs: Which important assumptions in relation to the activities to that cannot be influenced by the project or have been consciously defined as external factors. Must occur in order for the results/outputs to be obtained.

Manageable Factor	*Development Hypotheses*	
If these activities are carried out then results/outputs are obtained.	If these results/outputs are obtained then the project purpose is achieved.	If the project purpose is achieved then a contribution is added towards the overall goal.

1. Development objective The higher level objective towards which the project is expected to contribute. (Mention target groups)	**1. Indicators** Measures (direct or indirect) to verify to what extent the development objective is fulfilled. (Means of verification should be specified)	**1. External factors** Important events, conditions or decisions necessary for sustaining objectives in the long run.
2. Immediate objective The effect which is expected to be achieved as the result of the project. (Mention target groups)	**2. Indicators** Measures (direct or indirect) to verify to what extent the immediate objective is fulfilled. (Means of verification should be specified)	**2. External factors** Important events, conditions or decisions outside the control of the project, which must prevail for the development objective to be attained.

3. Outputs The results that the project management should be able to guarantee (Mention target groups)	**3. Indicators** Measures (direct or indirect) which verify to what extent the outputs are produced. (Means of verification should be specified).	**3. External factors** Important events conditions or decisions outside the control of the project management necessary for the achievement of the immediate objectives.
4. Activities The activities that have to be undertaken by the project in order to produce the outputs.	**4. Inputs** Goods and services necessary to undertake the activities.	**4. External factors** Important events, conditions or decisions outside the control of the project management necessary for the production of the outputs.

INDICATORS: SUMMARY CHARACTERISTICS

1. Objectively Verifiable Indicator (OVI)

An OVI or shortly a planning indicator should give a clear picture of the situation to be reached at the end of a certain period. The following points should be included in well defined objectively verifiable indicators:

Variable: The element to be measured (What?)

Quantity: The actual situation and situation to be reached (How much?)

Target group: The people to be affected by the project (Who?)

Place: The location concerned (Where?)

Period: The time concerned: at what time should the target have been reached (When?)

The indicator should be SMART:

2. Monitoring Indicator

A monitoring indicator measures the change which took place in the selected variables during a certain period. The indicator has to be:

Valid: Casual relation between what you want to know and what you want to measure.

Sensitive: reaction time between the change in the 'element' to be known and the indicator to be used should be short.

Measurable: Should be quantifiable

Simple: easy to measure and without many costs.

In order to select a proper monitoring indicator, you formulate a manager's question (MQ) which expresses exactly what you want to know. Check whether the MQ is formulated sufficiently gender specific.

Often you can deduce monitoring indicators from the planning indicators. However, sometimes you cannot use the planning indicator directly for monitoring (e.g. too costly, issue too sensitive) or the

MQ involves qualitative information (e.g. how is the users group functioning). In that case you have to formulate an indirect indicator.

3. Indirect Indicators

For defining indirect indicators we should proceed as follows:

(*a*) Identify the quantifiable elements in the manager's question.

(*b*) Analyze the variable, starting with the one which is easiest to measure, using the following checklist:

- Is the indicators valid e.g. is there a crucial relationship with the manager's questions?
- Can the variable be measured with sufficient accuracy?
- Is the indicator efficiently sensitive?
- Are the words used clear?
- Which aspects of the manager's question are not covered?

(*c*) Select the most suitable and cost-effective indicator(s) based on the analysis.

Once indicators have been specified, ENSURE THAT

1. They are specific in terms of quantity, quality, time, location and target group.
2. The means of verification is available (statistics, observation, records).
3. If not, check that the information can be generated at reasonable cost.
4. It is relevant as a measurement of the achievement of objectives.
5. The means of verification is reliable and up-to-date.
6. The collection, preparation and storage of information is an activity within the project and the necessary inputs for it are specific in the project management.

ASSUMPTIONS

Assumptions are external factors on which the intervention is not responsible, but on which the realization of the intermediate results, the project purpose and the over all objective depend. Assumptions answer the question: Which are the external factors that are not influenced by the intervention but affect the realization of the intervention significantly? In the logical framework, they are presented as follows:

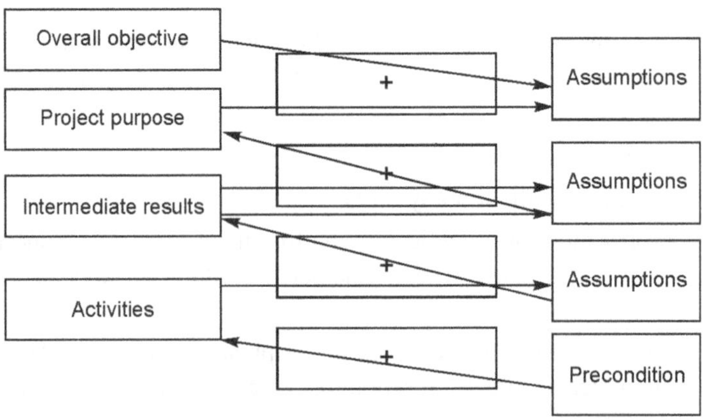

This scheme reads as follows:

- If the pre-conditions are complied with, then the activities will be started,
- If the activities are realized, and if the assumptions at the activity level are complied with, then the intermediate results will be realized,
- If the project purpose is realized, and if the assumptions at the project purpose level are complied with, then the project purpose will be realized.
- If the project purpose is realized, and if the assumptions at the project level are complied with, then the over all objective will be realized.

PROCEDURE TO DETERMINE THE ASSUMPTIONS AND PRECONDITIONS

1. Identify the diagram those 'objectives' that are not included in the intervention logic (first column), but that are important for the realization of the stated objectives in the intervention logic.
2. Place these objectives as external factors at the appropriate level.
3. Identify other external factors, not included in the diagram, but important for the success of the intervention.
4. Assess all external factors upon their importance and chance to be realized, using the algorithm.
5. This assessment leads to one of the following three conclusions:
    - The external factor can be left out as it is almost 100% certain to be realized,
    - The external factor will be kept as an assumption or a precondition.
    - The intervention should be redesigned.

Algorithm to assess external factors

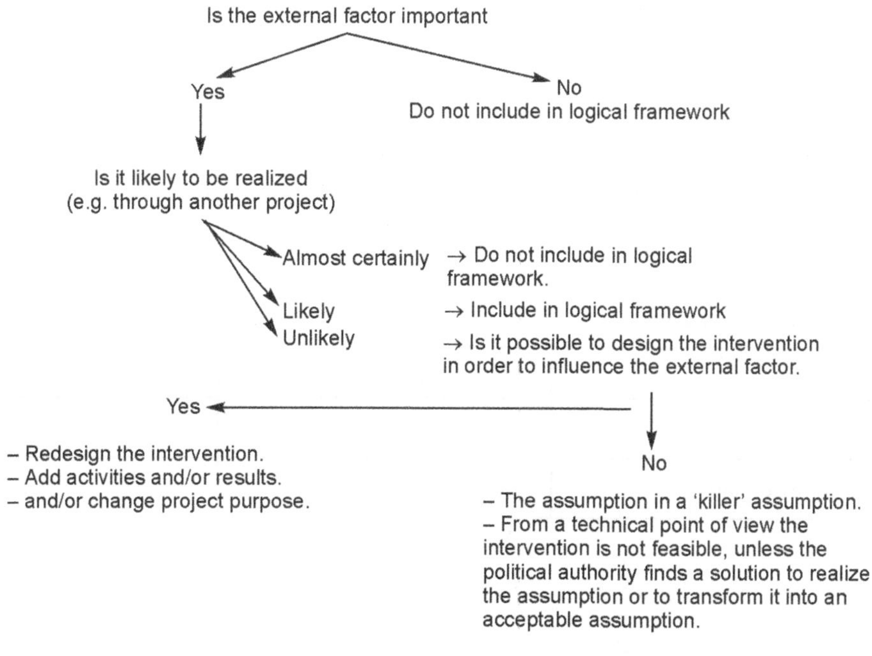

STEP-1: PARTICIPATION ANALYSIS

Lack of knowledge among the development planners about the people affected by development projects has proved to be a common cause of project problems, as evidenced in numerous evaluation reports and studies. As a first step, therefore, a comprehensive picture of the interest groups, the individuals and institutions involved has to be developed.

There are different interest groups, different motives and drives. A fundamental requirement of all development projects is that the objectives reflect the needs of the society and the interest groups, and not merely the internal needs of the organization.

In order to understand the problem, it must be listed, and the views of all the parties concerned, i.e. those likely to be affected by a possible development project in the area positively or negatively, directly or indirectly, should be listed.

Procedure

One has to identify all parties involved

1.1 Write down, even unsystematically, all persons, interest groups, and institutions and projects, which are located in the region, hold an influential position or may be affected by the problems. Indicate all external influence and interests of all parties involved.

1.2 Scan the groups and persons listed as to whether they consist of homogeneous units or whether sub-groups, sections or sub-units with specific problems or interests can be identified and listed separately; categorize them e.g. interest groups, individuals, organizations, authorities, etc.

1.3 Discuss whose interests and views are to be given priority when analyzing the problems. Specify gender. The planning team can decide on the criteria for analysis of all groups, institutions, etc.

1.4 When classifying into interest groups, participants etc., always proceed in steps, in the following order:

- Collect
- Classify
- Describe
- Analyze
- Evaluate

1.5 Divide the interest groups and institutions into participants and non-participants.

	Institutions	*Interest*
Participants		
Non-participants		

1.6 If the planning team feels it is expedient the group involved can also be divided.

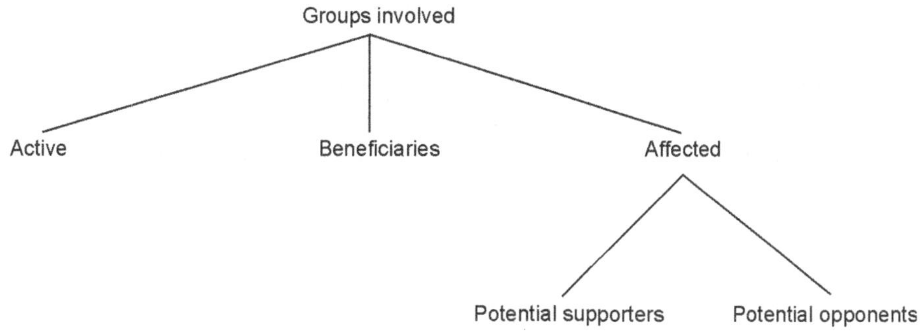

Based on the information available and the insight and experience of the participants, selection of the groups can be made and target groups could be identified. They could also decide on the criteria to be used in this analysis. If there is difference of opinion, the discussion should be discontinued for a while, and more information sought.

Take a closer look at some of the groups:

1.7 The planning team discusses whose interests and views are to be given priority when analyzing the problems. This leads to the second step and the question "What is the core problem?"

1.8 Separate in-depth analysis can be made of the internal situation in the institutions or interest groups and their relations with each other.

Make a more detailed analysis of these groups e.g. in terms of-

(*a*) **Problem:** The main problems affecting or facing the group (ecological, cultural etc.)

(*b*) **Interest:** The main needs and interests as seen from the group's point of view.

(*c*) **Potential:** The strengths and weaknesses of the group.

(*d*) **Linkages:** Main conflicts of interests, patterns of cooperation or dependency with other groups.

SET PRIORITIES

Decide whose interest and views are to be given priority when the analysis of the problems is carried out. This helps to build a planning perspective. It is more important to agree on whose interest and views are to be given priority when the analysis of the problem is carried out.

Relevant issues to have in mind are

- Which are the groups most in need of external assistance?
- Which interest groups should be supported in order to ensure positive development?
- What conflicts would occur by supporting given interest groups and what measures can be taken to avoid such conflicts?

Explanation of target groups/stakeholders

A basic principle, in all development projects is that they should be designed to satisfy the needs of people, not the internal needs of institutions. The affected groups can be sub-divided, e.g. into participants/non-participants, potential opponents/potential proponents, etc. There could be other groups, organizations, political authorities at different levels, represent motives and interests which may not necessarily coincide with those of the target group. Identifying inflict group is an important part of the project design and they should be indicated under external factors where applicable. If the project is only to reach its target beneficiaries indirectly through a local institution, then the project objective will normally best be defined in terms of the creation of upgrading of capacity to satisfy the recurrent needs of the intended beneficiaries on a sustained basis.

We should avoid un-specifiable terms as rural poor, unemployed workers, but use more specific terms.

The stakeholders/target groups to be specified

1. Specified in the indicators column at the level of development objective, immediate objective and output.
2. Precisely defined. If this is not possible, the opposition of the target group can be narrowed down e.g., according to one or more criteria.
   (*a*) Geographical area, where the majority of the population belongs to the target group.
   (*b*) Field of activity (e.g. farmers with a certain crop or income, landless labourers).
   (*c*) Economic situation, living conditions.
   (*d*) Needs, access to social services (health, education etc.)
   (*e*) Gender and age.
   (*f*) Class, caste, ethnicity, social status, etc.
3. Specified at the right project level. There may be different target groups at different levels in the Rural Project Management.

CHECK LIST

- Formulate vision, mission, goals, and objectives of the organization in a participatory manner.
- Draw up list of activities based on objectives and a financial plan and human resource plan to realize those activities implement the same in a participatory manner.
- When budgeting ensure that budgeted amounts match the actual requirements of the activities. Under budgeting will lead to lack of alignment of goals.
- Draw up a finance plan to ensure adequate cash flow.
- Draw up the operational budget to monitor the recurring expenditure and income effectively.
- Draw up the capital budget if required to ensure efficient utilization of the resources for the objectives.

INTRODUCING THE LOGICAL FRAMEWORK APPROACH

The logical framework approach (LFA) can be very useful for guiding project design and implementation. The basic ideas behind the LFA are simple and common for any design process.

1. Be as clear as possible about what you are trying to achieve and how it will be achieved.
2. Decide how will you know if you are achieving your objectives and put in place a monitoring system.
3. Make explicit the conditions (assumptions) outside the direct control of the project that are critical for the project so succeed and assess the risk for the project if these conditions fall to arise or change.

The LFA also has some limitations. The main criticism is that it can lead to a rigid and bureaucratically controlled project design that becomes disconnected from field realities and changing situations. However, the LFA is easy to use more adaptively, particularly if the original design is seen, at least in part, as needing future finalization and probably revision, and project management prioritizes annual reviews and logframe updating. So, in practice, a summarized logframe will be useful to provide an overview of the project and for those making decisions about project funding. For those using the logframe as a management tool, more detail will be needed. When facilitated well, the LFA is generally seen as very valuable by project stakeholders and leads to a better quality and shared understanding of needs, objectives and strategies by all involved. When possible, try to follow the basic ideas without forcing everyone to understand the full detail of the logframe matrix. Visually mapping out the process steps can make them clearer than using the four-column table format. It may also be a good idea to avoid some official terminology, finding local words instead. Some people may be scared off by terms like "logframe" and "objectively verifiable indicators".

Key steps in the logical framework approach

While most people are familiar with the logical framework matrix, the most important part of the LFA is actually the planning process that has been developed to improve the quality and clarity of project design. There are various versions of the steps in the LFA. The one presented below takes account of the specific nature of IFAD – supported rural development projects. The key steps to be undertaken – with well selected and diverse stakeholders are-

1. Establish the general scope or focus of the project
2. Agree on the specific planning framework, terminology and design process
3. Undertake a detailed situation analysis
4. Develop the project strategy (objective hierarchy, implementation arrangements and resources)
5. Identify and analyze the assumptions and risks for the chosen strategies, modifying the project design if assumptions are incorrect or risks are too high
6. Develop the monitoring and evaluation framework.

The logical framework matrix

The written output of the LFA is the logframe matrix. The standard matrix is a table with four rows and four columns. This matrix summarizes-

1. What the project should achieve, from the level of an overall goal down to specific activities.

2. The performance questions and indicators that will be used to monitor progress and overall achievement.
3. How these indicators will be monitored or where the data can be found.
4. The assumptions behind the logic of how activities will eventually contribute to the goal, plus associated risks for the project if assumptions turn out to be incorrect.

Below table shows a logical framework. Alternative, commonly found terms used in the matrix are given in parentheses. Note that inputs required for activities to be carried out are written at the activity level in the second column (performance questions and indicators) - the column is not for indicators. The table also suggests how to write the objectives in the hierarchy.

The logical framework matrix and how each level is written (alternative common terms in parentheses)

Objective Hierarchy *(Narrative summary, intervention logic)*	***Performance Questions and Indicators*** *(Objectively verifiable indicators, indicators, targets)*	***Monitoring Mechanisms*** *(Means of verification, sources of information)*	***Assumptions and Risks***
Goal (Overall objective, development objective) The long-term objective, change of state or improved situation towards which the project is making a contribution. **How to write it:** Put the verb in the past tense, as something already achieved over the long term.	Performance questions and indicators at goal level – high-level impacts.	How necessary information will be gathered.	For long-term sustainability of the project.
Purpose (Project development objective) The immediate project objective, the overall observable changes in performance, behaviour or resource status that should occur as a result of the project.	Performance questions and indicators for each purpose (component) lower-level impact and outcome indicators.	How necessary information will be gathered.	Assumptions in moving from purposes to goal.

How to write it: Put the verb in the present or past tense as if already achieved.			
Outputs (Results) The products, services or results that must be delivered by the project for the component objectives and purpose to be achieved. **How to write it:** Put the verb in the present or past, as already achieved.	Performance questions and indicators for each output-output indicators.	How necessary information will be gathered.	Assumptions in moving from outputs to purposes.
Activities The actions taken by the project that are required for delivery of the outputs. **How to write it:** Put the verb in the infinitive, as something to do.	Note: The needed inputs go here, not indicators for activities.		Assumptions in moving from activities to outputs.

A problem of concern in complex projects is the difficulty of including cross-cutting concerns in a linear objective hierarchy. For example, you may want to pay particular attention to women's empowerment in project activities. Setting up an output layer around gender equity may isolate gender, when what you want to do is to integrate gender into all activities. Yet you cannot ignore this output as distinct, since it risks leaving out indicators for assessing performance on the gender front. This dilemma can be overcome by including separate cross-cutting objectives or principles. Sometimes these fit into the logframe in an integrated manner. If not, they need to be included in the project document and preferably as an attachment to the matrix. Being explicit about these cross-cutting objectives or principles is important in order to include them not only in activities but also in M & E.

Three options for adjusting the structure of the logframe matrix

Type of Structure	*Description*	*Advantages*	*Disadvantages*
Standard objective hierarchy	Four levels: 1 x goal, 1 x purpose, any number of outputs, any number of activities per output.	– Is very simple. – Is commonly used and understood.	– Oversimplifies larger, multi-component projects. – Does not make project outcomes clear.
Multiple purposes	Four levels: 1 x goal, as many purposes as needed, any number of outputs per purpose, any number of activities per output.	– Maintains the standard four levels of the logframe matrix.	– The standard is one purpose, so this may cause confusion. – Confusion between purposes and outcomes can still occur.
Cascading logframes (objective hierarchies)	Several interlinked, standard four-level logframes; each project component written up in a separate logframe; the purpose level the component objective.	– Maintains the standard four levels of the logframe matrix. – Enables a focused, "sub-project" approach to management.	– Doesn't give an overview of cross-cutting objective. – Focusing on integrative impact is difficult. – Is more complex.
Extra layer(s)	Five levels: 1 x goal, 1 x purpose, any number of key outcomes (or component objectives), any number of activities per output.	– Makes a clear distinction between output, outcome and purpose levels facilitating M & E. – Is consistent with standard LFA. – Some donors already use it.	– More detail has to be included in the logframe matrix.

Recognizing the importance of outcomes

Your project may have one output that is formulated as "improve the capacity of the agricultural extension service and the skills of extension workers". Many projects use an indicator such as "number of extension workers trained". But if you want to manage for impact, you need to know the extent to which extension staff are using new skills in the field and, in turn, the extent to which farmers are developing and adopting improved agricultural practices. These are outcomes that occur after you have achieved outputs (number of extension agents trained) and are necessary in order to have impact (increased productivity and income for farmers). If your M & E data show that although many extension workers have been trained, farmers are not adopting improved practices, then you can question what might be going wrong with your strategy of improving the extension service through training. This is why monitoring change at the level of outcomes is so critical in managing for impact. So, for communication and reporting reasons, it is important not to limit the documentation of impact to only the goal level of the objective hierarchy. Most people who use the standard LFA and matrix focus on tangible outputs. Outcomes should be included as indicators at the purpose level, but this is rarely done well. This is partly because the logframe was originally designed to focus on controlling the delivery of tangible outputs to be produced, such as kilometers of road built or area of irrigation scheme constructed. The three ways of dealing with larger projects, mentioned above, all help make the outcome level more explicit and detailed and also easier to monitor and evaluate.

USING THE LOGICAL FRAMEWORK APPROACH

Step one: establish the general scope and focus of the project

The starting point for any project is to identify the general situation that will be improved, the likely primary and other stakeholders, the geographic scope of the project, the range of issues that will be addressed, and the likely length and expenditure of the project. Also find out what the community, government and potential funding agency's interests are in the project. This initial information provides for defining and guiding the detailed situation analysis and design steps. Some of this information will be outlined in the Country Strategic Opportunities Paper (COSOP). During this initial step, it is important to find out if the basic concept underpinning the project is feasible and if there is sufficient support from key stakeholders for it to be worthwhile to proceed to the next step.

Step two: Decide on the planning framework, terminology and design process

As already discussed, there are different planning frameworks and various approaches to the use of the LFA. In different countries, people will have had experience with different models and be used to a particular set of terms. It will help everyone if early on in the design process there is agreement about the approach to planning that will be followed, how the logframe will be used and what terminology will be used. Also define clearly what the design process will be, in terms of who will be involved, how and at what stage; what information needs to be gathered and how the final design will be checked with key stakeholders.

Weaving together a participatory design phase

- Establish a mentoring team – a group of committed, experienced and respected nationals who, on a voluntary basis, act as resource persons to advise the formulation process and champion the goals, strategies and approaches proposed by the project.
- Undertake a participatory stakeholder analysis through a process of brainstorming with groups/individual/institutions, grouping stakeholders, assessing their interests and impact on project success, assessing their influence and importance for project success, and outlining a strategy for their participation.
- Establish the design team with specialists from different professional sectors, relevant NGOs and government agency staff.
- Train the design team in the use of diagnostic participatory tools and in drawing implications for project design from qualitative discussions with groups of stakeholders.
- Review secondary data and key informant interviews.

- Formulate the study design and analysis plan based on the information gaps you have identified.
- Divide the project area into study zones, by identifying a number of relatively homogenous agro-ecological areas.
- Undertake village-level problem identification and needs assessment through focus-group meetings and household interviews:
  - Assess problems: discuss problems, issues and concerns of villagers; assess causes and effects; identify which issues could relate to the project being planned; agree on criteria for prioritizing problems; and priorities problems.
  - Analyze options: discuss strategies and options proposed/desired by the community to overcome the problem situation.
  - Analyze alternatives: agree on criteria for comparing options to overcome problems and realize visions, then identify and assess alternative strategies/options available to reach the desired objectives.
- Undertake a cross-cutting analysis, by agro-ecological zone and socio-economic stratum, to integrate analyses from different communities.
- Hold design workshops involving different levels of stakeholders to work together on the logframe matrix:
  - Summary of objectives (objective hierarchy): develop project concept, vision, mission, results and activities.
  - Indicators: together identify which indicators capture and measure the different levels of changes the project is anticipated to affect.
  - Means of verification: agree on the sources of information to be used for monitoring impact.
  - Important assumptions/external factors: discuss the attitudes, behaviours, processes, trends, natural hazards/disasters, etc. outside the control of the project that could affect it positively or negatively.
- Conduct continual surveys of primary stakeholder opinions to ensure that the consultation process and the interim results are as good as possible.
- Hold national-level project reality-check and planning workshops to which a wide range of (primary) stakeholders are invited and during which initial ideas are presented and debated to consider different realities.
- Draft the project proposal, based on workshop outputs, with a team of experts.
- Verify the draft project outline with the key stakeholders, particularly the intended primary stakeholders, in a series of discussions or workshops.

Step three: undertake a detailed situation analysis

Situation analysis involves learning as much as possible about the project context and the interests and needs of local people in order to design a relevant project. This learning is best done with several groups of stakeholders.

The standard LFA focuses project planning on developing a problem tree for the situation. A problem tree works well for simple situations. However, problem-based planning fits with a more mechanical approach to development where projects are designed to "fix" problems rather than to facilitate local development processes. Furthermore, people see their future in terms of visions and aspirations – not just as problems. Analyzing future visions helps identify opportunities for improvement and of successes that can be further developed.

A good situation analysis will combine information gathering and analysis about the local context, expert advice and participatory processes such as participatory appraisals, community meetings and multi-stakeholder workshops. A creative and learning-oriented situation analysis will combine several methods.

One result of a good situation analysis is that stakeholders have more insights about their situation and have better capacity to design a project. However, this will not be achieved in one community meeting. People's perspectives evolve as they debate and listen. After a community meeting, subsequent discussion in people's homes might have lead to adjustments if a meeting was held the following day. Take care that the situation analysis is designed as a series of events.

Updating the situation analysis is critical for the M & E system. Note that a situation analysis is not the same as a baseline survey. Both are information-gathering exercises. But a situation analysis is more open-ended in terms of the themes and questions that are analyzed, while a baseline survey only includes data that are needed to make impact-related comparisons. A baseline survey is undertaken after project design had been completed, while a situation analysis is undertaken as part of design.

Key themes, questions and methods for a thorough situation analysis with stakeholders

Stakeholders (stakeholder maps, institutional diagrams, secondary data).

- Who are the local people likely to benefit from the project?
- Who are the other key stakeholders?
- How do different stakeholder groups interact?
- What are the power relations between different groups?

Problems and Issues (rich picture, conceptual maps, focus group discussions, historical analysis, secondary data, matrix ranking)

- What problems or issues are central to the focus of the project?
- What are the main problems or concerns of the different stakeholder groups and how do these relate to the focus of the project?

Visions and Opportunities (rich pictures, role plays)

- What change would different stakeholder groups like to see the project bring about?
- Generally, what visions, hopes or dreams do different stakeholders have and are there implications for the project?
- What opportunities do stakeholders see for realizing their visions?

Biophysical setting (maps, transects, field visits, seasonal calendars)

- What are geographical characteristics of the project areas?
- What are the climatic conditions?
- What are the main forms of land use?
- What are the environmental problems or risks?

Organizations (institutional diagrams, network diagrams, flow charts, matrix ranking)

- What are the important government, business and NGO organizations?
- How effectively are these organizations performing?
- How are the different organizations linked together (power relations, communications, joint work, competitors)?

Infrastructure (resource maps)

- What are the key infrastructure issues for the area?

Law, Policy and Political Institutions (Rich pictures, institutional diagrams, historical analysis, focused interviews, secondary data)

- What legal factors are significant for the project?
- What government policies and programmes are significant?
- What are the main government and political structures and processes in the area?

Economic (wellbeing ranking, daily activity charts, seasonal calendars, livelihood profiles, secondary data).

- What is the economic situation of local people?
- What are the main forms of economic livelihood?
- What are the key characteristics of the local economy?
- What are the market opportunities and constraints?

Social and Cultural (historical analysis, focus group discussions, SWOT analysis)

- What are the main social and cultural conditions relevant to the project?

Step four: develop the project strategy

With a good understanding of the situation, you are now ready to start developing the project strategy. This explains clearly what everyone hopes to achieve and how it will be achieved. A project strategy includes the objective hierarchy, implementation arrangements and recourses required. This sub-section focuses on the objective hierarchy – column one of the logframe – central to the strategy. The objective hierarchy is a tree-type structure that maps out how activities and outputs contribute to the project purpose(s) and goal and the method description.

A project strategy will only work well if it is logical. This means that all the outputs required to achieve a particular purpose have been correctly identified and, in turn, that all the activities needed to deliver an output have been identified. For example, you cannot have as your output "production and certification of seeds of improved varieties", without also including "testing and setting up private production of seed" and "training of agriculture staff for certification" as activities. Once the objective hierarchy is drafted, the logic needs to be tested.

The standard LFA uses a very structured method of converting a problem tree into an objective tree or hierarchy. When working with project visions and in more complex situations where the problem tree becomes unwieldy in size, you could use a more open and iterative approach. The main steps in developing an objective hierarchy are outlined below with a detailed example.

1. **Define the project goal.** This should reflect the longer-term and highest-level impact to which the project will contribute.

2. **Identify the purpose(s).** This is what must be achieved by the project in order to contribute to the goal. The purpose level generally describes major changes in behaviour or capacity. Because a project can contribute to the goal in many ways, the stakeholders will need to decide what is most worthwhile and feasible for this particular project. It helps to establish criteria to help make these decisions. It is good practice to include a separate purpose for project management. Here, key project management tasks can be included as outputs, such as staff management, financial management, plant and equipment maintenance, and M & E.
3. **Establish necessary outputs.** For each purpose, identify what outputs are necessary for the purpose to be achieved. In other words, make the outputs fit the real needs and avoid outputs that are not absolutely necessary. Any purpose can be achieved in several ways. Think creatively and analyze the advantages and disadvantages of different options before making a choice.
4. **Identify activities.** Each output is delivered via a set of activities. At the initial project design stage, the best way of achieving purposes and outputs may be unclear, so activities may need future finalization and probably revision.
5. **Check the logic.** Once the objective hierarchy has been drafted, use the logic testing questions for checking and finalization.
6. Allocate resources required for activities and develop an overall budget.
7. Develop a work schedule for the main activities over the life of the project and establish key milestones.
8. Establish the management and operational arrangements, with key responsibilities and working procedures.

Logic testing questions

Level	*Logic Testing Questions*
Goal	– Does the goal express some future desired state or higher order impact towards which the project is contributing? – Does the goal help place the project in a wider context that provides the rationale for the project? – Is the goal narrow enough that it is meaningful given the scope of the project? Avoid goals expressed at an excessively general level. – Is the goal something owned and shared by relevant stakeholders?
Purpose (if a single purpose)	– Is the purpose a succinct statement of what the project will achieve overall? – Is the purpose realistic given the resources, time span and working context of the project?
Purposes (if multiple purposes) or outcome Or Component objective (if an extra level is included)	– Are the outcomes/component objectives the set of main outcomes necessary to achieve the purpose? In other words, if the outcomes/component objectives are achieved will the project purpose be achieved?

(Contd...)

	– Do the purposes/outcomes/component objectives reflect the highest level achievements of the project for which it can realistically be accountable? – Are the purposes/outcomes/component objective realistic for the project to achieve during its lifetime? – Is there a set of practical actions that can be carried out to achieve each purpose/outcome/component objective? – Is one of the purposes/outcomes/component objectives dedicated to effective project management?
Outputs	– Do the outputs together describe the set of achievements that must be realized for the outcome/component objective to be realized? In other words, if the outputs are achieved will the outcome/component objective be achieved? – Are any outputs unnecessary to achieve the outcome/ component objective or logically belong under another outcome/component objective? – Are the outputs realistic for the project to achieve during its lifetime? – Is there a set of practical actions that can be carried out to achieve each output?
Activities	– Do the set of activities for each output reflect the main actions that must occur for the outputs to be achieved? – Are any activities included that are unnecessary of achieving the outputs or that logically belong under another output? – Are there any activities that need to be split up and partly allocated to different outputs? – Are the activities all roughly equivalent in terms of their level of detail? In other words, are you sure that some activities are not more at an output level while others are at a task level? – Is the list of activities manageable (not too long)?
For all levels	– Are all levels understandable to project stakeholders and expressed as plainly and succinctly as possible? – Are any unnecessary means of achievement included? – Are there between three and about seven items for each of the (outcome/component objective, output and activity) levels?

Developing a good project strategy does not happen in one go from top to bottom. You will need to return to earlier steps as thinking becomes more detailed. For example, when you start thinking about the cost and practicality of some activities you might realize that some outputs and purposes might be unrealistic.

Common mistakes to avoid when formulating the objective hierarchy

- Defining overly ambitious goal/purposes, given local conditions and available resources and capacities.
- Overlooking key activities and outputs that are needed to achieve higher-level objectives (outcomes/purpose/goal)
- Poor logic as to why particular activities are needed for a certain output or particular outputs for a certain purpose.
- Objectives expressed too vaguely to know what will be achieved or how to implement ideas
- Inclusion of principles, such as "stakeholder participation" or "gender equity", as separate purposes or outputs, instead of integrated into project activities
- Confusion in the levels of the objective hierarchy

As far as possible, make each level in the objective hierarchy SMART. Remember that the logframe is only a summary of a more detailed description and justification for each level of the project strategy in the appraisal report. Try to make each statement in column one of the logframe as specific as possible. Additional targets can also be included as indicators in column two of the logframe. To avoid blueprint planning, remember that outputs and purposes are not only physical, such as roads, irrigation schemes or yield increases, but also include dialogue processes and capacity development. You can include approximate targets and explain that these will become more precise after the participatory planning processed at start-up that will lead to clearer understanding of primary stakeholder's priorities.

Ensuring you have SMART objectives

The goal, purpose, component objectives, outputs and activities should be SMART if they are to be impact oriented:

Specific

Measurable

Achievable

Relevant (to the project purpose and goal)

Time-framed

- What is achievable may need to be developed from experience.
- Good ideas take time to develop.
- Not everything that is wroth doing can be easily measured.

The project strategy is something with details that evolve over the life of the project. For example, at start-up a more detailed project strategy is necessary than for appraisal, and even more detail is required for an annual work plan and budget.

Developing a clear, logical and feasible project strategy is worth all the time and analysis that is invested. Very often project staff – understandably – are important to "get started". However, if actions are based on a shared clear understanding of the project strategy, then they will be more easily directed towards achieving the desired impact. Without this understanding, team members may end up doing good but isolated bits of work that do not reinforce each other.

Step Five: Identify and analyze assumptions and risks

Assumptions, in the fourth column of the logframe, are the logframe "orphan". They often receive little serious thought or time. Yet assumptions are the very backbone of the project strategy. They specify the necessary conditions (if-then relationships) outside the direct management control of the project that must exist for the project to achieve its objectives. They are fundamental to the overall logic of the project and therefore to project success. Ideally, think about assumptions as you develop and objective hierarchy and do this again with the full draft.

Assumptions are only important when they describe conditions that – if they do not occur – may jeopardize the project's success. Many logframe matrices only note assumptions that are extremely obvious, general and often very probable. **Assumptions column : the "rubbish bin"**

According to an M & E consultant, the assumptions column of the logframe is like "the rubbish bin where everything goes". Instead of dealing with them as an integral part of the project, design teams tend simply to throw all the institutional aspects in this column. This means that such issues are not dealt with by the project staff that then sees them as being beyond project control. More time is needed in the planning process to analyze the assumptions and think about what could be done with them.

Most projects recognize the importance of assumptions that show up as problems during project implementation. Many of these can be identified during project design, helping improve it. They are not recognized when a situation analysis is absent, has not been thorough or has not been analyzed well enough to tease out the underlying assumptions. For example:

- In one project, one of the main targets was "non-rice cropping area increased by 10%". It was only during implementation that the project became aware that the target group of small farmers did not have access to any additional land for planting such crops. Verdict: poor situation analysis.
- Another project had the output, "radio programmes developed and aired" and as an assumption "communities have access to radio media", communities did not, in fact, have radios. Verdict: poor situation analysis.

In both cases, the assumptions should have been checked out before the outputs were affirmed. If they had been, and it had turned out that the communities did not have necessary access to land or radios, the outputs would either have been thrown out or redesigned. For instance, in the latter case, outputs might be redrawn to provide radio access and the extra budget this would require.

Risks are the reverse of an assumption. One look at the assumptions for a project will give an idea of the level of risk that the project is taking. The more assumptions there are, the more improbable they are and the more they are out of the project's control. This makes the risk of project failure higher. One project had an assumption "the annual rainfall is above the annual average for the region." If project success is based on this assumption (which may have been developed in haste without much thought), then it is certainly a high-risk project. Good M & E needs clear, valid assumptions. When a certain objective is not realized or problems occur, you will often find a faulty assumption is the cause. Part of good M & E means keeping a close check on the validity of assumptions. Here are few tips to make assumptions a useful management tool:

- Think of assumptions first as risks. When identifying assumptions, you might find it helpful to start by thinking of possible risks to the project. For example, if you think that a risk for the project is "non-delivery of contracted services on time by project partners", then this would appear in the logframe matrix as "project partners will comply with their contracts on time".

- Consider assumptions about: Performance of pubic agencies, performance of private organizations, performance of NGOs/CBOs, performance of contractors/consultants, performance of funding agencies, policy environment, natural events, world or domestic markets and prices, and war/civil disturbance.
- You cannot observe large number of assumptions. Limit the number of assumptions to only those that are most critical for success. After listing all possible assumptions, filter out those that are not important to project success and those that are almost certain so don't demand monitoring. A useful method for assessing the importance of assumptions is through the use of a risk assessment analysis.
- Focus on those assumptions about whose probability you are uncertain. Such assumptions need to be monitored as they may seriously endanger the project if they turn out not to be true. Examples of such assumptions from project logframes include: "primary stakeholders will be effective in the management of their newly acquired land", "climate fluctuates within normal ranges" and "community abides by fishery regulations on size of nets".
- Check that the assumptions are clearly outside the control of the project. Use a decision tree for this. The process of formulating assumptions is very important. It helps in checking that the project strategy is on course to achieve its purpose, having considered in this design as many components as possible that assumed factors might affect. If you realize that assumptions can fall within the control of the project, you can use them to indicate additional outputs and activities in the logframe matrix.

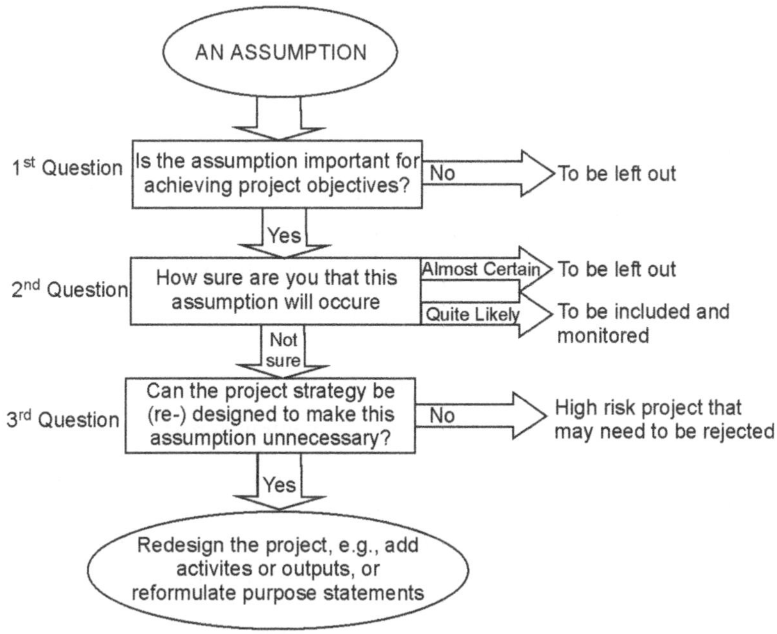

Figure-1: Deciding which assumptions are important to keep the project strategy on course.

- If important assumptions are very unlikely to be true, then these are "killer assumptions". The project must be redesigned to remove these assumptions. An example of a killer assumption is: "training of extension agents will lead to more uptake of new technologies by farmers". This cause-effect assumption needs to be dealt with by the project because it is, in fact, very unlikely that lack of knowledge is the key constraint for extension agents (you don't know if you have enough people whom you could train nor if they are the right people). It is also extremely likely that farmers face many other constraints to the uptake of technologies, not just extension agent's knowledge.
- Revisit you assumptions regularly, at least during the annual review, to adjust or remove those that are no longer valid and add those than have emerged. A reflective participatory project will formulate new assumptions as the strategy changes and initial results become clear. Compare your M & E data to the assumptions to see if there are contradictions that need to be removed. For example, you might assume that a 25% increase in household income would lead to less illegal firewood collection. When the monitoring data show that incomes are up by 35% and such firewood collection is still at the same level, then you need to rethink the project logic if you want to reduce deforestation. Increased local purchasing power could be stimulating the demand for more firewood. You can probably conclude that "increasing incomes" is not the best strategy for "reducing illegal firewood collection".

Step Six: Develop the monitoring and evaluation framework

The final step is to develop the monitoring and evaluation framework for the project.

From a logframe matrix to an annual work plan and budget

Translating a project strategy, as mentioned in the logframe matrix, into an operational annual work plan that is clear to project staff and partner organizations transforms ideas into actions. An operational plan is detailed enough when staff and implementing organizations know what they are expected to do, when and how.

WHAT IS THE AWPB?

The most important operational and planning tool of a project is the Annual Work Plan and Budget (AWPB). The AWPB guides daily implementation and includes:

- *Work plan*: a logframe-based description of each activity/output/indicator per component;
- *Schedule or time plan*: specifying when activities are to take place and in what order;
- *Budget*: identifying the cost of each output and activity per component;
- *Personnel plan*: identifying responsibilities, additional staff needs, staff training;
- *Material/equipment plan*: requirements for each output and activity per component, including procurement.

The AWPB describes the annual commitment of the project towards the communities, the government and NGOs. The AWPB is normally integrated into ongoing government budget processes. With that, the AWPB has acquired legal endorsement and forms the formal base for implementation and release of funds.

The AWPB process is usually initiated before the fiscal year ends and is based on experience gained at the field level during implementation. With the detailed AWPB, the importance of the project appraisal report fades away over the project's lifetime. After the first year, it is no longer useful for planning, except for general guidance on objectives, principles and approaches. The project appraisal report does, however, remain an important evaluation reference point, as AWPBs do not include references to long-term objectives and general principles.

The AWPB sits within the framework of the loan agreement, which can be amended when required. Changes come from the experiences of all project participants, who prepare the AWPB usually relies on the project appraisal report, updating details such as prices and actual requirements. Subsequent AWPBs are best when prepared during a partipatory review and planning workshop process. Communities and project and partner staff jointly review performance of the past year. The outcomes of these discussions form the basis for participatory, goal-oriented planning for the next AWPB.

In an increasing number of projects, AWPBs are preceded by participatory appraisals during which primary stakeholders with the guidance of project staff, identify their community's needs, resources and priorities. These form the basis for "community action plans" that are the building blocks for higher-level plans (e.g., district or ward) from which the project derives its AWPB.

The AWPB not only guides the project for a year but is also the mechanism by which the project can review the experiences of the previous year and make modifications accordingly. It adapts the project's operational plan to the current situation and specifies for the year: the outputs to be achieved, the activities to be undertaken to achieve these outputs, the resources required to undertake the activities and the costs of these resources as well as the institutions with financial responsibility.

REPAIRING THE AWPB

To prepare the AWPB, information is drawn from the project appraisal report, the loan agreement, any specific strategic plans, and plans and reports of previous years. AWPBs are produced for each level of participants in the project, starting with the project primary stakeholders according to their needs and demands using a bottom-up participatory process. At the highest level, preparation of the AWPB should be made just before government funding allocations for the following fiscal year, to give a clear indication of the funds required by the project. To develop an AWPB, here are some basic steps:

1. Take the activities from the revised project logframe matrix and list them in the first column of the work plan. List them in terms of which activity is needed in order to do others. Clarify them further and add sub-activities, if needed.
2. For each (sub) activity, specify the following: milestone – what is to be done by when, who is responsible for implementing it and for checking it, when it should start and finish, staff requirements in terms of person-months, quantity of material and equipment needed, cost and cost category and important assumptions.
3. Check the plan by ensuring that the total cost is within the budget and that people are not overloaded or forgotten in terms of responsibilities (or that there are gaps or contradictions). Also make sure that timing is realistic and consistent. You cannot have the same person or piece of equipment scheduled at the same time.
4. Do the above with the main stakeholders to ensure a shared sense of responsibility.

5. Compile the final consensus into the AWPB document and send this to the appropriate body for approval, including a "no objection" from the cooperating institution.

The AWPB is the basis for more detailed operational planning: work plans per project component, per staff member, per month/quarter/half-year, etc. Some projects use Gantt charts to show when activities are to happen during the year. However, these charts do not show other important information, such as responsibility and resources, so other charts are also needed.

PARTICIPATORY REVISION OF THE BUDGET AND PROJECT STRATEGY

Even simply integrating the budget with the logframe can prove difficult. At a participatory workshop on developing the logframe, the participants were in a hurry simply to plug in the numbers and leave. Project staff had to encourage them to justify the expenses as part of the wider strategy and activities. Not surprisingly, the budget was far beyond the resources available. To reduce the budget they had to review their thinking process and identify to see activities which most contribute to the outcomes they wanted to see. This process of backtracking helped the participants explain and justify why the activities were important and what would not be undertaken if not for external resources.

Example table of contents for an AWPB

Topic	*Description*
1. Introduction implementation to date	Summary of project objectives, area and components that focuses on the strategy to reduce poverty. Describe any critical issues or recommendations resulting from changes in policy, government directives or supervision missions.
2. Analysis of	Description of progress made, problems experienced, adequacy/ inadequacy of project inputs, lessons learned for each level of logframe. Indicate any adjustments needed to the logframe and justify them.
3. Budget summary	Consolidated budget: summarized per project component, per output, per district/facilitation unit and at national and overall project levels. Explain how components are to be financed by different stakeholders: government, primary stakeholders, funding agencies, as well as what each stakeholder is contributing to each component.
4. Overall work plan	For each component, an explanation of what is to be funded, rationale, strategy, expected outputs and any changes from last year's AWPB, outlined following the logframe format. Explain which of these relate to needs prioritized by primary stakeholders and which needs are left out and why. Summarize the process to be followed for primary stakeholder participation in the coming year.
5. Output/activity plans	Plans for each component, including what is needed in terms of project support and coordination and training activities for project/partner staff and primary stakeholders; how plan implementation is to be monitored?

6. Procurement plan	Types of facilities and equipment to be purchased, quantities, cost, destination and description of purpose.
7. Contracted services plan	Technical assistance, NGO and private sector services to be contracted.
8. Required plan and budget	Output/activity budget: definition of the input requirements for carrying out the activities, by component and by expenditure category. This is directly related to the work plan.
9. Overall schedule (Gant chart)	The period during which activities are to be undertaken and outputs to be achieved, who is responsible and key milestones for the year.
Appendices	Outlines of formats: output/activity plan, output/activity budget, indicators and monitoring schedule, contracted services monitoring, training activities monitoring, implementation progress monitoring, financial status, project status summary, credit analysis, project outputs summary and calendar of activities.

Approaches to Project Formulation

Chapter 4

Before submitting a final project proposal, a concept paper is required to be submitted to funding agency.

FORMAT FOR THE CONCEPT PAPER

The concept paper should be précised, brief and clear preferably in 3-4 pages.

1. Title of the concept paper
2. Organizations profile (name, legal status, etc.)
3. Project Design
   - (*i*) State the problem, opportunity or issue the concept paper addresses.
   - (*ii*) Briefly discuss the key or root causes of the problem or issue.
   - (*iii*) Whom does the problem or issue affect, where does it occur? Make explicit any relevant issues that are differentiated by gender.
   - (*iv*) List the strategic objectives the project is expected to achieve.
   - (*v*) Describe the proposed project strategy or the package of activities that you expect will achieve the objectives, and address the problem and its causes. Provide a rationale and justification for this strategy.
   - (*vi*) State the expected timeframe for the project (months/years).

Capacity Analysis

- (*i*) Who will be responsible for implementing and monitoring the project (e.g. Project Implementing Agency (PIA) in case of watershed development projects.)
- (*ii*) Discuss the capacity or competencies of the implementing agency and its partners to implement, monitor and evaluate the proposed intervention (partner may be village panchayat, village youth and women groups or any other voluntary organization).

Budget

- (*i*) If known, discuss the potential funding sources of this project and the likelihood of gaining their support.
- (*ii*) Provide an estimated monetary value (in Rupees for national and in Dollars for international funding) for the entire budget of the project.

(*iii*) Estimate the additional funds necessary for further intervention in the project.

Submission

Submit the concept paper to the agency alongwith required documents, progress reports etc.

Difference between a concept paper and a project proposal

	Concept Paper	*Project Proposal*
Main Purpose	A way to initiate and test ideas or concepts for a project before investing in extensive project design activities and, ultimately a full proposal.	A tool to receive approval and funding for a project. Distills a clear and precise description of the outcomes of the project design process and decisions.
Content	Focuses on problem or opportunity analysis, objectives and a feasible intervention strategy, includes a preliminary results framework: may include a preliminary proframe in some cases.	Includes fully developed sections or chapters describing various aspects of the project, in addition to information contained in the concept note. A proframe, results framework, performance indicator, tracking table, implementation schedules, monitoring and evaluation strategies are included.
When	First step of project design. Existing knowledge on rapid assessment and analysis informs the telescoped project design.	Last step of the project design process.
Requirement of resources	Prepared by in-house staff's knowledge.	Requires investment of resources appropriate to the time frame and scope. Consultants or advisors may be called for assistance in the larger projects.

PROJECT FORMULATION

Based on project planning, project may be formulated as per the profarma of the funding agencies and guidelines there of. The profarma deviate from one to another while a sketch is given below about the typical profarma as follows:

Part-1 (Project Framework)

1. Title of the project
2. Location
3. Background information
4. Intended beneficiaries
5. Goal (the higher order objective to which the project contributes)
6. Purpose (the desired impact of the project)
7. Developmental justification (reasons for undertaking the project)
8. Project activities
9. Duration of the project
10. Project participation (in project design, management, monitoring and evaluation)
11. Project management (How the project will be managed, responsibility of implementation, monitoring and evaluation).
12. Project sustainability (How will the activities be sustained after the support for the project is discontinued)
13. Budget: (The calculation of the budget needs to be based on list of inputs needed to carry out the activities and the prices and costs currently applicable in the project area. Give a budget in Rs. for national agencies and US dollars to international agencies as convenient or quote the prevailing exchange rates to the US dollars.)

Head	*Year-1*	*Year-2 and so on*
(*i*) Salary		
(*ii*) Equipment		
(*iii*) Travel		
(*iv*) Vehicle, fuel, maintenance		
(*v*) Raw material for training		
(*vi*) Stipend to trainees		
(*vii*) Recurring (telephone etc.)		
(*viii*) Secretarial (reporting etc.)		
(*ix*) Any others		

Few agencies require budgets to be submitted under recurring and non-recurring heads.

14. Justification of the budget (item wise)
15. Contribution from NGO
16. Contribution from community

Part-2 (Institutional Framework)

1. Name of the organization
2. Address with Phone No.
3. Legal Status
   (*i*) Societies Registration Act/any other: No. & Date
   (*ii*) Whether registered under FCRA: No. & Date
   (*iii*) Whether registered under 80G of the Income Tax Act.
4. Name and designation of the chief functionary
5. Brief bio-data of project functionaries
6. Present activities of the organization
7. Bank A/C No. and Bank
8. Any other specific information

Part-3 (Enclosures)

1. Registration certificate
   (*i*) Societies Registration Act/any other Act
   (*ii*) FCRA, if applying to international agencies
   (*iii*) 80G of the Income Tax Act, if receiving tax exempted donations
2. Certified bye-laws
3. Audited statement of accounts
4. Annual reports
5. Any other relevant document

STAKEHOLDER'S ANALYSIS

Stakeholders are individuals, groups, institutions important to the success of the project. Some obvious examples of stakeholders for a watershed development project are the women who benefit from the project and who have given up their previous time in organizing programmes, and the NGO who develop and implement the project. Their ownership of the project is central to its ultimate success. But who else is important to the project?

In most situation, a variety of stakeholders are likely to have some level of interest in or influence over a project, their expectations, or what resources they commit. Influence refers to the power that stakeholders have over a project such as their decision-making authority, or their ability to influence project activities or stakeholders in a positive or negative way.

An expanded list of stakeholders for the social development project includes the following:

- Beneficiaries
- People's elected representatives (Sarpanch, MLA and others)
- District level officers: District Collector, Chief Medical Officer for health project, Chief Development Officer for a development project and others.

- Funding agency or donors
- Project volunteers
- Other project partners or NGOs

WHY TO DO STAKEHOLDER ANALYSIS?

A stakeholder analysis helps implementing agency and partners think carefully about who is important to your project and their level of interest or influence. From this analysis we can decide how they should be involved in various stages of the project cycle. Stakeholder analysis helps you to do the following:

(*i*) Create and enhance right relationship among stakeholders that enable joint sponsorship and encourage cooperation within a project.

(*ii*) Engage stakeholders appropriately so that they can participate meaningfully at all stages. This requires finding flexible and appropriate ways to work together. Examples include using partner's extensive knowledge of an area to develop a concept paper or holding joint meetings to identify strategies and objectives. Meaningful anticipation increases ownership and a higher likelihood of success. Do not try to involve every stakeholders in all the activities, involve them as per their expertise.

(*iii*) Reveal assumptions and potential risks within the project. Understanding these risks and assumptions early allows you to design and manage your project in order to reduce these potential threats or concerns. For example, a project that encourage women to form SHGs and obtain credit on concessional rates might result in loss of business for local money lenders so they may actively discourage activities and obstacle in SHG management. High-quality stakeholder analysis would reveal this potential risk to project success.

Recognizing this possible threat, the project management team can take steps to ensure project success- perhaps by meeting with local money lenders and involving them in the project in some way or empowering women to cope up with these threats.

Project functionaries must be aware that stakeholder analysis involves sensitive information about power and influence, there may be some hidden and private interests. For example, some stakeholders may only be interested in the political benefits and high profile a project brings in their community. In other cases stakeholders may be most interested in the project's financial and material resources.

HOW TO DO STAKEHOLDER ANALYSIS?

Project management team perform the comprehensive stakeholder analysis depending upon needs. With experience the project staff will become skilled at putting together an analysis that is appropriately short. The project team may understate the following steps for stakeholder analysis.

Step-1: Identify the main purpose of analysis

Work with your design team members to define the purpose of the stakeholder analysis. One reason might be to make sure you have identified the most important stakeholders that ought to be involved in assessment and analysis activities and, later, in decision-making for project objectives and strategy. Another purpose might be that you want to study the relationship between stakeholders in order to minimize and threat to those relationships that a project might pose. In the earlier example, the relationship between women and the local money lenders might need attention during project design.

Step-2: Identify stakeholders for the project

After you establish the purpose, you can brainstorm a list of key stakeholders for your project at various levels: local, regional and national. Be as specific as possible: name individuals rather than referring to vague labels. In a new area and project, a more formal approach such as interviews with key informants may be useful. Once you finish brainstorming your list, use the following checklist to help ensure that all potential stakeholders will be identified:

Step-3: Assess stakeholder's interests, influence and relationship

After the identification of stakeholders, the next step is to list them in a table to further investigate their roles, relations, interests, influence, relative power and capacity to participate in the project, and resource requirements to involve stakeholders.

THE DIFFERENCE BETWEEN ASSESSMENT AND ANALYSIS

Assessment can be visualized as a broad, "horizontal" process where a wide number of issues are explored. It shows the breadth of the situation in a particular area. Assessment is more open-ended in terms of questions and issues to be studied. The issues, problems, and opportunities uncovered by an assessment are then prioritized in readiness for further analysis.

Analysis can be visualized as a deep, "vertical" process where prioritized issues are probed in depth. Analysis investigates the underlying causes and effects of specific problems or issues and involves reflection and examination.

UNDERSTANDING THE DIFFERENCE

A chief functionary of NGO reviews his staff through report to see 'how well he is doing in project work, rapport building, training and official work' is assessment. But if he discovers that he is doing poorly in field, so he meets with the field incharge to thoroughly explore the reasons and causes for this situation (this is analysis). The importance of accurate assessments cannot be overstated. An assessment that is incomplete, inaccurate or provides misleading data may lead to inappropriate emergency responses and costly delays.

Chapter 5

Project Design

Project design is the formal framework which establishes in advance the intent, the work plan, the means of ascertaining progress and the assumptions on which the project is based. The premise of design is simply that 'thinking a project through' will improve its chances of achieving something and that such effort needs to be invested before the project starts.

A good project document will answer the following questions:

1. **What** is the project expected to accomplish, if completed successfully and on time?
2. **Why** is the project being undertaken? What are the reasons for it? What is the project's underlying rationale?
3. **How** is the project to be implemented? What work is necessary in order to achieve?
4. **Who** is primarily responsible for the project implementation?
5. **Who** are the intended beneficiaries, the target group, who are expected to benefit from the project?
6. With in what period of **time** is the project to be carried out and the objective to be attained?
7. **What resources** are necessary to achieve the objective?
8. **What external factors** are necessary for project success?

A well-designed project is usually characterized by a project document which is logical and complete the format outlined in these guidelines provides the planner with a place to put each item of information, and permits verification that all the essential points have been covered.

The process usually begins with the identification of a problem, followed by formulation of objectives, which spell out the decision, action or change in a target group or area which is expected to occur as a direct result of the undertaking.

DESIGN COMPONENTS—OBJECTIVES, OUTPUTS, ACTIVITIES AND INPUTS

(*a*) Immediate objective expresses the particular effect which the project is expected to achieve, if completed successfully and on time. Example- by 2007, the Swaranajayanti Gram Swaraj Yojna of Ministry of Rural Development, Government of India will be capable of imparting training to 2 crore youths and develop them as Swarojgaris.

(*b*) Development objective describes the programming level beyond the immediate objective, the reason for the project and the impact toward which the project efforts are directed.

Normally, progress toward the development objective will depend on a number of related projects, each meeting its own immediate objective.

(*c*) Inputs are the resources, goods or services to be provided by the beneficiary country, by the International Labour Organization, UNDP or by other agency.

(*d*) Activities are the actions necessary to transform inputs into outputs. This category should, for example, answer "What will the project staff actually do?" Example- Training, conducting survey, organizing health camps.

(*e*) Outputs are the products that can reasonably be expected from good management of the inputs and activities. Example- Human resource, funds, research reports.

In this manner there is a "logical hierarchy" of "means-ends" or "cause and effect" relationship connecting the various levels; each level is necessary for advancement to the one following. The clarification of this relationship or linkage is the basic of the design concept.

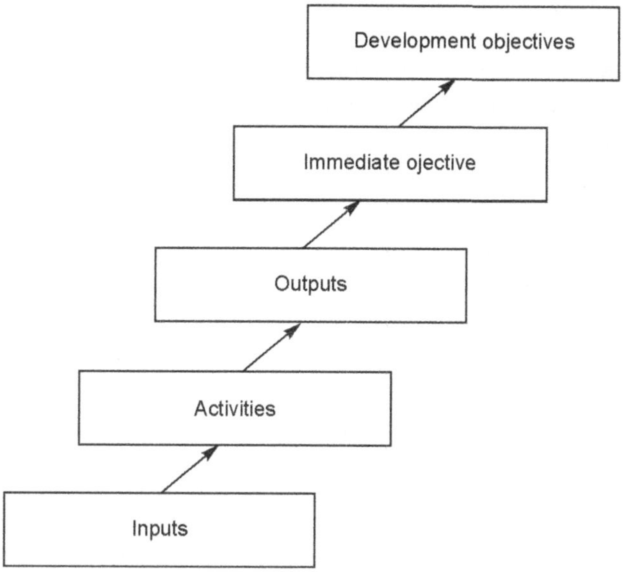

DESIGNING A PROJECT

A project document prepared along the following outline provides a solid foundation for subsequent implementation. It will also serve as a valid basis for evaluation, since prior management about what the project can and should be able to achieve is the only fair standard against which its results can be measured.

The order of designing a project document suggested below is somewhat arbitrary, and it is quite possible that the designer may prepare the various sections in a different order.

1. Background and Context

The first part of the project document will normally consist of a narrative statement, describing the problem or situation which has been observed and which seems to call for action by the donor. The statement of background and context, which should be brief, serves to set the stage, to "frame the problem" for which a solution is sought. It should also describe any past efforts, especially by the donor, to address the problem and the results. It should not describe or seek to justify the project being proposed. There will be ample opportunity to do that further on.

2. The Target Group (intended beneficiaries)

For whose benefit is the project being conducted? What population group or groups are expected to be better off, either directly or in the longer run, as a result of the project?

Many themes, such as livelihood, poverty alleviation, livestock management, etc. are conceived with broad target groups in mind. When it comes to designing individual projects, however, the specific target groups often are not clearly enough identified. As a result, it may be discovered at the end of the project that relatively few advantages, actually accrued to the intended beneficiaries. Therefore, sound project design requires the identification of the target group and of the measures which will be used to assess the project's impact on them. For example if state's leather industry is being rendered obsolete by technological change, and a project is designed to open up new employment opportunities for the redundant workers, the project designer needs to clearly identify the target group (by number, location, skills etc.). This will make it possible to construct the project so as to maximize the employment-certain effect on behalf of relundant leather workers, rather than creating a number of jobs only to discover later that they had been taken up by employed workers who wanted to change fields.

While descriptions such as "the rural poor" or "underemployed workers" may be appropriate for statements of policy etc., they are clearly inadequate for individual project documents. A precise description of the target group will help ensure that the benefits of a given project to indeed flow to them. If specific identification is not feasible, the composition of target group may be narrowed down according to one or more of the following criteria-

(*a*) geographical area, where a predominant proportion of the population belongs to the target group.

(*b*) Field of activity/farmers with a certain crop or income, landless labourers, artisans.

(*c*) Access – or lack of access – to certain services (health, education, etc.)

(*d*) Nutritional status, asset measures (landholding, shelter, livestock) etc.

In most cases, the direct recipient of the project assistance will not be identical to the target group, but rather a government or non-government agency or organization, with the expectation of improving the latter's ability to help the target group.

3. Objectives

What specific effect is the project expected to achieve within its lifetime and what impact is it intended to have on the target group?

Formulating the Objective

A project idea arises when a problem or situation is observed which seems to invite donor action. A rough formulation of the objective can often be arrived at by "inverting" the problem.

Problem: The government is unable to carry out manpower requirement studies without outside assistance. This impedes the development of suitable manpower policies. More than a third of the rural labour population is semi or underemployed.

Inversion: Government is able to carry out manpower requirement studies without assistance. With the assistance of experts, NGOs and others, effective policies are developed. As a result, fewer people are underemployed.

Means and Ends

An objective is a simple expression of desired ends. In formulating an objective, we should not confuse ends with means. Such terms as "to promote", "to coordinate", "to guide", etc. denote means rather than ends and should not be used when stating objectives, in order to avoid confusion between those project elements which are causes and those which are effects.

Not: 'to assist the government in developing a capability to carry out manpower studies'. But: The government's capability to carry out manpower studies will be established by 2007. At the objective level one is not so much interested in the approaches being used those are in any event described under "outputs" and "activities" as in the effect the project is expected to have. "To assist", etc. are means to those ends, not ends in themselves.

Multiple Objectives

As a general rule, the project should be formulated in terms of single development objectives often denote ambiguity or the presence of means, rather than ends.

When there are multiple objectives at either level, such objectives will either complement each other or compete with each other. Only under carefully controlled circumstances can two or more competing objectives peacefully co-exist.

Consider the example of a project intended to increase agricultural production while at the same time expanding rural employment. If a capital intensive strategy were applied, increased production might be achieved but rural employment opportunities might not improve, conversely. If a labour intensive strategy were used, employment opportunities might expand at the expense of production. In such a situation, the project planner would need to: (*a*) explicitly define the trade off relationship and identify optimum trade-off point; and (*b*) devise separate progress measures for both the production and the employment targets.

By contrast, complementary objectives can exist and will generally create fewer problems for the planner. For instance a project which combines both handicraft and literacy training, with neither the prerequisite of the other but taking place concurrently, might fit into this category.

However, two (or more) objectives are proposed at a single a closer examination may reveal that one is really a pre-requisite of the other. That is to say, there would be no change of achieving the second until the first has been achieved. It is not acceptable to compress two such steps into a one-sentence statement: certain words or phrases will often reveal that separate steps have been compressed into a single statement, as in the following examples:

- research institute able to carry out human resource studies in order to develop training policies;
- improve the income of the target group by increasing employment;
- create a better understanding of the effects of population pressure on land ownership through establishment of a research centre.

Such design elements must be started separately in logical order.

THE DEVELOPMENT OBJECTIVES

"What is the reason for the project, the broader sectoral objective towards which the efforts of the project are directed? Why is the project being undertaken?"

A single project cannot normally be expected to bring about the achievement of a development objective, given the enormity of the problems usually being addressed in relation to the resources available. Rather, a project can be expected to contribute toward the attainment of the development objective by removing basic constraints or contributing one or more necessary elements. Yet the identification of this higher level is important. It serves to check on the economic, political and social relevance of the immediate objective (and hence the project), the appropriateness of the project in the light of donor's area of competence, and conformity with existing plans.

If carried out to the extreme, the development objective could presumably be expressed in terms of "higher over-all quality of life" or something equally amorphous. However, a single project is unlikely to have a measurable impact on such a broad objective (although it might have an impact on some specific aspects, such as income, job satisfaction, unemployment, etc.).

Once the development objective has been formulated, verify that it:

(*a*) reflects the reason for the project, the programming level beyond the immediate objective;

(*b*) Comprises a single objective or a group of compatible objectives; it does not contain two or more objectives which are no different hierarchical levels;

(*c*) Is so stated that progress towards it can be verified.

THE IMMEDIATE OBJECTIVE

"What specific effect is the project to achieve within its lifetime, or directly thereafter? If the project is completed successfully, what improvements or changes are expected in the group, organization or area toward which the project is directed?"

The immediate objective is the situation that is expected to prevail at the end of the project. This level of the project design obviously is of crucial importance, since it will determine the magnitude of the inputs, activities and planned outputs, as well as the process or approach to be employed. The problem may be an obvious and pressing one: the best way for the donor to contribute in a significant way to its solution is seldom as obvious.

The statement of immediate objective should name the party to whom the project is directed, and state the effect which is sought by the "end of the project". For example, the trainees will be able to need the production norms by next year.

Once the immediate objective has been formulated, verify that-

(*a*) the statement says what effect will have been achieved if the project is completed successfully and on schedule;

(*b*) the project is stated in terms of a single immediate objective, not a collection of sequentially linked targets; alternatively, if the project has two or more objectives, their interrelation, trade-offs, etc. are clearly identified;

(*c*) the immediate objective is stated in terms of ends, not of means;

(*d*) there is a reasonable expectation that the achievement of immediate objective will made meaningful contribution towards the attainment of the development objective; and

(*e*) the direct recipient of project assistance(and, if different, the project's ultimate target group) has been clearly identified by this point.

INDICATORS

What evidence, measures or indicators will demonstrate that the project's immediate objective has been achieved? What are the observable facts which will provide evidence of progress towards the development objective?

To put it another way, how will the project designer, or anyone else, know whether the project is effective and is having the desired impact on the target group?

Indicators represent a logical extension of the previous steps. The objectives are expressions of the project's aim: the indicators are tools to further clarify and more preciously define the objectives and the desired impact upon the intended beneficiaries. This is necessary because only rarely will a project objective, even when formulated as described above, be free of terms which are open to personal interpretation; worlds such as "improved", "made viable", "enhanced" etc. for example, all call for subjective judgment on the part of the reader.

In the past, such changes often defied measurement not-because no changes occurred but because the planner had not made clearly what meaning was attached to such words, i.e. what specifically would constitute evidence of achievement. Indicators are meant to perform this role. Not only the objective statement itself, but almost any objective appearing in a statement of objective ("comprehensive", "viable" etc.) will have to be qualified by selected indicators to specify the expected changes. Evidence of such changes may not "prove", but will demonstrate that the objectives are being met. To say that the effect of the project cannot be measured is very close to admitting that the project is not expected to have a noticeable effect.

The most frequently cited example of an indicator is the clinical thermometer which records body temperature and serves as one possible measure of health or illness. Under certain circumstances, it can serve as an indicator of a patient's response to treatment. Direct indicators reflect changes sought by and directly attributable to the project. In the case of a rural health project, an indicator might read as follows: 2000 working days lost through T.B. in 2003, 1550 working days lost in 2004.

When a planner is confronted by conditions which are not directly quantifiable, or for which data are unavailable or cannot be gathered economically, he may need to resort to indirect (proxy) indicators.

Most development projects aim at bringing about changes of quality as well as changes of quantity. Project planners often believe that the qualitative changes they are seeking will be "non-quantifiable". True, qualities changes can be more difficult to measure, but suitable indicators can visually be found nevertheless. Teacher's report cards are a case in point, as are nutritional statistics or most measures relating to various aspects of basic needs satisfaction.

THE NEED FOR MULTIPLE INDICATORS

Several indicators are better than one. Seldom can any one indicator convey a comprehensive picture of change. Much as the independent evidence of unrelated witnesses is considered necessary to establish the facts, so several indicators, each reflecting a different fact of change, are needed to corroborate achievement.

For instance, in the case of a vocational training project established to alleviate persistent manpower shortage in the country, success can not be gauged simply on the basis of increases in the number of technicians trained per year. The degree of achievement could be confirmed by including indicators which reflect such factors as whether- (*a*) a significant percentage of graduates are actually placed in suitable positions; (*b*) the training meets the requirements of the employers; (*c*) There are adequate incentives for the teaching staff to limit turnover to an acceptable level (*d*) Future budgets for the school are sufficient to maintain the plant and replace worn-out equipment; (*e*) the incentives for graduates are such that the number and quality of applicants for admissions to school will remain sufficiently high to maintain the desired standards (*f*) Shortages of trained manpower reported by the employment exchanges progressively diminish; and (*g*) production delays attributed by the industry association to manpower deficiencies decline. These measures, taken together, would clearly be more likely to reflect the achievement of the project objective than a mere counting of the number of graduates.

SELECTING INDICATORS

Several factors need to be kept in mind when selecting indicators. They should be:

(*a*) **Specific:** Indicators should be specific in terms of magnitude and time. Terms such as "an increased number" are of little value as a part of an indicator since it doesn't specify what sort of increase is called for. After all the planner might have in mind a change from 100 to 110 or a change from 100 to 400. Furthermore when an increase to a specific number is called for say, 10 training centres in operation by 2005 – it is necessary to indicate how many such offices exist at the beginning of the project.

(*b*) **Independent:** Each development and immediate objective must have its own set of indicators. Since development and immediate objectives will be different, and each indicator is expected to reflect evidence of an achievement, it follows that the same indicator cannot normally be used for more than one objective.

(*c*) **Factual:** Each indicator should refer to fact rather than objective impression. It should have the same meaning to a project advocate and an informed sceptic.

(*d*) **Valid:** The indicators taken together should reflect the effect of the project rather than the effect of external factors.

(*e*) **Based on obtainable data:** Indicators should draw upon data that are readily available or that will be collected as a part of the project administration.

SOURCE(S) OF INDICATOR DATA

The availability of indicator data, especially on the immediate objective, is of paramount importance. Immediate objective indicators for which data are not readily obtainable or for which no specific collection arrangements are made as part of the implementation process, usually are of little value. As a matter of fact, experience has shown that data which are to be collected exclusively for the purpose of measuring progress somehow often do not get collected.

As part of the indicator section, explain how, when and where the data for each of the indicators are to be obtained. It is the responsibility of the designer to verify that the required data can in fact be made available when needed, or that arrangements for the collection of the necessary data are made part of the project design.

Once the indicators have been selected and the data sources identified, make the following checks, at the development objective level, verify that:

(*a*) The indicators selected are such that, if fulfilled, progress will have been made towards the attainment of the development objectives;

(*b*) the indicators are verifiable and specific in terms of target group, quantity, quality and time;

(*c*) the indicators are not only restatement of the outputs;

(*d*) the objective (as reflected by the indicators) can be achieved in the proposed time span, given the outputs;

(*e*) each indicator is traceable to an output or output assumption. In the event, this linkage is not apparent, it is explained in the project document;

(*f*) the document makes it clear when, where and how the indicator data will be obtained.

OUTPUTS

"What kind and how many of outputs will need to be produced with the inputs provided and activities undertaken in order that the immediate objective might be achieved?" Outputs are the products of completed activities. As such outputs differ substantially from the objective, which is the effect of the project hopes to achieve. As a rule of thumb, if the production or realization of certain elements is under normal circumstances largely within the power of project management, and provided that the requested funds, personnel or facilities are made available, it is in all probability is an output and not an objective.

Many planners also find it difficult to distinguish between outputs and activities; the following examples of outputs may help clarify the difference:

'Guidelines on equipment selection prepared' not 'guidelines on equipment selection being prepared'.

'20 persons trained in carpet weaving' not '20 persons being trained in carpet weaving'.

Note that the outputs result from the completed actions of the project team.

Many outputs may need to be produced well before the end of the project; in those instances, give the scheduled completion dates. If certain outputs are to be produced over the entire period of the project as in the case of a continuous fellowship programme, state how many are to be produced at the end of year 1, year 2, etc.

State the outputs, then verify that:

(*a*) Outputs are so stated that their realization can be verified, in terms of quantity and time;

(*b*) Outputs are stated as the result of activities rather than as activities proper;

(*c*) All key inputs necessary for achieving the immediate objective are listed;

(*d*) each output can be traced upward to the immediate objective level.

ACTIVITIES

"What activities need to be undertaken in order to produce the desired outputs?" These are the actions, the research, the tasks to be carried out by the project staff. Activities usually describe what project management does, the 'means' by which 'inputs' are transformed into 'outputs'. For each output, then, there will normally be one or more activities.

State the activities; then verify that:

(*a*) Activities are so stated that their implementation can be verified, in terms of quantity and time;

(*b*) Activities are stated in terms of actions being undertaken rather than as completed outputs;

(*c*) All key activities necessary for achieving the outputs are listed;

(*d*) There are no activities listed whose effects can not be traced upward to the output level.

Most projects require a work plan or detailed implementation schedule. Whenever such a document is prepared during the design stage, it can be used in place of this list of activities does not replace a work plan or implementation schedule.

INPUTS

"What money, personnel, materials, services, etc. are to be provided by the donor, funding agency and/or the government? Major inputs by all key parties should be identified. They should convey a realistic picture of what is to be provided by the donor, government.

Inputs should normally be listed by source (funding agency, recipient country) and other donors and should show, as appropriate:

- Type (experts, equipment, fellowships, etc.)
- Number or amount
- Length or duration of assignment
- Cost
- Qualification or field of specialization.
- Date by which to be provided (not as soon as possible)
- Try to fix a realistic data
- Purpose for which provided.

The listing of inputs should include all personnel resources. For the Chief Project Officer and other positions, a complete job description is often required as part of the project document, but as a minimum, the project document should contain a short statement of basic qualifications and functions for each position.

If the type of expertise required is not fully known at the time the project document is prepared, give whatever information is available and indicate on what basis the personnel inputs have been computed.

Whenever there is a sizeable equipment component or a subcontracting component for equipment, supplies and related services under negotiation, and in all cases where the total amount is more. However, all inputs which are essential to an understanding of the project should be itemized, e.g.-

- 3 motorcycles for weekly visits to social marketing centres, including operating expenditure over the length of the project: 1,50,000
- Printing charges (12th month of the project) for publication of manual: 12,000

List the key inputs; then check that inputs are stated in terms which can be traced to activities rather than passive resources.

INSTITUTIONAL FRAMEWORK

"What will be the institutional framework of the project in the recipient organization and how will it contribute to the successful implementation of the project?"

(*a*) provide a resume of pertinent information regarding the organizations's physical location, purposes, programmes, physical, financial and staff resources, as well as its place within the overall government machinery;

(*b*) identify and describe other agencies or organizations or projects which will have indirect role in the implementation of the project and explain the nature and significance of their relationship to the project;

(*c*) give the location of the project's headquarter and, where relevant, describe the geographic area within which the project will operate and the reasons for its selection;

(*d*) explain the arrangements that will be made for achieving the necessary, coordination among and between the agencies/projects/areas concerned;

(*e*) provide where the establishment of a coordinating body for the project is envisioned, details about its location, structure, membership, functions and modalities of operation.

PRIOR OBLIGATIONS AND PRE-REQUISITES

"What prior obligations and pre-requisites are necessary for the successful implementation of the project?"

The description should specify the actions – and only those actions – which would have to be undertaken by the government on the one hand, and by the donor on the other, prior to carrying out project activities, and indicate the dates by which they will have to be completed.

The description should normally be in two parts. The first part, captioned 'prior obligations', should list those actions whose fulfillment is necessary for efficient and effective project implementation, but is not a condition for donor assistance.

The description of prior obligations and/or pre-requisites should in be particular cover:

(*a*) legislative and other actions concerned with the establishment of the institutional framework of the project;

(*b*) budgetary or other actions concerned with the mobilization and delivery of government inputs in the required quantities and of the required quality on a timely basis;

(*c*) selection, preparation and release of national staff who need advanced education or training under fellowship arrangements prior to carrying out project activities;

(*d*) the provision of documents, statistics, and other information required for the project.

Assumptions

"What events, conditions or decisions outside the control of the project are necessary for the success of the project?"

External factors largely outside the control of project management, but important to the success of the project, should be stated in the form of assumptions, e.g. qualified volunteers available in sufficient numbers. In most instances, it would still be necessary to add the reasons which lead the planner to believe that the assumption will materialize.

Why state assumptions? Why call attention to uncertainties inherent in the project? Primarily because project may stand or fall on the basis of such external factors. The planner can reduce the uncertainty in which the project will operate (and establish the bounds of managerial responsibility) by specifying the situations which must be 'taken as given' if the project is to achieve its objectives, but over which the participants (donor, government) have little or no control. Furthermore, stating such assumptions doesn't imply that the project's design is effective, only that the designer is being realistic. A single project is only one of many forces at play, and usually a relatively small one at that uncertainties about at every level of the project: the project components are by themselves unlikely to bring about progress from each design level to the next. These factors are necessary but only with the addition of the assumptions are the conditions established which are both necessary and sufficient for progress to the next level, for instance, the project may be intended to complement a programme of the government, of another UN agency, or of a bilateral donor or other donor. The very fact of stating such expectations concerning 'third parties' will start the project off on a sound and more realistic foundation.

The assumptions identified in the project document should be:

(i) **Well founded:** After stating each assumption, the planner may wish to add why the assumption has a good chance of materializing, e.g. legislation to reduce import duty on raw material for handloom industry by 25% will pass by 1 January. The Minister of Commerce, Minister of Labour have announced their support, the trade union has made an official representation, and a parliamentary drafting committee has been established.

This suggests that some checking is often required before an assumption can be stated. For example, high chronic underemployment in an area where a rural labour intensive road project is planned does not necessarily mean that sufficient manpower will always be available; it could turn out that key project phases requiring peak manpower levels coincide with the harvesting or marriage season.

(ii) **Precise:** The assumptions should be stated in operational terms rather than nebulous hopes. Thus: not "Researchers will have access to all necessary data" but "The project's data cell will provide the necessary statistical data by 1 January."

Stating assumptions in this manner may also serve to alert the project's management to opportunities that may arise to make recommendations or exert influence, when appropriate, in order to increase the probability of an assumption materializing.

(iii) **Highly probable:** This point is critical. A project based on a set of assumptions which are unlikely to materialize is in trouble before it starts. Obviously some assumptions may be more important than others, ranging from the highly desirable to the absolutely indispensable. It is quite unlikely that a project which is based on several essential assumptions, each of which has only a limited chance of being realized, will be successful.

Note: under assumptions do not list (a) prior obligations and pre requisites or (b) inputs to be provided by one of the partners to the project; these are not things over which the partners to the project have no control.

It should never be assumed that the target group wants the project. Reasonable efforts should always be made to confirm this beforehand. This is not to suggest that the target group is bound to accept the eventual recommendations or findings of the project, but merely that the target group or their spokesmen or people's elected representatives agree that the project should take place. If such an assumption were made and turned out to be untrue, the potential contribution of the project would likely be nil.

A. Assumptions (Immediate objective to development objective)

What events, conditions or decisions outside the control of the project are necessary so that the achievement of the immediate objective will contribute to the attainment of the development objective?

B. Assumptions (outputs to immediate objective)

List the assumptions necessary so that the immediate objective will be achieved once the outputs have been produced.

C. Assumptions (activities to outputs)

List the assumptions, in addition to the activities listed which are necessary for the production of the outputs.

D. Assumptions (inputs to activities)

List the assumptions necessary in order for the activities to be undertaken once the inputs are available. Once the assumptions have been listed, verify that:

(*a*) Planned performance, at each level, together with the assumptions, create the necessary and sufficient conditions for progress to the next level;

(*b*) Each assumption has a strong probability of materializing;

(*c*) Whenever possible, assumptions are stated in operational terms so that project management can recommend or inspire action by others to increase the probability of an assumption materializing.

PROJECT RATIONALE

While designing a project proposal it is optional to formulate project rationale. At this point, in the project document, the planner may wish to explain the reasons for recommending a particular approach or strategy. He may wish to discuss why, under the circumstances, the proposed solution is considered more timely or acceptable than some obvious alternatives. The planner may wish to add information essential to an understanding of the project, or to develop any aspect of the previous steps which requires further amplification. He may wish to discuss why it is the organization that should be conducting this project, or describe how the project fits into a unified, integrated, coordinated or multi-disciplinary approach.

This section is optional; it may be used, however, if the balance of the project document does not adequately convey the reasoning underlying the recommended approach.

PROJECT DOCUMENT OUTLINE

The inter-relation of the various design components can be seen at a glance in the Project Document Outline (Form-1). Use of this form is optional but can be helpful in organizing various design components and in putting them into their perspective, thereby making it easier to prepare the document narrative.

The information presented in the outline must obviously be limited to key aspects in summary form. For example, for a human resource input, the following entry might appear:

Training specialist to develop curriculum (by Feb. 20): Rs.80,000

The outline (Form-1) showing the questions appropriate to each section appears overleaf, followed by a completed outline for a typical project of International Labour Organization (ILO).

PROJECT DOCUMENT OUTLINE

Form-1

Project Title: Country: Length:

Narrrative Summary	*Objective Verifiable Indicators*	*Important Assumptions*
1. Development or Higher-Level Objective: What is the reason for the project, the broader sectoral objective towards which the efforts of the project or programme are directed? Why is the project being undertaken? Who are the intended beneficiaries? What impact is being sought?	1.1 Indicators of Project Impact: What are the means of verifying the accomplishment of the development (or higher-level) objective? How will project management, or anyone else, know that the project is making the hoped – for contribution towards the achievement of the objective at this level?	
2. Immediate Objective: What specific effect is the project to achieve within its lifetime, i.e., if the project is completed successfully, what improvements or changes could be expected in the group, organization or areas towards which the project is directed?	2.1 Indicators of Objective Achievement (End of Project Status): What evidence, measures or indications will confirm that the project's immediate objective is being or has been achieved? What are the objectively verifiable conditions or situations which are expected to exist if the project achieves its immediate objective?	2.2 Immediate to Development or Higher-Level Objective: What are the events, conditions or decisions outside the control of the project which must prevail in order that the achievement of the immediate objective may contribute to the attainment of the Development or Higher-Level Objective?

(Contd...)

3. Outputs: What outputs (kind and number) will need to be produced (with the inputs provided and activities undertaken) in order for the immediate objective to be achieved?	3.1 Outputs to immediate objective: What are the events, conditions or decisions outside the control of project management which, together with the project outputs, are necessary for the achievement of the immediate objective?
4. Activities: What activities need to be undertaken by the project team in order to produce the desired outputs?	4.1 Activities to outputs: What are the events, conditions or decisions outside the control of project management which, together with the project activities, are necessary for the production of the outputs?
5. Inputs: What goods and services (personnel, equipment, training, etc.) are to be provided by the (*a*) government, (*b*) funding agency, or (*c*) other donors, to permit undertaking the necessary activities which in turn are expected to produce the scheduled outputs?	5.1 Inputs to Activities: What are the events, conditions or decisions outside the control of the project management which are necessary in order for the activities to be undertaken once the inputs are available?

REPORTING AND MONITORING SCHEDULES AND EVALUATION PLAN

Reporting

List the various reports (financial, progress and terminal) which the project management is required to submit during and at the completion of the project; alternatively, state where the relevant instructions are to be found. Since these requirements vary widely, depending on the source of funding. If appropriate, the staff time and other costs of preparing these reports should be provided for in the project itself.

Monitoring

To the extent known at the outset, identify any special monitoring requirements (e.g. technical reviews) to be met during the life of the project.

Evaluation

Every project document should include an evaluation plan containing the following information:

(a) Frequency and timing

The following represents the minimum schedule for evaluations of technical cooperation projects:

- For projects under 18 month's duration, on completion of the project;
- For projects of 18-30 month's duration, near the mid-point of implementation and also upon completion.
- For projects in excess of 30 months, every 12 months and also upon completion.

More frequent evaluations may be necessary under certain circumstance (for example in the case of a pilot due for early replication, need to make advance decision on extension, change of circumstances surrounding the project non-realization of key assumptions, etc.) and can of course be scheduled accordingly.

The evaluation report should take account of existing reporting and monitoring requirements and key decision points in order to avoid duplication of effort and to allow one exercise to contribute to the other. An evaluation carried out before some key funding decision, a tripartite monitoring review, a programme review or the visit of a technical mission will be more meaningful than one which takes place after such events.

(b) Evaluation participants

The composition of the group depends on the type of project, setting, individual functions, staff capabilities, etc. The following guidelines are proposed for consideration:

Minimum participation

- Project management team;
- Representative of government department directly concerned with the project,
- Representative of the funding agency,
- Technical expert/specialist (including activists, journalists, academician or researcher).

Suggested additional participants

- People's elected representatives of the local areas, representative of the target group.

(c) Parties responsible for the collection of data

Required for the evaluation, including any outside assistance or funding needed.

(d) Orientation and training required

Project functionaries who will normally have the primary responsibility for conducting evaluations, should be familiar with the concept when the time comes for evaluation. The same may not be true of the other participants in the evaluation such as government officials, outside contractors, or employer and people's representatives. If pre-evaluation training is judged desirable, estimate of costs and timing should be included.

Note: The over-all evaluation plan, i.e., the scope, frequency and required resources, must remain appropriate to the size, cost, importance and complexity of the project. A sample evaluation plan for a 36 month's project is shown below:

Sample Evaluation Plan

(a) Frequency and timing

The project is to be the subject of an evaluation at the end of year-1, year-2 and at the end of the project. In the event, consideration is given to extending the project beyond the original 3 year period, an evaluation will be conducted before such a decision is to be reached.

(b) Evaluation participants

It is intended that the following may participate:

- Representative of the labour department,
- Representative of DRDA
- Representative of funding agency.
- Chairman/secretary of the implementing agency.

Also to be invited:

- Advisor of the concerned project.
- People's elected representative of the panchayat/block/district.

(c) Parties responsible for the collection of data

Project management will have primary responsibility for the collection of data necessary for the evaluation of the project.

(d) Orientation and training required

The project management team has received adequate training in the application of the evaluation methodology. If required, additional training programme will be organized for the capacity building of the staff.

Design Review

Before finalizing the design, make sure that the following factors have been covered to your satisfaction:

(*a*) The inputs, activities, outputs and immediate objective, together with the assumptions on each level, will create the necessary and sufficient conditions to bring about progress to the next level.

(*b*) The 'logic of the project' is sound: if the requested inputs are provided, the proposed activities are undertaken, the outputs are produced, and the assumptions prevail, there is likely to be observable progress toward the objective, as reflected by the indicators. The project makes sense.

(*c*) The scale of the project is large enough to have some impact on the problem described.

(*d*) Lessons learned in previous projects in the same technical and/or geographical area have been taken into account.

(*e*) The project document shows how the project is related to national or regional development priorities.

(*f*) The target group is identified.

(*g*) If the project is a 'first phase', the document provides some information on the 'second phase'.

(*h*) Withdrawal of donor on the completion of the project will not place unrealistic strain on the recipient organization.

(*i*) If this is a 'pilot project', the cost and feasibility of eventual replication have been taken into consideration.

(*j*) The document makes clear why the implementing organization and donor should be conducting the project.

(*k*) Adequate provision (source, cost, time) has been made for the collection of necessary baseline and performance (evaluation) data. The cost and effort required to collect these data are reasonable.

1. AN OVERVIEW OF LINKING PROJECT DESIGN, ANNUAL PLANNING AND MONITORING & EVALUATION (M & E)

When you 'manage for impact', project design, annual planning and M & E become linked process. Your starting point for implementation is the initial project design as outlined in the project appraisal report. But design is an ongoing process for the life of the project. Continually adapting the project strategy in response to new understanding and to changing contexts is key in maximizing impact on rural poverty. So, good project design is as important for managers and M & E staff as for the initial design team.

Key aspects of a project's design are built into the project loan/grant agreement. Changing these can be difficult and time consuming. Thus it is critical that the initial design be as high quality as possible. In addition, the initial design team must build in flexibility to allow changes at project start-up when the design is revised.

1.1. Project design as an ongoing process

Why is change to the project design necessary? First, many projects start up to several years after initial design, during which the context will have changed. The project cycle includes many steps that lead to start-up, each of which takes time. Second, the initial design of supported projects is undertaken with limited time and resources. Many of the implementing partners will not have been identified and so there will have been limited participation in the process. This means that a comprehensive participatory process of reviewing and, where necessary, improving project design is critical at start-up. After start-up, the two main opportunities for improving the project design are: (1) on an annual basis as part of the annual progress review and planning process and (2) during the mid-term review (MTR). Table 1 lists the design and adaptation tasks during the project's lifetime, showing how (re-) design is ongoing.

Table 1: Design and adaptation tasks at key moments during the project lifetime

Moment in Project Life	*Design Tasks*
Initial design phase	• Access feasibility, scope and rationale of project. • Determine the goal objectives. • Outline main project outputs and key activities. • Outline project implementation process and structures. • Outline the M & E system. • Develop the budget and specify staffing levels.
Start-up phase	• Develop understanding of project goals and objectives with key stakeholders. • Review and revise the initial design.

(*Contd...*)

	• Design and plan work in sufficient detail to allow for implementation. • Develop a detailed operational M & E system.
Annual review of the work plan and budget	• Check if the outputs, purpose-level objectives and goal remain relevant; adjust. • Decide what activities and tasks are necessary to deliver outputs.
Supervision (recurrent)	• Discuss overall progress of the project. • Decide on changes that should be made in the annual work plan. • Assess any potential changes in the overall design that require loan agreement negotiations.
End of the early implementation phase	• Review overall project strategy in light of early implementation experience. • Develop recommendations for the work plan in the next phase. • Negotiate any significant changes to project design for the next phase.
Mid-term review (or reviews between phases if the project has a flexible lending mechanism)	• Review achievement of outputs and progress towards the purpose(s) and goal. • Assess appropriateness of the overall strategy. • Redesign the project as necessary.
Beginning of the phase-out period	• Identify the priorities of final activities in order to maximize impact. • Review and adjust strategies with a view to sustained impact.

1.2 Good practices for project design

There are six good practices in any design process of a development intervention. They are critical during formulation and start-up and when any revision of the project is undertaken, such as during annual and mid-term reviews.

1. Involve all relevant stakeholders in participatory processes of project design.
2. Undertake a thorough situation analysis, together with primary stakeholders, to learn as much as possible about the project context as a basis for designing a project strategy and implementation processes that are relevant.
3. Develop a logical and feasible project strategy that clearly expresses what will be achieved (goal and purposes) and how it will be achieved (outputs and activities).
4. Agree and focus on cross-cutting issues of poverty, gender and participation.

5. Plan for long-term capacity development and sustainability to ensure that the project contributes to the empowerment and self-reliance of local people and institutions.
6. Build in opportunities and activities that support learning and enable adaptation of the project strategy during implementation.

1.3 Using the logical framework approach

International agencies have required that projects be designed using the Logical Framework Approach (LFA). This process was originally developed in the 1970s to improve the quality and clarity of project design. The LFA process is based on participation of key stakeholders, including primary stakeholders. The project design that results from the LFA process is summarized in a table that is referred to as the logical framework matrix, or logframe. While the LFA has become widely accepted as useful for project planning, it also has some clearly recognized problems. So the standard LFA planning process has been improved in different ways over the years. Flexible and critical use of the LFA means:

- Recognizing that development is not mechanical by building options and opportunities for adaptation into the design;
- Valuing outcomes (achievements between tangible outputs and long-term impacts) by making them explicit in the logframe;
- Avoiding over-simplification of large projects or programmes by using multiple purposes, a cascading logframe or a five-layer logframe;
- Including people's visions and aspirations and identifying opportunities during the planning rather than focusing only on problem analysis;
- Recognizing that quantifiable indicators and qualitative information, such as opinions and stories of change, are needed for M & E;
- Guarding against bureaucratic control by reporting more on outcomes, (interim) impacts and planned improvements – and less on activities and outputs;
- Avoiding token use of the logframe matrix by ensuring it represents the shared vision for the development intervention, by using it as a management tool and by keeping it updated;
- Tracking assumptions as part of M & E to help guide the project strategy.

Note that a project can be designed well in different ways – and that the LFA is only one of these ways. Also, using the LFA is certainly no guarantee of ending up with a good project design. You need to be both critical and creative to achieve a design process that is appropriate for the context.

1.4 Linking project design with the annual work plan and budget

The project logframe will show the main activities for the life of the project. Each year the implementers need to identify which activities are needed for the coming year and prepare a budget. The logframe is the basis for the annual work plan and budget (AWPB). For the logframe to be useful, it must be sufficiently detailed and, in particular, updated to reflect the current situation of the project. For example, the original logframe may have included outputs or even components that are no longer appropriate and have been dropped. How the project appraisal report is translated into operational plans varies enormously across projects, although all have annual plans. Some have an overall operational plan with milestones that look at key implementation over the project's lifetime, which can help translate the logframe into annual clusters of activity. Others have 'project implementation manuals' that detail operations. Some have two – or three – year operational plans, alongside annual plans.

1.5 Linking M & E to project design

Developing M & E starts long before start-up. Initial project design strongly influences the ease with which M & E is implemented later on through, for example:

- The relationships and commitment established with partners and local people, particularly the intended primary stakeholders;
- The logic and feasibility of the project strategy;
- The resources allocated to M & E (funding, time, expertise);
- The degree of inbuilt flexibility that allows M & E findings to have a steering function;
- Any operational details of M & E that might be established during initial design.

During project formulation, a broad M & E framework should be developed and included in the formulation and appraisal documents. This framework provides: (*a*) Sufficient detail to enable budgeting and allocation of technical expertise, (*b*) an overview of how M & E will be undertaken, and (*c*) some guidance for project staff about how M & E should be set up during start-up. The M & E framework complements the highly summarized M & E information that is the logframe. Much of what is developed for the M & E system during the initial project design phase will only be indicate of the final plan and will need to be revised and refined during start-up.

2. DESIGNING FOR LEARNING, EMPOWERMENT AND SUSTAINABILITY

Designing a good rural development project requires careful attention to the social processes and institutional development that will enable learning and the empowerment of primary stakeholders and lead to sustained benefits.

2.1 Involve stakeholders in project design processes

Projects without good stakeholder consultation are setting themselves up for failure. Those that do consult widely increase their chances of success. Involving stakeholders in project design is important specifically for:

- Inspiring them to identify, manage and control their own development aspirations, and so empower themselves;
- Ensuring the project goals and objectives will be relevant and, as a result, meet the real needs of the rural poor;
- Ensuring the project strategy is appropriate to local circumstances;
- Building the partnerships, ownership and commitment needed for effective implementation.

Local participation early on can also be cost-effective in the long run. If the investment hadn't been made up front, much money would have to have been spent later for one-way information campaigns before and during project implementation.

The first step in project design is to conduct an initial stakeholder analysis. This requires listing potential stakeholders (individuals, social groups and organizations), prioritizing who must be involved (and not everyone who it would be nice to involve) and agreeing with them on how they can best be involved. This is the basis for being able to understand their needs.

Stakeholder participation in design is not limited to working with local communities or valuing their views above others. The idea of a 'community' that one consults is quite simplistic and can cause problems. For example, if implementing partners or project staff consult a community, will all local voices be heard? Which ones will unintentionally be forgotten or ignored? Also, what is good for one community is not necessarily good for another or for its region. So which community will you listen to if they have differing opinions? Understanding differences within and between local communities means, listening and listening again – and working together. Only then can we gain insights into local relationships and interests. Some people think that illiteracy and geographic isolation of target groups makes participation impossible. But many examples show how including the poorest, most isolated and illiterate of groups is possible with some creativity and time. Good participatory processes involve sharing perspectives and negotiating differences. Stakeholders can be involved in many ways, including comprehensive participatory rural appraisal (PRA) processes, informal discussions and planning workshops. However, people's physical presence is not enough. Some very poorly designed projects have included many local people who did not participate freely. Ensuring high-quality participation is key and will require creating project structures that can respond to people's requests.

2.2 Plan for learning and adaptation during implementation

Any project will require many adjustments during its life. Do not overly detail a project strategy, as this hinders adjustments during implementation. Here are some ideas for a design team to build learning opportunities and change into the design-

- Design the process, as well as objectives, at the higher levels. Identify the forums and processes that will be used to involve stakeholders in project review and adaptation, and build in flexibility to respond to unplanned opportunities. Local communities had a strong sense of group action. When local youths saw what the project was beginning to develop, they started to participate voluntarily in certain aspects, lending a hand with seedling protection, community health and water supplies. The project was able to involve them in implementation and M & E, and so gained valuable support and informal feedback on the field situation.
- Focus on clear goals (impacts) and purposes (outcomes), rather than over-specifying activities and outputs. Project design teams commonly over-specify activities and spend time on the overall goal, then they fill the in-between steps with hastily formulated purpose (s) or outcomes. Yet these interim levels are the most important part of 'managing for impact' so require most of the attention. This approach can also have secondary benefits. Project management and the cooperating institution were given the authority to adjust the components and outputs in the design to respond to locally expressed targets. This more flexible design also increased the involvement and ownership of the project by the primary stakeholders.
- Be explicit about uncertainty. Instead of trying to force specificity, explain what you simply do not yet know, such as exactly how communities will want to administer local development funds. Explain what is unknown and how and when project management should be clear on the issues. This means suggested targets should be approximate. State quantitative targets as being approximate and describe how the project could revise them, if necessary. The logframe should be regarded as indicative, as it will need to be reworked by its stakeholders in the course of implementation.

- Build in mini-research phases at key moments. Not all issues of relevance to a project can be anticipated ahead of time. List as an activity and budget for 'focused studies' to answer questions about the project context that may arise. For example, if the project is testing a new kind of micro-credit scheme, then before this is expanded a focused and detailed interim evaluation is needed.
- Make it explicit that the project strategy and logframe matrix should be revised each year. Annual adjustments to the logframe are increasingly accepted and expected. A project design can indicate when and with whom this will take place.
- Make 'adaptive management' a key function in the terms of reference for senior management and partner contracts. When hiring managers and selecting partners, select those who can balance uncertainty with being clear about poverty reduction goals.
- Budget for experimentation and for the unexpected. If the project is testing a new approach, then the budget should reflect this and more money should be allocated to later years when there is more certainty about expanding the approach. Also leave a portion of the budget and staff time for activities that do not fit into established categories. In some companies that must innovate to survive, researchers can spend 10% of their time on activities of their own choosing. This allows them to respond to unexpected opportunities.

Chapter 6

Programme Design

Program design is very significant part of the rural project management. A good programme design leads to successful implementation and fruitful results for community. International development and relief agencies have offered consultancy services by consultancy organizations like DFID offered services of Price Water house Coopers in the design of the PACS programme. International Labour Organization had devised well structured programme design instructions. Based on these guidelines, a programme design is elaborated on the programme for the elimination and rehabilitation of child labour. Programme design differs from agency to agency, however, there are twelve steps in programme design. These are the logical steps which may be needed to follow in preparing good summary outlines for action programme-

STEP-1: PROBLEM ANALYSIS

Introduction

The first step is always the most important. Action programme aims to improve a bad situation, or find a solution to a problem. When you plan to undertake an action programme the first thing to do is to find out more information about the problem you wish to address. If your problem analysis is poor or wrong, so will be the design of action programme. Good information about the situation is also vital in assessing what impact your porgramme has had on the well being of working children. Good problem analysis should lead to good programme design and good evaluation.

1. What is problem analysis?

Problem analysis consists of answering three questions:

1.1 What is the nature and extent of the problem?

This means finding out about:

(*a*) **The nature of the problem.** What is the exact problem or situation which the children face? How does this situation affect them? What are their main needs? What are the factors behind the problem?

(*b*) **The extent of the child labour problem and distribution of those affected.** How many children are in this situation and where do they live? What is their age, sex, class and ethnic distribution?

(*c*) **The family and social context.** What are the children's cultural, social and economic characteristics? What is their family and community setting?

(*d*) **The wider socio-economic context that gives rise to the problem** e.g. problems of urbanization and a growing street children population; growing poverty due to problems of economic restructuring and external debt, etc.

1.2 Analysis of existing responses to the problem

Part of the purpose of problem analysis is to assess existing welfare and development measures that have an impact on the lives of the target group. This involves looking at:

(*a*) **Legislative and policy responses.** What laws (e.g. minimum age legislation) and policies affect these children and in what ways? How effective are they? Which measures have worked and which have not ? Why?

(*b*) **Programme response.** What programmes exist to address these problems and what approaches do they use? How efficient are they and what is their coverage? What has worked and what has not? Why?

(*c*) **The various actors.** Government agencies and NGOs and their programmes and capability.

1.3 Assessment of unmet needs

The aim of assessing existing response to working children's various needs is in part to identify the most effective approaches and also to highlight possible failures and problems of present services. This involves looking at:

(*a*) **Gaps between problems and responses.** What are the gaps between the problem and the programme responses to it? Which of these gaps are most important?

(*b*) **The changes over time.** What are the trends in the children's condition? How have the responses to their situation changed? Are the responses becoming more or less effective in addressing the children's problems?

(*c*) What is needed to reduce the gaps between problem and responses? What type of action programme would be most effective? What should be the criteria of success? What alternative approaches are there? What is already being done which is useful, and what else should be done?

2. How to conduct problem analysis

There are many ways of gathering information on working children. First you should look at what has already been published on the problem by government agencies, NGOs, the mass media, religious groups, etc. Then you should count all the people involved with the problem ,especially working children.

For each of these sources of information on the problem there are different methods of obtaining the information you need . There are three main methods of enquiry-Observation-Survey-Interviewing. The most effective results can be obtained by using a mixture of these techniques. Local university may be able to help you design your investigation and help train local interviewers.

The important thing is to take sufficient time to do a thorough analysis of the situation and problem. You need to look, listen and learn, especially from working children.

STEP-2: DECIDE ON YOUR STRATEGY

The Program Strategy must make clear what you want to do, for whom and with whom . We can distinguish two types of strategy for helping working children.

DIRECT SUPPORT is one type of approach and means the programme worked directly with children and their families, through the provision of services such as education and training, health care, protected work, etc., or direct support to governments through, for example, technical assistance in drafting a policy document. Many programmes, though, concern themselves with a second type of intervention called. INSTITUTIONAL DEVELOPMENT i.e. strengthening NGO or government organizations to deliver better services to children and their families. The intention is to improve their capability through, for example, training personnel in programme design and implementation, so that at a later stage they can deliver higher quality services to the target group.

Institutional development programmes have a multiplier effect i.e. more people will be reached. The multiplier effect can be very considerable from, for example, training in enforcement practices relating to child labour legislation, or through a training of the trainers programme. Often both approaches will be combined. For example a programme might work initially with a group of say 500 child workers providing them with a comprehensive range of services in the short term (i.e. direct support.) then it might move on to improve the capability of government through the development of child labour units to initiate and coordinate policies and programmes (i.e. national development).

With institutional development programmes, it is very important to distinguish between what the programme staff will do and what the institution will be capable of doing - training staff who leave, or who do not pass on their skills, or having experts take over and run an organization rather than develop its staff- leaves institutions worse off and is therefore self-defeating.

STEP-3: DECIDE ON WHO IS TO BENEFIT

One of the first things you want to know of an action programme is– who is to benefit? In child labour programmes, working children are naturally the TARGET GROUP or INTENDED BENEFICIARIES. Programmes should be aimed at meeting their needs.

It is important to define target groups precisely if the activities of the project are to be properly focussed and if we are to answer the obvious question: "Did the programme help those it was supposed to help?" Here it is important to avoid vague general descriptions such as "child labour". It is much better to give a precise size, location and social /economic/cultural characteristics of the target group.

Examples of target groups could include:

(*a*) Children employed in specific industries;

(*b*) Children working in the informal sector;

(*c*) Children engaged in street trade;

(*d*) Working children in agricultural setting;

(*e*) Children engaged in construction; and

(*f*) Children particularly at risk because their work is hide.

(*g*) Children working in hazardous industries.

In selecting the target group it is important to recognize certain biases-those in favour of boys in "visible" activities. Programme designers counter these biases by selecting target beneficiaries from the "invisible" sectors such as domestic and agricultural work, where girls often predominate, or where low income or caste groups are the subject of the worse excesses of child labour. Another bias that designers need to guard against is the "top-disown" approach which views working children and their families as passive. At this stage, wherever practicable, children themselves and the community in which they live should be consulted over the programme proposal. Put simply: Do they want the programme? Does it meet their needs? Is this the best possible strategy? By involving them at this preparatory stage you not only avoid some very serious design pitfalls, but you also increase the chances of success by developing a sense of ownership of the programme. Community participation is then an important feature of the design process.

STEP-4: CHOOSE YOUR PARTNERS

Reacting children at risk demands co-operation between a range of agencies, both public and private. Given the scale of the problem it makes little sense if agencies compete over scarce resources. Only a partnership at local, national and global levels can hope to effectively combat child labour. A very important aspect of the programme strategy is then choosing of partners with whom the programme will work. This is called the national framework.

Programmes should not be conceived in isolation, nor do they operate in a vacuum. How effective a programme is will depend crucially on the relationships it forges with its target beneficiaries and partners? At a practical level this will require effective coordination. If the programme is, for example government/NGO partnership, it will be important to clarify roles and responsibilities in advance-where are the lines of authority? What are the channels of communication/do people have clear job descriptions? If the programme is targeted at governments. Then it is important that various social ministers coordinate their efforts through, for instance, a child labour unit or similar mechanism.

STEP-5: SET YOUR OBJECTIVES

An objective is a simple expression of what you hope to achieve and can usually be arrived at by turning the problem on its head (or inverting it), as in the example below:

Example: Direct Support Action programme

Problem: There are 1,000 child workers under the age of fourteen currently working in factories in the carpet weaving industry .

Inversion into immediate objective: 1,000 child workers under the age of twelve currently working in factories in the carpet weaving industry will be removed from working and absorbed into full- time education.

These are two types of objectives:

1. The Development Objective

The development objective is ultimate aim of a programme. Why is it being undertaken? There is usually only one development objective in all child labour projects. This is the elimination of child labour. This is a long term goal, and will by definition, be beyond any one programmes scope and timescale . The keyword here is to contribute.

2. The Immediate Objective

The immediate objective is the situation that is expected to be present at the end of the programme .As a general rule immediate objectives should be kept to a minimum (from one to three). The keyword here is to achieve. In formulating the immediate objective the designer should precisely name who will directly benefit from the programme and state the effect, in the measurable terms, which is sought at the end. This will help to facilitate the evaluation of the action programme. In formulating the immediate objective it is helpful to refer to the strategy of the programme: is it an institutional development programme, direct support programme or combination of both? It is also important to be realistic. Avoid setting objectives that are beyond your resources. Poor formulation of immediate objectives is the single greatest cause of poor design and therefore of programme failure. Again, this is another reason for good problem analysis, as this help to clarify your objective . Here are some examples of formulated immediate objectives:

Example: Direct Support Programme

At the end of the programme 300 children under 14 years in the district Bhadohi will have been removed from hazardous industries and absorbed into an experimental non-formal education programme.

Example : Institutional Development Programme

At the end of the programme the Ministry of Labour will have established a child labour unit with the facility to formulate and co- ordinate government child labour policies, planning and programmes.

STEP-6: DECIDE ON WHAT YOUR PROGRAMME WILL PRODUCE

The products which result from the programme activities are called outputs. The keyword is to produce. Again, be precise. Examples are:

1. X number of school places provided;
2. X number of boys and girls provided with non -formal education;
3. X number provided with skill training;
4. X number of boys and girls benefitting from nutrition, health and other types of services, including protected work and shelter, etc;
5. X number of labour inspectors, government officials or NGO workers, including volunteers, trained;
6. This, or that, type of planning, coordinating structure established, e.g., Child labour unit.

In a typical institutional development programme outputs take the from of staff trained , reports produced, materials produced, as in the example below:

Example

Objective: To have strengthened the facility of the Ministry of Labour in the carpet industry.

Outputs

By the end of the programme fifty labour inspectors will have been trained in child labour matters; a manual for labour inspectors on child labour will have been produced;

Reports produced on the working conditions in factories using child labour in carpet industry.

STEP-7: DECIDE ON YOUR ACTIVITIES

Activities are the actions undertaken to produce the desired outputs i.e. what will be done, not the results themselves. Activities transform inputs of the programme into outputs. The keyword is to do. Producing one output usually requires that you undertake a number of activities. Giving an overview of activities helps to explain and justify the request for specific resources. It is important not to confuse activities with outputs, though they may look similar. In the case of institutional development projects, activities are undertaken for and with the direct recipients. In DS projects, activities are undertaken for and with the target group.

To produce the outputs set out in the above example the project will need to undertake a number of activities. It will:

- Organize five workshops for labour inspectors;
- Develop training materials and field test these in workshops;
- Commission a consultant, based at the local university, to investigate child labour in the unregulated sector. Other examples of action programme activities are:
- Developing a workman;
- Preparing training manuals;
- Carrying out surveys;
- Developing curricula and materials;
- Conducting advocacy campaigns;
- Conducting seminars and conferences.

A good way to set out your activities is through a work plan.

STEP-8: DEFINE WHAT YOU NEED

You will require many things to carry out your action programme. First you will require a variety of resources- funds, equipment, expertise, people, etc.- these are needed to carry out your activities and are called inputs. Again be precise and realistic. You need to be clear who will be responsible for providing what. Inputs should be specified by:

- Type
- Quantity
- Duration
- Cost

When you estimate the costs make sure you always list the inputs that your organization can provide in terms of staff, etc; and be clear about what you want from outside agencies or the donor. Do not ask for a lump sum to be spent for unclear purposes. Ask for concrete inputs.

Example

Bad Input: Rs.200,000 for equipments.

Good Inputs: Rs, 1,00,000 for a photocopier capable of running 300 copies per week.

There will be other needs which have to be satisfied before your action programme starts. These we call pre-conditions. There is the interest and co-operation of the target group. This should not be assumed. Beyond this, pre-condition could include the co-operation of the government, and the use of its resources to reach and deliver services to working children. Yet another example might be the establishment of a steering group to co-ordinate, monitor and help evaluate the action programme.

STEP-9: DECIDE HOW YOU WILL MONITOR AND EVALUATE

It is important to think right at the beginning about how and when the programme will provide reports on progress, and how it will be evaluated. In good design it is essential to state the reporting, monitoring and evaluation procedures. For example:

- When will progress report be prepared (e.g., every six or twelve months);
- When will the programme be evaluated (e.g., part way through, at the end; some time after the end of the project);
- How will the programme be evaluated (e.g., using internal and/or external people);
- Who will take part in the evaluation (e.g., programme staff, beneficiaries, external funding agencies).

STEP-10: PREPARE A PRELIMINARY BUDGET

Preliminary Budget

The calculation of the budget need to be based on the list of inputs needed to carry out the activities and on the prices and costs currently applicable in the project area. Give a budget estimate by year, in rupees, or US dollars as convenient. You should also quote the prevailing currency exchange rate to the US $.

The main budget heads will be:

- Personnel;
- Local travel if any;
- Training;
- Equipment;
- Raw material;
- Miscellaneous e.g., telephone, reporting costs etc.

STEP-11: WRITE A SUMMARY OUTLINE FOR ACTION PROGRAMME ON CHILD LABOUR

What needs to be included?

A Summary outline must be brief (suggested length about three pages plus a budget sheet). It consists of the following essential components:

- A clear precise title, indicating work to be done;
- An exact location for the programme activities;

- Background and justification, including a description of the identified problems, the programme's strategy to address the problems;
- The target groups including characteristics and size;
- A brief description of the executing institution and the main partners, also including monitoring and evaluation procedures to be adopted by the institution;
- Development and immediate objectives;
- Main outputs;
- Main activities;
- Major inputs and preconditions; and
- A preliminary budget estimate with justification.

STEP-12. MAKE A FINAL CHECK OF YOUR PROPOSAL

A final checklist – some useful hints

Having completed your summary outline for action programme on child labour you need to go over it to make sure that the proposal is complete and coherent and worth undertaking. This is the appraisal stage. Check in particular the linkages between the components, i.e., if the requested inputs are provided, the planned activities carried out and the outputs produced, is it likely that the stated immediate objectives will be achieved? You may find the following checklist helpful:

1. Background and context

Does this section reflect-

- The preparatory work on analysis of the child labour problems(s);
- The analysis of alternative strategies and the justification for following the one proposed;
- How the programme fits in with national priorities and strategies relating to child labour;
- How lessons learned in past child labour programmes have been taken into consideration.

2. Target groups/partners and strategy

- Has the target group been identified precisely enough so one can see later if they benefitted;
- Have you identified your partners and their capability;
- Have you clearly defined the strategy of the project-institutional development, direct support or both;
- In the case of an institutional development project, have the direct recipients been distinguished from the target group.

3. The development objective

- Has the immediate objective been formulated in such a way that there is a reasonable expectation that the project will make a contribution to it.

4. The immediate objective

Some tests to be applied:

- Is it really an objective rather than an activity or output.
- Does it reflect the strategy of the programme, institutional development or direct support.
- Are the objectives precise and measurable enough to be used as criteria for the success of the programme when it comes to evaluation.
- Are the objectives such that information about them will be available before and after the programme.

5. Outputs

- Do they properly reflect the main focus of the programme
- Are they necessary for the immediate objective
- Are they quantified and is it clear what will be produced by whom and when.

6. Activities

- In the case of institutional development is there a clear distinction between what the programme itself will do and what the institution concerned is expected to become capable of doing.
- Are they sufficient to produce the planned outputs.
- Has the timing been specified.

7. Inputs

- Are they all there, both local and national and perhaps international.
- Have you been realistic about timing.
- Have you been realistic about the required qualifications of key personnel.
- Are funds for reporting, monitoring and evaluation included in the budget.

8. Pre-conditions

- Are you clear about the pre-conditions for the action programme to start e.g. government support.

9. Monitoring and evaluation

- How will you monitor progress.
- Are you clear about the reports that will be needed.
- How will you evaluate the effects of your programme.

Chapter 7

Implementation

Implementation is a highly complex process and it involves relationship amongst several systems and variables. Fullan and Pomfret (1977) have done a thorough review of research on implementation and have suggested four major categories to be considered in this connection. The first category consists of characteristics of the innovation. They found two as the main important characteristics which are relevant for implementation. One is explicitness of the innovation, indicating various dimensions about the nature of the innovation (who is involved in sponsoring and accepting when the innovation is to be implemented and how). Low explicitness results in confusion in the user, lack of clarity and frustration, which leads to a degree of implementation. The second category which has been found to be important is the perceived complexity of the innovation. The more innovation is perceived as complex by the user for whom it is intended the lower is its implementation likely to be.

The second category relates to strategies and tactics. These refer to the methods employed to introduce and implement innovations. Implementation involves the process of re-socialization of key factors, and so to the strategic and tactics that support and facilitate this process are very relevant to implementation. They suggest four main strategies in this connection. These are: in-service training, resource support (provision of time, materials and other facilities needed for effective implementation), feedback mechanism (developing an interactive network to take corrective action for effective implementation), and participation.

The third category relates to characteristics of the adopting unit. They have identified four main characteristics relevant to implementation: adoption process (as a problem solving process), organizational climate of the adopting unit, environmental support provided to the adopting unit, and various demographic factors about which a large number of studies have been reported.

The last category significant for implementation relates to the characteristics of macro socio-political units including design issue, incentive system, evaluation and political complexity.

Implementation may be regarded as a process by which a set of predetermined activities is carried out in a planned manner, with a view to achieve certain established objectives. Emphasizing the importance of implementation, the late Prime Minister J.L. Nehru, once pointedly remarked, "We in the Planning Commission and other concerned have grown more experienced and more expert in planning. But the real question is not planning; but implementing the plans............. I fear we are no quite as expert at implementation as at planning."

APPROACHES

There are two approaches-

(*i*) **Traditional approach:** It is characterised by a mechanical view of planning and development in which implementation is simply a tool of the powerful (donors, planners, politicians). Employees are seen variously as cogs in a machine or troublesome but necessary raw materials. Project beneficiaries are seen as either clients (to be sold an idea) or employees (to be instructed).

(*ii*) On the other hand, the open approach attempts to make people important, thinking in terms of 'instigators' and 'actors' rather than planners and clients. In a development situation an approach is needed which encourages and foster decreasing dependence and increasing self-reliance and the open is suited to this.

Most of the activities of the NGOs are project based supported by national and international agencies, however, NGOs may adopt implementation strategies on their own accord.

1. Planning for Implementation

An implementation plan should specify what is to be done? Who is to do? When it is to be done? And how it is to be done? To begin with, a plan should be divided into a number of activities and for every activity implementation systems should be developed as per its peculiar requirement and characteristics.

(*i*) *Plan for primary work effort*:

It includes:

- Estimation of requirement of manpower, infrastructure, people's participation, identification of community leader.
- Arrangement for staff, finance etc.
- Allocation of funds, jobs responsibilities and cooperative intervention.
- Other decision making and administrative activities.

(*ii*) *Time plan*: The estimated time required for each activity assuming the availability of manpower decided as date, month, year as to when each work will begin and finish. Programme Evaluation and Review Techniques (PERT) and Critical Path Methods (CPM) could be used to be taken to match requirements with availability in each time period both in terms of quantum and pattern. Frankly review and utilize the result of feedback for improvement.

2. Developing Support for Implementation

The support for the implementation of a programme of change requires a great deal of support from several sources. The main support comes from administrative and managerial groups. Moulik (1979) has suggested four main elements in the implementation structure-

(*i*) The Central Organization (*ii*) Outside Intervenor Systems (OIS) (*iii*) Person who volunteer to work in such a system, the independent volunteer cadre in which a youth is offered to volunteer his services (*iv*) and the target group where implementation of a programme is being effectively done. Support from all four such groups or agencies would be necessary for effective implementation.

In India, planning structure is well knitted from Planning Commission at the centre, to Village Planning Committee at the village/grassroot level, but the implementation is left on the mercy of functionaries. Even in almost all the programmes NGOs have been involved at the grassroots level but these NGOs even don't find the support from all actors.

3. Participation

Now-a-days contribution from the community is a pre-requirement of an NGO to get support from funding agencies. The participation must be ensured by NGOs in all the stages of implementation. This may be done through P.R.A., formation of implementation/users groups at grass-root level.

(*i*) **Attention to the process:** Implementation is a difficult process which involves people working in teams for achieving some results. Enough attention needs to be given to the various processes of persons working with each other and developing collaborative relationships, increasing the capability of the user organizations of people to cope with problems as they arise, establishing norm of openness so that problems and difficulties can be discussed and solution worked out with effort, creativity for searching unconventional ways of dealing with problems, and self-reliance and attitude which may help people to work on their own rather than expect solutions from and depend on outside people or agencies. In the absence of full attention to such process aspects, implementation is likely to run into great difficulties. The more the attention, energy and time invested earlier in the life of the project in the process issues, the more time and energy would be available for effective and fast implementation later in the project.

(*ii*) **Developing feedback and evaluation system:** For effective implementation it is necessary to have effective systems of getting feedback on the progress of the project, its contribution to the problems, fidelity of its implementation (to what extent it continues the objectives and the design originally planned) and review mechanisms to consider various factors which contribute to the development as well as the problems faced by the project.

Norms of openness helps in making the feedback effective, such mechanisms of feedback and review also help the organizations and people to membership in project implementing agency, etc.

4. Input Resource Planning: It includes

(*i*) Identification of scarce input.

(*ii*) Determination of total requirement of each category of inputs.

(*iii*) Breaking the total requirement into period wise components in line with the time plan formulated.

(*iv*) Realistic forecasts of likely availability for each period and specification of assumptions underlies these forecasts.

(*v*) Comparison of requirement with availability for each period.

5. Project Organization

Both for the implementation plan as well as for executing the project, organization should be developed, responsibilities for various task clearly assigned filling key positions with adequately skilled and experienced persons on time is also important. It is also better to spell out the monitoring and management information systems to be used during implementation and to develop the necessary report formats.

6. Building Backward & Forward Linkages

This is necessary to complete the project in time and to derive full benefits from the interrelated projects e.g. training etc. Drawing electically on several sources of idea, Robert Chambers and his colleagues have developed a system for programming and controlling of implementation of projects. The backward and forward linkages should be chalked out in advance.

FACTORS AFFECTING IMPLEMENTATION

A number of technical, economic and other factors affect the implementation of a development programme. Knowledge about the nature, magnitude of the effect of each of these factors is necessary for development managers to be able to implement and manage the programme efficiently and effectively. Similarly knowledge is also necessary for development policy makers and planners of NGOs to formulate realistic policies and plans for development.

1. Technical Factor

A project format can accommodate diverse activities or endeavours. An enormous variety of development activities may usefully be cast in project form. From technical point of view, projects of NGOs may be as diverse as irrigation, livestock, development, health, education etc. Every project is aimed at producing some output which may be an asset, or a commodity, or a function by which inputs are transformed into outputs. Production function involved is technical in nature.

It is necessary for functionaries of NGOs to know the nature and form of the production process and the factors affecting it so as to be able to manipulate it to produce the desired results. Skilled and experienced technical staff with enthusiasm are essential for specifying the crucial technical factors involved in the implementation of a project.

2. Economic and Financial Factors

The economic factors affecting a project are relevant from the point of view of the society as a whole where as financial analysis takes the viewpoint of the individual participants.

Financial analysis reveals the need for investment, credit, stipend to trainees, honoraria etc. and other incentives for the successful implementation of the project. On the other hand, economic analysis allows us to decide whether labour and other inputs to be used in the project should be remunerated at market prices or at shadow prices.

3. Commercial Factors

The commercial factors affecting the implementation of a project include the arrangements for marketing the output produced by the project and arrangements for the supply of inputs and credit needed to build and operate the project.

On the output side a careful analysis of the proposed market for the project's production is essential to ensure that there will be an effective demand at remunerative prices. On the input side, appropriate arrangements must be made for the project participants to secure the supplies of raw material and infrastructure. Facilities of credit to farmers, artisans and trainees to purchase various tools, raw materials etc. should be made to ensure successful implementation of a project.

4. Socio-cultural Factors

The socio-cultural factors affecting the implementation of a project include the stratification of the project participants based on caste and religion, social customs and traditions, mores and taboos, distribution of project benefits among the clientele of the project, impact on environment and quality of life in general. Many projects have failed because they didn't meet the social objectives of their clientele. V.K.R.V. Rao has rightly attributed the failure of planning due to "its lack of cohesion with social factors and the impediments imposed by the social and cultural forces."

5. Political Factors

NGOs have faced many challenges in implementing their projects due to political outfits. Many NGOs, left the area, few fought with politicians and few compromised and accepted subordination. With the decentralization, people's elected representatives have been given due place in planning and implementation viz. selection of beneficiaries. Sometimes these NGOs act to satisfy their vested interests. So, NGOs have to keep political considerations in mind and act on people's participation.

6. Managerial Factor

Managerial skills are a necessary input for NGOs for the optimal use of resources, resource mobilization, information management, monitoring system, assessment of the needs of project participants. It is unfortunate with the NGOs, that most of NGOs have no professional development manager, for the very reason that support to NGOs is project based and expectations of these professional managers are greater.

7. People's Participation

The implementation of area specific development project is very difficult without the active and wide-spread participation of its clientele. Sometime community is project partner to NGOs and NGOs have become 'corporate partner' to funding agencies. Many factors may motivate people to participate in a project or refrain from participating. It is necessary to find out factors and design specific strategy to enlist their participation.

In few areas, NGOs have been successful in enlisting the support and participation of local community in the implementation of development projects. But that is more because of the charismatic personality of the project leader and less because of any institutional innovations that can be replicated in a large scale elsewhere. Rauanan Weitz has distilled some simple thumb rules for enlisting people's participation. These are:

(*i*) Create a human relationship.

(*ii*) Know the traditions and social customs of the project participants.

(*iii*) Introduce programme gradually and adapt them to the ability of the target population to enable it to absorb the change involved.

(*iv*) Get yourself a partner from amongst the local leaders.

(*v*) Encourage and promote development leadership among both the project employees and the local people.

8. Integration and Coordination

Many government and non-government agencies are undertaking development programmes at the grass-root, same time for the same area and same beneficiaries. It is essential that different development programmes under way in an area be integrated and coordinated for optimum results, otherwise it creates over lapping, duplication and wastage of scarce resources.

METHODS FOR EFFECTIVE IMPLEMENTATION

Project involves many activities, project functionaries should use methods for effective implementation to complete in time and budget.

Bar charts

First developed by Henry L. Gantt, it is sometimes referred as Gantt chart. Bar chart is a pictorial representation showing various activities involved in a project. The chart has two coordinate axes; one axis represents the activities and the other axis represents the time required for completion of the individual activities.

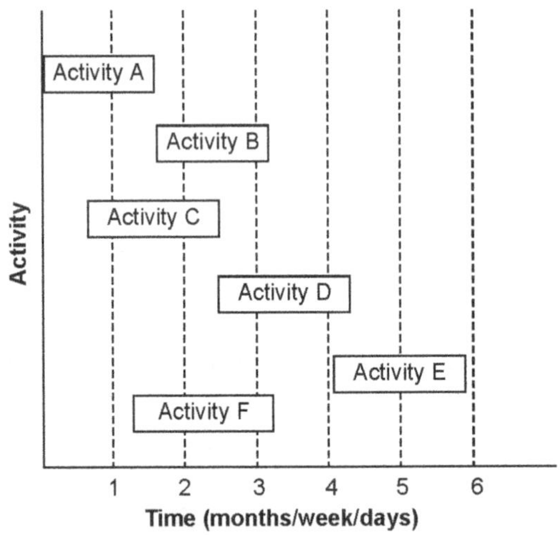

A typical bar chart

The axis represents activities, involved in a project, are drawn in the form of bars, and the length of the bar represents the time taken for the completion of each activity.

In the projects, there are some activities required to be taken up simultaneously, while some are required to be taken up only after completion of other activities and there may also some activities, which are independent.

Consider the example of construction of a training centre. The following are some of the activities involved in the construction of a training centre:

Activities	*Time Required*
Digging of foundation	3 Weeks
Pouring foundation concrete	1 Week
Construction of walls	10 Weeks
Construction of roof slab	3 Weeks
Land leveling	4 Weeks
Fixing of doors and windows	1 Week
Digging of well	2 Weeks
Plastering and finishing of walls	2 Weeks
Electrification	1 Week
Total	27 weeks

The above activities can be depicted in a bar chart after identifying their logical sequence. If water required for the construction work is not available at the project site, the activity 'digging of well' takes priority. Let us assume that water required for the construction work is not available at the project site and it is also not easy to procure water from outside. Under these circumstances consider the following two activities-

- Digging of foundation, and
- Digging of well.

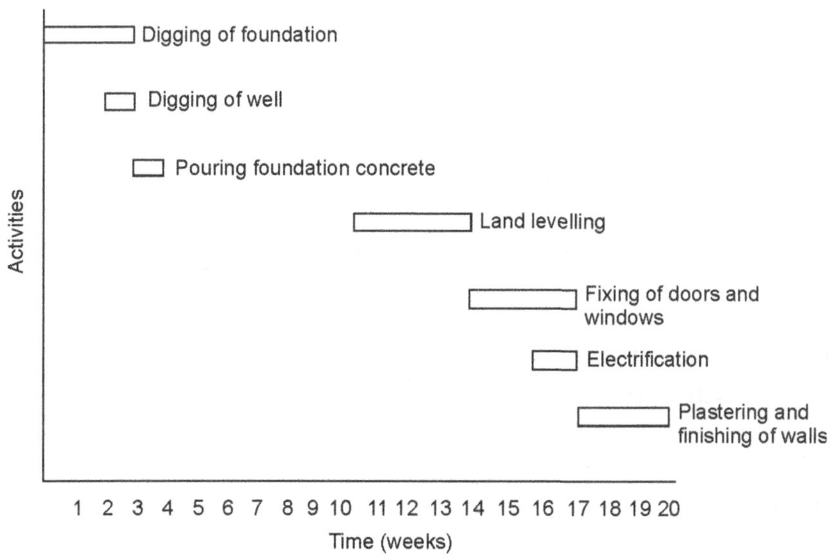

Fig. Bar chart showing construction of a training centre

Though digging of well seems to be the first activity that should be started since requirement of water is essential for the construction work, digging of foundation activity need not wait till the digging of well is completed. Water is required only for brick and concrete work and hence both the activities viz. digging of well and foundation can be done at the some time.

As we see from the bar chart, the total time required for the completion of the project is 20 weeks.

Network based scheduling

For a rural development project having large number of activities, the project scheduling becomes very complex. Network scheduling techniques can keep away from time over-run and cost over-run. These are:

Critical Path Method (CPM) and Programme Evaluation Review Technique (PERT). CPM was developed in the year 1957 by Morgan R. Walker of Du Pont and James E. Kelly of Ramington Rand.

Activity: An activity is an identifiable job that has a beginning and an end. An activity consumes resources like time, human resource, money and material like organizing health camps in villages, farmers training may be called activity. An activity is represented by straight arrow with circles at both the end. The direction of the arrow indicates the direction of flow of the project. The length of the arrow doesn't represent duration of activity. Circle in the beginning of arrow represents the starting point of activity, while circle placed at end of the arrow represents the finishing point of activity.

The symbol of the activity and its duration is represented as under:

Activity	*Symbol*	*Activity Time*	*Symbolic Representation*
Farmers training	A	6 days	$\bullet\overset{A}{\underset{6}{\text{——}}}\bullet$
SHG training	B	5 days	$\bullet\overset{B}{\underset{5}{\text{——}}}\bullet$

Event: An event (also called as 'node') is the beginning or end of an activity. It represents a specific point in time through circle. An event does not consume resource.

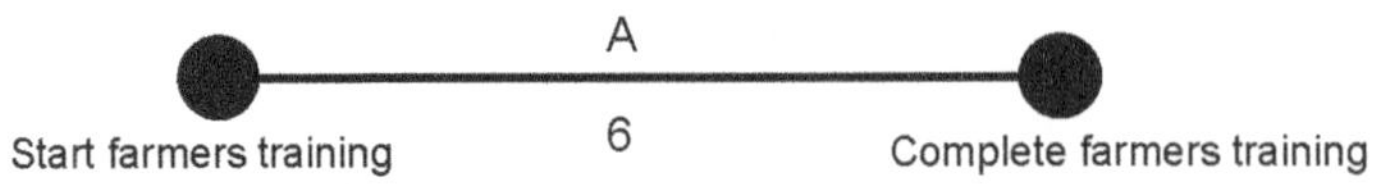

Relationship among activities: Activities of the project are interrelated in relationships.

Concurrent Activities: The activities that can be carried out concurrently are called concurrent activities. As in earlier case, fixing of doors and windows and electrification are concurrent activities and can be carried out concurrently since they do not depend on each other.

Preceding Activity: The activity that occurs immediately before a given activity, is preceding activity.

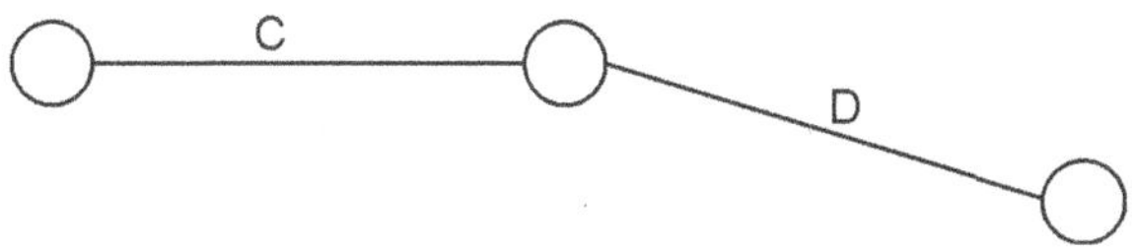

Activity 'C' is the preceding activity for activity 'D'.

Dummy Activity: Dummy activity is an imaginary activity included in a network. Since it is not a real activity, it does not consume resources but it is included in a network to maintain the network logic and to avoid ambiguity. It is represented by a dotted arrow, as below:

Critical Path Method (CPM): A network represents logical sequence of activities having many paths starting from the initial event and leading to the last. If duration of all the activities that lie on a particular path are added, it gives the duration of that path. The path with longest duration is called critical path and the activities that lie on the critical path are called critical activities. It is the critical path that sets the overall duration of the project. For example in the construction of training centre, the longest duration is 27 weeks and is a critical path. The main function of PERT and CPM is to determine and control the time required to complete a project, the main benefit is time saved through the scheduling of tasks, both initially and as the project progresses. Since time and cost are closely related, saving time usually leads to savings in costs. In addition, both PERT and CPM have been adapted and applied explicitly to costs. They can, for example, be used to develop an optimum cost-efficiency schedule that can help managers to determine the savings and costs involved in achieving a shorter production schedule. Using extra labour to reduce the duration of an activity, for instance, may cost more than the bonus for early completion. Other extensions of PERT and CPM, such as pinpointing problem areas, improving communication, and comparing alternative actions, also enhance their usefulness.

Proper analysis of cost incurred on a project in terms of environment degrading and social dilemmas have led agitations against those projects. There have been responsive causalities over these agitations and there have been deadlocks on such projects.

Monitoring

Chapter 8

Monitoring is a continuing function that aims primarily to provide functionaries and main stakeholders with regular feedback and early indications of progress or lack of thereof in the achievement of intended results. Monitoring tracks the actual performance or situation against what was planned or expected according to pre-determined standards. Monitoring generally involve collecting and analyzing data on implementation process, strategies and results and recommending corrective measures.

Monitoring may be participatory or non-participatory. Participatory monitoring is a process in which the project recipients become actively involved in the implementation and regular checking of the project progress or lack of it.

HOW TO DESIGN A PARTICIPATORY MONITORING PLAN

An important lesson in the implementation of the M & E strategy teaches that the design of a Participatory Monitoring Plan from the beginning of a project contributes greatly to more effective implementation. Thus, once the design of the projects is over, it is advisable to hold a workshop on How to Design a Participatory Monitoring Plan. The workshop should help with the stakeholder's commitment to the accomplishment of the main Project Results (outputs, outcomes and impacts).

Seven Steps of a Participatory Monitoring Plan

<table>
<tr><th>A Participatory Monitoring Plan</th><th colspan="5">RESULTS BASED MANAGEMENT</th></tr>
<tr><td rowspan="8">Basic Components</td><td>Stakeholder Consensus on Type of Results</td><td colspan="2">Outputs</td><td>Outcomes</td><td>Impacts</td></tr>
<tr><td>Stakeholders Consensus on Indicators</td><td colspan="4">Qualitative/Quantitative indicators</td></tr>
<tr><td rowspan="2">Definition of Data Collection To Monitor the Type of Results</td><td rowspan="2">Type of Data When By Whom Where</td><td>Baselines</td><td>Benchmarks</td><td>Targets</td></tr>
<tr><td colspan="3">Case Studies, Documentaries, Surveys, Focal Groups, Informal Meetings</td></tr>
<tr><td>Reporting Requirement</td><td colspan="2">Formats</td><td>Frequency</td><td>Distribution</td></tr>
<tr><td>Responsibilities</td><td colspan="4">Sub-programme Implementers (Standing Committees) UNDP/NGOs GOI States/CBOs</td></tr>
<tr><td>Schedule</td><td colspan="4">Crucial M & E activities for the life of the sub-programme</td></tr>
<tr><td>Budget</td><td colspan="4">For Monitoring form 1 to 5 % of the project or sub-programme budget</td></tr>
</table>

PLANNING FOR MONITORING

Planning for monitoring generally takes place at the programme design stage and yearly thereafter. A plan for monitoring may focus on projects and programmes as well as resulting development changes (outcomes). Programme managers are responsible for designing monitoring arrangements that are appropriate for the nature of the outcome, programme and project. A few examples of different kinds of monitoring arrangements are provided below:

- If the outcome being monitored is the enhancement of livelihoods at the village level, a more participatory approach may be required.
- If the outcome involves a high degree policy advice, the monitoring plan should include means of following the policy formulation process in the country.
- If the outcome involves high degree of advocacy, monitoring might need to capture changes in perceptions (as revealed through client surveys or focus groups rather than physical changes as revealed through field visits to project sites) when planning for monitoring to assess progress, functionaries may take following steps.
    1. **Assess needs:** This is done by assessing the nature of the outcome and/or the programmes and projects that are expected to contribute to outcome. What information is needed to assess that outcome? What elements are most important to keep track of? What would indicate progress or success?
    2. **Assess current monitoring:** To assess current monitoring (or proposed monitoring for new projects), look at the monitoring tools being used in all of the projects and programmes to contribute to a given outcome. Are these tools providing the necessary information? Do they involve the keys partners? Is monitoring focusing on key issues for efficiency? Are there possibilities for greater efficiency and coordination? This will help to identify gaps in the analysis as compared with the needs for this information.
    3. **Review monitoring scope or tools:** Is there a need for additional or specific monitoring scope or tools to suit the programme or project? For example, large or complex programmes may require more details about implementation, downstream projects may require additional participation by beneficiaries, and innovative pilot projects may generate specific lessons learned that should be captured through monitoring.
    4. **Adapt and/or design monitoring mechanisms:** The mechanisms used should provide sufficient analysis on outcomes and close the gap, if any, between the available and the required information. For example, if steering mechanisms are being used to monitor, be sure to include partners working in the same outcome area. Or, if an outcome involves a large number of partners, add tools such as stakeholder meetings.

An outcome monitoring plan drawn up by the programme management helps to ensure that the organization continuously collects information on the outcome and periodically analyzes it to chart progress: Organizations that establish an outcome monitoring plan must be sure to include information on the outcome indicators so that (*a*) indicators are not selected unless data is likely to be available and (*b*) data will be available for the indicators that are selected.

It is recommended that an outcome monitoring plan, identify the following:

- Outcome to which the indicators apply;

- Outcome indicator(s);
- Data source(s)
- Method and frequency of coolection and analysis.

The plan may also identify who will be responsible for data collection and analysis and who will use the resulting information. Table below provides a sample format that suggests how indicators might fit into an outcome monitoring plan.

Table: How indicators might fit into an outcome monitoring plan

Outcome	*Outcome Indicator(s)*	*Data Source(s)*	*Method of Data Collection/ Analysis*	*Frequency of Data Collection/ Analysis*	*Who is Responsible*	*Who will Use the Information*

When planning data collection and analysis using indicators, Programme Managers may realize that data are not immediately available. In such cases, Programme Managers should plan to collect data through alternative instruments and/or approaches, such as:

Awareness/attitude surveys and questionnaires;

Expert panels;

Key informant interviews;

Focus groups;

Mapping techniques.

Attitude surveys allow for some quantification of qualitative change. For example, the proportion of people who perceive of local government management as "participatory" has gone up from 40 percent to 65 percent over a certain period of time. This statistics provides some measure of the degree of qualitative change.

KEY PRINCIPLES FOR DATA COLLECTION AND ANALYSIS USING INDICATORS

Rationale

Build a conceptual framework into which ideas can be placed, giving definition, orientation and direction to available information and to your own ideas about the project or programme. This means a credible chain of results in terms of outcome, outputs and partnerships.

Statement of purpose or problem

What is it that you plan to investigate? Define problems and issues, look for signals that have clear meaning, establish agreements with beneficiaries and partners. This involves the definition of the development problems at the SRF Sub-Goal level.

Questions to be answered

When the data collection is finished, what are the major questions to which reasonable answers can be expected? What evidence can be used to verify the level of achievement of the indicators?

Statement of outcome

Spell out the particular outcome(s) you will monitor, set targets that are realistic and keep in mind data sources and monitoring responsibilities.

Design and procedure

State who will be the subject of your interviews, surveys and focus groups and describe how they will be selected. Explain the conditions under which the data will be collected, what measuring instruments or data-gathering instruments will be used, and how the data will be analyzed and interpreted. Look for data that is easily available and avoid major data collection.

Assumptions

What assumptions have you made about the nature of the issues you are investigating, about your methods and measurements, or about the relations of the investigation to other problems or situations?

Limitations

What limitations exist in your methods or approach to internal and external validity?

Delimitations

On what basis have you narrowed the scope of data collection and analysis? Did you focus only on the selected aspects of the problems or outcome, certain areas of interest or a limited range of subjects?

Definition of terms

List and define the principal terms you will use, particularly where terms have different meanings to different people. Emphasis should be placed on operational and/or behavioural definitions.

Involving stakeholders

The organization in direct consultation with the senior management – should establish mechanisms for sharing information generated from indicators with primary stakeholders. This is particularly true for outcome indicators. This ensures that the analysis of progress is locally relevant using local knowledge, while fostering "ownership" and building groups decision-making skills. It is worth nothing, however, that stakeholder or partner participation in the analysis of the indicator data may significantly alter the interpretation of that data.

Participatory observation and in-depth participatory reviews with implementation partners and beneficiaries are integral to visual on-site verification of results-which is a reliable form of assessment. More "top down" and less participatory approaches to assessment may be used to achieve analytical rigor, independence, technical quality, uniformity and comparability. Ultimately, of course, the information gained through the analysis of indicators feeds into evaluations. This data helps assess process towards outputs and outcomes, and includes a measure of stakeholder satisfaction with results.

USING INDICATORS FOR MONITORING

Results-oriented monitoring of development performance involves looking at results at the level of outputs, outcomes and, eventually, impact. Table below shows how indicators are used for each type of results and who the primary user of the indicator is.

Type of Result	*What is Measured*	*Indicators*	*Primary Level of Use*
Output	Effort, or goods and services generated by projects and programmes.	Implementation of activities.	Project Management
Outcome	Effectiveness or results in terms of access, usage and stakeholder satisfaction from goods and services generated by projects, programmes, partners and soft assistance.	Use of outputs and sustained production of benefits.	Programme Management
Impact	Effectiveness, or results in terms of the combined effect of a combination of outcome activities that improve development conditions at a national level.	Use of outcomes and sustained positive development change.	Senior Management

Indicators are used periodically to validate partner's perceptions of progress and achievement to keep projects and programmes on track and to provide early warning signals of problems in progress. Indicators only **indicate**; they do not **explain**. Any interpretation of indicators is done through qualitative analysis.

For output indicators, the programme manager uses day-to-day monitoring to verify progress, as well as field visits and reports and/or information received from the project management, The Annual Project Report(APR) is too infrequent to allow early action in case there are delays or problems in the production of outputs.

For outcome indicators, annual monitoring is more appropriate and is accomplished through input from the technical project experts in the APR, discussions at the Steering Committee and the Annual Review. Since outcomes are less tangible than outputs, indicators are indispensable for an informed analysis of progress.

For impact indicators (also called situational indicators), discussion may take place annually if information is available but is often done less frequently.

Elements of Implementation Monitoring

(Traditionally used for projects)

(*i*) Description of the problems or situation before the intervention;

(*ii*) Benchmarks for activities and immediate outputs;

(*iii*) Data collection on inputs, activities and immediate outputs;

(*iv*) Systematic reporting on provision of inputs, etc.;

(*v*) Directly linked to a discrete intervention; (or series of interventions).

(*vi*) Designed to provide information on administrative, implementation and management issues as opposed to broader development effectiveness issues.

Elements of Outcome Monitoring

(Used for a range of interventions and strategies)

(*i*) Base line data to describe the problem or situation before the intervention;

(*ii*) Indicators for outcome;

(*iii*) Data collection on outputs and how/whether they contribute towards achievement of outcomes;

(*iv*) More focus on perceptions of change among stakeholders and more focus on "soft" assistance;

(*v*) Systematic reporting with more qualitative and quantitative information on the progress of outcomes;

(*vi*) Done in conjunction with strategic partners;

(*vii*) Captures information on success or failure of partnership strategy in achieving desired outcomes.

Monitoring consists of continuous collection of data on what is ongoing in the project and its effect, in order to assess progress towards the project's objectives. Monitoring focuses on transforming inputs, through activities, into outputs. It is essential for management to make regular progress reports on programme implementation that inputs are being made available as planned and activities are taking place in line with work plan and that outputs are being produced on schedule. It is also important to know what changes, if any, have taken place in the above and more importantly the reasons for any changes management must always be in a position to adopt the programme to new needs and conditions which couldn't have been foreseen at the design stage. If necessary the programme document should be revised, thus facilitating subsequent evaluation.

According to Inaytullah (1980) it is important to distinguish between the concepts of 'monitoring' and 'evaluation', although both terms are used to indicate a set of related activities concerned with the gathering of information about the performance and effectiveness of a programme/project. The Word Bank document defines monitoring as, "The gathering of information on the utilisation of project inputs, on unfolding of project activities, on timely generation of project outputs and on circumstances that are critical to the effective implementation of the project" (Cernea and Tepping, 1977).

The document issued by United Nations on monitoring and evaluation defines the concept of monitoring as follows: "the term monitoring usually refers to the process of routine periodic outputs undertaken during programme implementation. Monitoring is normally concerned with the procurement, delivery and utilisation of programme resources, adherence to work schedules or progress made in the production of out puts" (United Nations,1978). Both of these agencies agree that monitoring deals with the relationship between the input and outputs of the programme and that it lost during the period of implementation of the programme . Both agree that the function of monitoring is to provide early warnings concerning any short falls in inputs or outputs in order to enable the programme management to undertake timely corrective action. Monitoring is a process of generating low entropy messages at both the ends of a development process. The poor and the 'poverty -alleviators'. How do we do it? Is it inevitable that we must state precisely what we know what we didn't besides what we prepared to disown before we even think of developing a line of communication with poor?

THEOREMS OF MONITORING

Prof. Anil Kumar Gupta had developed few theorems on monitoring. These are as follows-

1. Banks did not monitor in which seasons, spaces or ecological contexts, what sectorial enterprises will be most viable, land development banks have disbursed loan on the purchase of light commercial vehicle.
   - Programmes on cooperatives didn't monitor who became members initially but dropped out subsequently, whether there existed a pattern in the population of drop outs, whether cooperatives of unequal inflect forget the cooperation/collusion amongst the better off and that too at public cost, whether cooperatives had regular general body meetings, whether development was really a positive sum game etc.
   - Government didn't monitor the NGOs at the time of registration under Societies Registration Act while it deny registration under FCRA for certain reasons.
2. **Monitoring access implies designing counters and not corridors**
   - We first design a system with back doors and side-windows, then monitor the access at the front window. Finding not enough people or not enough of the 'target type' we expect.
   - The indifferent excluded ones to organize themselves. To generate pressure/demand, from those who failed to get the services, on the delivery system which failed to deliver became the dominant morale of the development story.
   - Whenever resources were scarce, queuing was inevitable. How to define eligibility rules for standing on the que, through whom to monitor date on exclusion.
   - Those who infact managed to elbow out the rest.
   - Those who could not participate.
   - Those who could not participate despite knowing all the pros and also the cons (many families refused to take loan under IRDP).
   - Those who were not eligible either because they had too much of resources or too little.

The issue really is that when implicitly be design, the corridors in the form of scope for negotiating the possible meaning of a policy are allowed, access across counters (i.e. the delivery windows) gets distorted. To monitor the effectiveness of counters, one has also to monitor defining precise rules of queing. The exclusion will have to be monitored through those where are normatively desired to be in the queue.

3. Monitoring 'deviance' to build self-decision potential of developmental organization is sins quo non of building up organic learning system.

One of the implications of ece-specific planning is to have a wide range of variety in both organization design, policy content and delivery systems. However, tendency of centralized monitoring systems to concentrate on uniform standard indicators reinforces risk-averse complaint behaviour amongst the functionaries of organizations.

At the same time, it is inevitable that there would be minority in various organizations specially NGOs which will deviate from the norms. In our obsession with failures we seldom seem to be capable of anticipating success.

The question then arises, how to spot, sustain, and strengthen organizational insurgents? If a miniscule minority in different bureaucratic organizations demonstrated that not only its sensitivity to the problem of poor but also recognized the power of other peers having nexus with vested interests to thwart its efforts how to ensure that such a minority in the NGOs will not be annihilated?

How to generate a critical network, which will provide morale and material support to such deviants and also enable that their strategic coalition, tactical retreats, etc. Perhaps only a network of such deviance could sustain each other by providing critical feed back, monitoring their errors, extracting lesson of each failure and morale of each success. Unlike the already existing coalitions of vested interests within and outside NGOs.

4. Development on cheap is a bane of our poverty alleviating programmes poor people monitor our interrelations behind these programmes by looking at the investment in the monitoring process. It is not rare to visit a village and be confronted with question "What is your scheme? What do you want to give? How many cases do you want? Why don't you leave us on our fate? etc."

At the same time there are many who are just different.

The cost at which we want to develop them and the costs that they have already paid for surviving so long very seldom match.

5. Monitoring context changes the content– There is a famous story of Birbal, who when asked to shorten a line without rubbing it, drew a longer line adjacent to it. Very often we monitor the content without even realizing the enormous variety of difference in the meaning which may emerge because of the differences in the context. NGOs many times forge dependency amongst the poor when concentration is placed on physical investments rather than on capacity building.

It is important to realize that be monitoring the context i.e., the setting in which a programme had to be implemented, we would inevitably design better policies, programmes and projects, but the reverse was not true. The tendency is that often we monitored only the content. The result was that despite highly heterogeneous implementation of the policy, solution often was more of the same. Context comprises, most importantly, the centours of coping mechanisms of poor. How little we know of them was apparent from the stylized statements as poverty littered all over the plan documents.

6. Participation– Often in the name of decentralization and implementation bureaucratic machinery chose to organize camps to demonstrate its apparent anxiety to deliver results through people's participation. But what do these camps and campaigns really achieve?

- The participation ends where it should begin.
- Routine is converted into celebration.
- People are immobilized in normal times such that camp generates a greater need for still another camp.

- People often interpreted the camps as a sign of helplessness on the part of senior officials who failed to galvanize their machinery to act in the absence of it.

There is a need to systematically catalogue such attempts to seek participation of people.

It has been observed that monitoring is performed by independent consultants, officials and agencies providing support. Monitoring need further exploration. These are as follows-

1. **How to create capacity building in groups of poor to monitor the leaders–** Very often the poor recognized the need for literate and articulated leader who in their view could be able to understand the logic of bureaucratic system. These leaders sometimes after repeated interactions with bureaucratic functionaries, themselves start realizing the futility of having detailed interactions with their peers.

   Soon, these leaders loose the confidence of poor but the later have very limited capacity to dislodge them. This scenario represents a very familiar experience of NGOs. Most social interventionists have neglected the need of instituting processes of accountability and openness in leader-follower interface.

   Risk, recourses and skills are considered three basics on which any development activity has to be modeled. Often modern management interventions presume need for de skilling as the basic of any organized activity. Specialization in skills traditionally was a source of multiple leadership. Since rural social structures require multiple skills for survival, specialists in one skill became natural leader of the tasks groups around that skill. Need for pursuing propositions remained, if viable collectivities of poor had to emerge. Question is, shall we the interventionists, agree to be monitored ourselves?

2. **How to generate capacity amongst poor to monitor government programmes?**

   Organizational leaders often pass on blame for inefficient and ineffective functioning of development programmes on the lowest rung of bureaucracy. Credit unlike blame, seldom trickle down. In the process, the distrust amongst leaders and followers in public organizations transcends the organizational boundaries and is manifested in the relation between organizational functionaries and the poor clients.

   How do we identify role for desired target group to monitor the extent to which programme reached following subsets of target group-

   (*a*) Desired bit devoid of technological as resource potential for using the project/programme resource.

   (*b*) People with potential but not belonging to the normatively defined category of desired group.

   (*c*) People neither having potential nor belonging to the desired group.

Government's efforts for generating potential amongst the desired target group would also need to e monitored to test the intentions of planners.

3. **How to monitor access to common property resources (CPRs) as well as public goods.** How to ensure that the poor excluded ones didn't pay costs of free riding by the powerful ones?

4. **Will markets act as monitors–** Those who believe in equilibrium economics assume that markets monitor better, we should get what and where depending upon the demand and

supply. Is not it true that market forces often in coalition with bureaucratic forces and state power lead to a system whereby only certain types of needs of only certain classes of rural society in only certain regions were responded to?

5. **How to monitor 'the monitor'–** Very often the development interventions as well as the developmental programme managers become incapable of being monitored by the people. It is very crucial that if people were to become partners in developmental experiments, they must have incentives and capacity to monitor the 9interventionist. It has enormous learning advantage for both the sides. In addition to being a very important means of generating valid knowledge in a social setting, the process of mutual monitoring or what could be called as a surveillance mechanism also ensured genuine democratic culture. Unless and until leaders in a group were subjected to these mechanisms, it is quite. Likely that they would become autocratic and insensitive to the interest of the poorer members. First step in this process was to demystify our own assumed expertise in the matter.

   Generally, organizations programme or activity whichever is being monitored become a facilitators for monitor, while is their right of NGOs to keep vigil on monitor.

6. How to monitor that development intermediaries don't infiltrate resources meant for poor?

   In a survey at Sarguja district, it was found that most of the available resources meant for the poor have gone in the hands of rich and dominant people. This has been done intentionally by the government officials due to idleness and arm chair implementation of the schemes. Had their been regular monitoring by the government authorities and the people's representatives, the resources would have not been grabbed by the rich and dominant people of the area. Regular weekly and fortnightly honestly may solve this problem.

NATIONAL AND INTERNATIONAL MONITORING SYSTEM

Monitoring of a project depend on the aptitude of the funding agency. Some prefer through themselves, some through other institution, consultants. Sometimes beneficiaries are taken into belief in the monitoring process. Korten suggests that voluntary organizations and people's organizations must act directly to increase access to information and enhance people's ability to make rational-choices toward a sustainable future. Voluntary organizations working at international levels should collaborate in developing a system to monitor the plans and actions of development donors, financial institutions, and MNCs. National voluntary organizations must create similar systems to monitor and make known the plans and actions of national governments and corporations. The purpose is to ensure that the people have access to the relevant information to access social and environmental impacts and to take necessary actions to protect their interests. There should also be broad based historical assessment at national and regional levels of the social and environmental impact of foreign assistance and trade and corporate investment policies for creating greater understanding of the dynamics of the international system and of the issues at stake.

Organization and methodology for monitoring– We need to focus our attention on the organization and methodology for monitoring. The monitoring should not only identify the bottlenecks in the implementation of the programme, but also collect data to assess and evaluate the impact of the programme concurrently. A clear cut distinction should be made between concurrent evaluation and ex-post evaluation. Ex-post evaluation doesn't influence the success or failure of the programme as originally planned. A monitoring system which include concurrent evaluation also is concurrent to and co-terminus with the programme. However, comprehensive ex-post evaluation prevents the repeat of mistakes in new programmes stemming from earlier ones.

Devising formats-considerations of goal hierarchy– The data elements can be derived logically by studying the programme 'Goal Hierarchy'. The superordinate goal or goals of an organization are normally broken-up into intermediate goals which are further divided into more concrete sub-tools which finally end up in the physical tasks to be done. The identified inputs and outputs of these activities are the data elements to be measured and monitored, and report formats, quarterly or monthly or both, are evolved.

The data elements may be arranged according to sector classification for the convenience of field officer, the emphasis is on the achievement and impacts and top management should not concern itself unduly with the mechanics of field level operators.

In addition a monthly progress report covering relevant money expenditure may be evolved. A quarterly critical narrative report giving problems encountered and corrective action taken and highlighting innovative type of activities undertaken at the district/block level, is useful. The latter should be used for the transfer of knowledge and technology across blocks or districts.

Impact information and measures for impact assessment– To discover if a successfully implemented activity generates the kind of effect envisaged while planning there should be two kinds of information flow i.e. (*a*) On the progress of activities and (*b*) On the fulfillment of objectives and the impact created by them.

Suitable measures for assessing the impact of the programme will have to be evolved in accordance with the objectives of the programmes.

Data Flow and Analysis

Data flow depends on the organizational structure of the implementing agency. It should be arranged to meet the requirements of distributing work loads, acquiring an estimate knowledge of Districts/Blocks in order to provide a closer link between them and the centre, providing a timely feedback to District/Blocks and improving motivation through this feed back at the District/Block levels.

Monitoring at different levels and the need for field visits

To be effective, monitoring of a programme should be decentralized. It should be undertaken at all levels, from the lowest to the highest, of programme operation. The units reporting on progress of implementation of programmes or schemes may need to be strengthened through training of staff in the techniques of monitoring and through additional staff. The data base should also be strengthened. It must be clearly understood that the information requirements at different levels are not the same, ranging from detailed information at the District/Block level to less detailed information at the state/central level.

Information received on performance should be supplemented by frequent visits by the persons responsible for monitoring to the location of the programme, since a personal approach is more effective than correspondence. These visits would also provide guidance in the filling up of performance and reduce the time log in the receipt of information. The frequency of these visits may be red letter when the progress reporting staff at lower levels becomes conscious of the need for prompt reporting.

Feedback to the field: Feed back notes to all programme districts/block should include aspects such as promptness in reporting and performance in various sectors, the clarification of discrepancies revealed in analysis, identification of the top and bottom 20% districts/blocks in each sector, suggestions form sector experts and specific queries regarding activities.

Analytical techniques

The collection of information at various levels of monitoring has to be put into a systematic form and analyzed. In choosing the techniques formalizing the data, two important criteria have to be kept in mind, i.e. the resulting interpretation should be useful for managerial decision making and it should be uncomplicated and use a minimum of time and effort.

Safeguards against malfunctioning of a monitoring system

Good design in a monitoring system should guard against situations such as reports are not being received in time and errors in reporting. When reports are not received on time, analysis of physical and financial achievements cannot be made. A remedy to this situation may be a feed back assuming 'nil' achievement for the relevant period for the defaulting district/block which might shame the district/block into reporting regularly. Target changes should be incorporated into the monitoring system only after the approval of the sanctioning committee and the issue of a formal order to the implementing agency.

The identifying of reporting errors by transcribing of data into data base cards and by charting in different ways, and the subsequent reconciliation of discrepancies, is time consuming. Care should be taken in reporting. Similarly, when data inflow is punched into cards for computer processing complex verification schemes are needed to avoid errors.

Monitoring and participatory monitoring

Monitoring is a continuing activity that aims primarily to provide project management and stakeholders with early indications of progress, or lack thereof, in the achievement of objectives. Participatory monitoring is a process in which the project recipients become actively involved in the implementation and regular checking of the project progress or lack of it.

Evaluation and participatory evaluation

Evaluation is a time-bound exercise that attempts to assess, systematically and objectively, the relevance/ performance and success of a programme/project.

Participatory evaluation is the active collective assessment and examination of a project by all stakeholders, in which project recipient, become not just mere objects of evaluation but also agents of evaluation.

Focus on monitoring

Since monitoring is fundamental to the achievement and demonstration of results, it should be systematically and objectively focused on the relevance, performance and success of ongoing development interventions. Thus, monitoring and evaluation share the same three criteria as essential focus. These criteria are:

Relevance

It is the degree to which the objectives of a programme or project remain valid and pertinent either as originally planned or as subsequently modified owing to changing circumstances within the immediate context and external environment of that programme or project.

Evaluations must consider the relevance of programme and projects to-

- Development issues at the local, national, regional and global levels;
- Target groups, whose needs and constraints must be clearly identified relative to their gender, socio-economic status and geographical location;
- Direct beneficiaries, which may be the government, the private sector and/or CSOs, which are responsible not only for implementing the programme or project but, more significantly, for sustaining its positive results;

Performance

It looks at the progress that is being made by a programme or project relative to its main results (outputs, outcomes and impacts).

There are three criteria for evaluating performance-

- Effectiveness- It is the extent to which a programme or project achieves or produces its desired outcomes and impacts.
- Efficiency- It is the optimal transformation of outputs into outcomes and impacts.
- Timeliness- It is the accomplishment of results on time.

Success

The three criteria of success are impact, sustainability and contribution to capacity building.

Impact

It refers to the results of a programme or project that are assessed with reference to outcomes and impacts. In this context, outcomes and impacts represent changes in a situation, whether planned or unplanned, positive or negative, that a programme or project brings about. For evaluations to be significant in the context of results-based management, a programme or project, should contain baseline data and indicators.

Sustainability

It is the durability of positive programme or project results after the termination of the technical cooperation channeled through the programme or project. Static sustainability refers to the continuous flow of the same benefits that were set in motion by the completed programme or project to the same target groups. Dynamic sustainability refers to the use in, or adoption of, programme or project results to, a different context or a changing environment by the original target groups and/or other groups.

Contribution to capacity building

It is the extent to which a programme or project enables target groups to be self-reliant and makes it possible for government institutions, the private sector and CSOs to use positive experiences with the programme or project in addressing broader development issues.

Evaluation

Chapter 9

"Evaluation is a complex process which seeks to identify the factors which are related to the performance and effectiveness of a programme/project in order to determine its feasibility to develop more effective projects and programmes in future." What distinguishes evaluation from monitoring is that it goes beyond collection of data on relationships between programme inputs and outputs and seeks to determine the effects and impact of the programme.

Following the United Nations concept Prof. Udai Pareekh suggests three types of evaluation: Pre-programme evaluation, ongoing evaluation and ex-post evaluation. The concept of monitoring and evaluation are interrelated and in a way evaluation as an ongoing process includes monitoring. Evaluation should be joint effort to collect feedback and take corrective action. Evaluation not only helps the implementers in increasing the effectiveness of their programmes, but also all other individuals involved in designing and implementing the programme.

Project evaluation is the ex-post analysis of an executed project determining the real benefits and effective costs. By comparing the expected project results (ex-ante) with the real results (ex-post), project evaluation tests the hypotheses established during the appraisal exercise. Project appraisal is the ex-ante of a proposed project, identifying and valuing the expected costs and benefits. It should be emphasized that evaluation is preferably not a once only post-project exercise, but a continuing management activity. Project evaluation is the most specialized planning process which involves systematic objectives and comprehensive appraisal of development programme for projects. It implies an assessment of a project as its operational technique, economic, financial and managerial efficiency. Project evaluation refers to the procedure of fact finding about the results of planned social action. Evaluation is an essential aid to policy to assess its success or failure and to find out further lines of improvement.

BASIS OF EVALUATION

(*i*) Evaluation on the basis of benefits: A project is evaluated on the basis of benefits accruing from it. Benefits refer to the addition to flow of output accruing from a project. These are:
- (*a*) Tangible and intangible benefits.
- (*b*) Real and nominal benefits
- (*c*) Direct and indirect benefits.

(*ii*) Evaluation on the basis of costs:
- (*a*) Real and nominal cost
- (*b*) Primary and secondary cost

A FRAMEWORK FOR MONITORING/EVALUATION

(*i*) The selection of variables to be evaluated. Following the decision of what type of evaluation is to be carried out, agreement should be reached with the end-user(s) of the evaluation, on the variables to be evaluated. There is usually a limit to the resources available for monitoring/evaluation and therefore it may be necessary to make a careful selection of the variables. The variable with the highest priority for evaluation features:

(*a*) Critically important for the success of the project.

(*b*) Capable of being influenced by subsequent management decisions.

(*c*) Uncertain performance in the given situation.

(*d*) Requiring a relatively lower cost for evaluation than other variables with the previous three features.

(*ii*) Alternative evaluation designs

(*a*) Design one: Case study with the measurement and no control group. This design only compares the actual project performance with the planned performance.

(*b*) Design two: A case study with two measurements and no control group. One measurement is before implementation and the other after implementation. This design requires qualitative analysis to help overcome problems of changes due to factors out side the project's activities.

(*c*) Design three: A case study with one measurement and a control group. Data are collected on similar control and project groups, before, during and after the implementation of the project. This is the best evaluation design but also the most costly.

(*iii*) Data collection, processing and presentation: There are basically four sources of data: existing statistics, project reports, surveys specific to evaluation requirements and key informants (i.e. opinion leaders, people's elected representatives etc.).

Processing is often the bottleneck with the monitoring/evaluation framework, and the resources available for processing should help to determine the amount of data collected. The form and content of presentation should meet the needs and capabilities of the users of evaluation reports e.g. action oriented, easily understandable and refined in the light of previous discussions with appropriate levels of management.

There are 5 indicators which can express some helpful ideas for designing and implementing a programme evaluation:

1. Why evaluate?

There are two reasons:

(*i*) for funding agency to present and analyse programme outcome.

(*ii*) for the NGO/programme staff to identify what worked and what didn't work? So that in future programme may be improved.

2. What should be evaluated?

Good evolution looks at the process of the programmes and productivity of the programme.

3. What does cumulative evaluation include?

While formative evaluation examines programme operation, cumulative evaluation identifies programme outcome or results.

Evaluation during the programme is formative evaluation and evaluation at the end of the programme is cumulative, formative evaluation checks progress towards programme's goals and problems on a frequent basis (such as weekly or monthly).

4. What are some important things in conducting evaluation?

There are three indicators which are used as a guideline for evaluating a development project:

(*i*) The project staff responsible for implementing the project should not be treated as an object of the evaluation but they should be associated with the evaluation work.

(*ii*) For in-depth information, the outside evaluator should establish good rapport with project staff, this will facilitate proper and adequate evaluation.

(*iii*) Participatory evaluation techniques should be adopted to have a view of opinion leaders, people's elected representatives and beneficiaries.

5. What should the final report of evaluation include?

A final report usually combines and integrates the formative and summative evaluations. It analyses the relationship between what happened during the programme operation and the programme's outcome. A good evaluation report might include following:

(*i*) Brief description of the programme.

(*ii*) Narrative summary of the activities (problem, success which occurred during the programme).

(*iii*) Results of formative or summative evaluation.

(*iv*) Analysis of factors which helped to achieve the goal.

(*v*) Analysis of factors which hindered the programme reaching its goal.

(*vi*) Concrete recommendations with alternatives.

Dimensions: Haque et. al.(1977) have suggested four main dimensions of the criteria for the evaluation of rural development programmes. They are as follows:

1. The basic institution which would include the contribution of the programme to the development of a basic institution which becomes the forum for systematic deliberation of the target group on all issues that concern them.
2. Economic criteria, which include five main criteria, viz. economic benefit, distributional equality, collective accumulation, horizontal expansion, and developing linkages.
3. Attitudinal criteria, which have six main criteria, viz., sense of solidarity, democratic values, spirit of cooperation, collective spirit, creative spirit and spirit of collective self-reliance.
4. Self administration and momentum, which include experience in economic and social administration, generation of internal cadres and indigenous momentum.

It is suggested that the aggregation of all these criteria's should result in qualitative change in the social consciousness of the target group, and enhancement of its political power. Thus a synergy of effort should lead to a major thrust and change in the target group.

MODELS OF EVALUATION

Evaluation is currently being considered as important and several models of evaluation have been developed by Prof. Udai Pareekh, Bhola (1979), Burton & Rogers (1976). These are as follows:

1. The CIPP model: CIPP (Content, Input, Process and Product) model adopts the criteria of internal and external validity, reliability, objectivity, relevance, importance, scope, credibility, timeliness, persuasiveness and efficiency.
2. The discrepancy model defines evaluation as the art of describing a discrepancy between the expectation and performance of a programme. Five different types of discrepancies can be located in programme implementation relating to the design of the programme, its installation, the process used to implement it, its product and its cost.
3. While the foregoing models focus more on the achievement of the goals of the programme, Scriven (1979) has made a significant distinction between formative and summative evaluation. The former is for implementers, and latter for the consumers. The purpose for the formative evaluation is to evaluate the process involved in forming the programme-organizational strategies, curriculum development, motivational techniques, instructional material, etc. the purpose of summative evaluation is to sum up the effect of the whole programme and find out the impact made.

EVALUATING A PROJECT

Evaluation critically examines actual or potential results in order to improve the effectiveness of continuing projects and to provide guidance for the planning of new ones. Evaluation represents an attempt to learn form the collective experience of persons knowledgeable about or involved in the project. Some projects go ahead roughly as planned, and present few worries for their managers; other encounter unforeseen difficulties and never reach their objective, even after exceptional efforts on the part of the staff.

Evaluation should be a constructive discussion among interested parties, a collaborative effort rather than a judicial review. Only if those involved in the evaluation understand the proper approach to the exercise from the outset can the time and effort devoted to the process yield the desired benefits.

Evaluation can take many forms depending on the specific purpose and objective of the evaluation and whether it is carried out by outside consultant, donor representatives, in-house personnel, the project staff or a combination of any of these.

The intensity and depth of an evaluation and a description of the aspects to be addressed will normally be established through the terms of reference. Although evaluations carried out by any of the above groups are likely to address the same basic questions, supplemented by such others as might be determined by the evaluation objectives, the following guidelines are designed for evaluations carried out by the project management. In applying this process, project management becomes both the primary agent and the main user of evaluation. Within certain limits, the selection of evaluation team under these circumstances is likewise management's prerogative, although the value of the exercise will normally be enhanced by involving a number of persons connected with the project and representing varied viewpoints, experiences and skills. Brand representation will usually result in a more comprehensive review of project status, promote a better understanding of the project and facilitate the implementation of decisions taken. Finally, of course, the review represents a valuable learning experience for the participants.

The evaluation process normally can be divided into three phases:

1. Preparation for evaluation
2. Conduct of evaluation
3. Preparation of report and recommendations.

1. PREPARATION FOR EVALUATION

Evaluation worksheet: Unless specifically provided for otherwise, it is the responsibility of the project manager to arrange for the collection of certain data relating both to the achievement of stated objective (as reflected by selected indicators) and project performance (as reflected by inputs received, activities undertaken and outputs produced). About a month before the event, the team should prepare an "evaluation worksheet" for the use. Much of the information can simply be copied directly from the project document or from the optional project document outline. Objectives, assumptions, indicators, etc. should not be altered at this stage, either in order to reflect the current status or in anticipation of the evaluation findings.

Evaluation Worksheet

Development objective

(*a*) What is the development objective?

(*b*) What indicators of development objective attainment were identified in the design?

(*c*) Have any facts been observed which tend to confirm that the project is making a contribution towards the attainment of the development objectives?

(*d*) Unless covered under (*c*) above, state whether the project is having, or likely to have, the desired impact on the target group (intended beneficiaries).

Immediate objectives

(*a*) What is the immediate objective?

(*b*) What indicators confirm achievement of the immediate objective?

(*c*) For each such indicator, what data have been collected? What facts have been observed which tend to confirm that the immediate objective is being or has been achieved?

(*d*) What major assumptions were identified as necessary for the achievement of the development objective?

(*e*) For each assumption, show whether it has materialized, remains valid or is no longer valid.

Output

(*a*) List planned outputs.

(*b*) For each output, identify portion scheduled or intended for completion during period covered by report.

(*c*) For all outputs, list present status.

(*d*) What major assumptions were identified as necessary for the achievement of the immediate objective?

(*e*) For each assumption, show whether it has materialized, remains valid or is no longer valid.

Activities

(*a*) List scheduled major activities.

(*b*) For each activity identify portion scheduled or intended for completion during period covered by this report.

(*c*) For all activities list present status.

(*d*) What major assumptions were identified as necessary for the production of the output?

(*e*) For each assumption, show whether it has materialized, remains valid or is no longer valid.

Inputs

(*a*) List planned inputs.

(*b*) For each planned input, identify portion scheduled or intended for provision during the period covered by this report.

(*c*) For inputs, show those provided to date.

(*d*) What major assumptions were identified as necessary for undertaking of the activities?

(*e*) For each assumption, show whether it has materialized, remains valid or is no longer valid.

2. CONDUCT OF EVALUATION: PROGRESS ANALYSIS

The evaluation worksheet and project document outline, should be submitted to the members of the evaluation team as early as possible in advance of the evaluation review. The group should first agree on whether the worksheet correctly reflects the design as a whole and the previously established objectives, indicators and assumptions, and whether performance to date has been adequately reflected. Once agreement on this has been reached, the evaluation team can compare the results with the projections through the application of following distinct but inter-related analytical tests.

2.1 Effectiveness

To what extent has the project achieved, or is likely to achieve, its objectives?

Has the project made an anticipated progress towards the realization of the scheduled outputs? Judging likely that the immediate objective will be achieved? Similarly, does the available evidence suggest that a meaningful contribution towards the attainment of development objective will be made and that there will be desired impact on the target group? Obviously, some changes in outputs from those originally planned can be expected in the type of projects undertaken by donor. By the same token, accomplishment of indicator targets may vary from projections. Any divergence from plans is not automatically a sign of trouble. However, substantial short-falls or the need to make major downward revisions in the case of continuing projects should give cause for reflection. The question is to be asked at this point is whether the objectives have been achieved or if there is a reasonable expectation that projections will be met and, if not, whether the objectives are still attainable.

2.2 Efficiency

Do the expected project results continue to justify the cost?

The present methodology permits only limited measurement of efficiency by ascertaining whether the balance between inputs on one hand and outputs and immediate objective achievement on the other remains essentially as originally planned. A conscious decision was presumably made during the design phase that the expense was appropriate in relation to the results expected. In the event that extensive changes of inputs, outputs or the immediate objective are needed, or in case the project schedule is changed significantly and as a result costs increase. This balance needs to be addressed.

2.3 Relevance (significance)

Does the project continue to make sense?

There is the basic question whether, under the circumstances prevailing at the time of the evaluation, the original objective is still as relevant as when as essentially proposed. The relevance test, though frequently neglected, is of the utmost importance in view of changes which frequently occur between planning and implementation. Political, economic or other factors or the effect the project has had during its initial implementation period will often change the setting and rationale to an extent that the expansion, extension or cancellation of the project becomes warranted. The test in this instance is a determination whether the project's immediate and development objectives are still worth pursuing.

2.4 Continuing validity of the project design

"Is the design itself still logical and coherent? Is there a reasonable expectation that the planned inputs, activities and outputs, together with the appropriate assumptions, will lead to the achievement of the objectives?"

If the answer is negative, the project will almost certainly fail to have the desired effect, even though some fruitful result may come from the outputs produced. In many events, the project obviously is heading for serious trouble and needs to be carefully re-examined.

If on the one hand it is found that the inputs were delivered more or less as producing the expected outputs, one may conclude that the project's technical, managerial and other constraints have been successfully overcome. If the outputs, in turn, had the anticipated effect at the immediate objective level, the hypothesis underlying the project probably were valid and appropriate.

If, on the other hand, there have been significant deviations from expectations, the reasons need to be determined. They might be the result of internal problems, a faulty hypothesis, an unexpected external factor, or an incorrect assumption.

2.5 Unanticipated effects

"Is this project having any significant, unexpected effects, whether beneficial or detrimental?"

Despite, the best efforts of planners, projects often have unexpected results, especially in the uncertain socio-economic environment in which organizations such as ILO, UNDP and other donors and implementing agencies operate. The process of periodic evaluation provides the occasion for identifying major unexpected factors and, in the case of continuing projects, considering appropriate action to maximize (or minimize) these effects. Is there any evidence of unanticipated effects which should be considered in planning future projects?

2.6 Identification of alternatives

"Is there or would there have been a more effective or more efficient way to approach the problems being addressed by this project?"

Problems can be addressed in a number of ways. Health conditions might be improved through employment, productivity through health care, nutrition through family planning, etc. The choice is difficult one. While it is perhaps somewhat unreasonable to expect management to opt for a different strategy during a project's implementation, the questions of alternative approaches to a given problem should certainly receive serious thought as a project nears its end. Based on past experience, which approach to the problems might have met with greater success or could have been at lower cost?

This information will be especially valuable when follow-up activities or similar problems are elsewhere being considered.

2.7 Casualty

"What factors affected project performance?"

By now the review will have considered a large number of factors which have either contributed to or retarded project progress. Their identification is indispensable for deriving both short range (or feedback into the project) and long range (for future planning) benefits from the exercise?"

The evaluation report form includes a check list of factors which may have effected project performance in a negative or positive way. The participants in the review are called upon to determine for each factor whether performance has been negative, as anticipated or superior, and also indicate if the factor has played an important role in project performance. All factors judged to be not applicable should be so marked. Pertinent factors which do not appear on the check list should be added in the spaces provided, as should any clarifying or explanatory comments.

Marking these factors may prove difficult, since the participants in the review are likely to have different perspectives. The discourse in itself can have a beneficial effect. There also may be a tendency to frankly identify shortcomings of performance, and then mark the factor "as anticipated". While this may seem the expedient thing to do as that moment. It is likely to delay initiating remedial action and fail to provide lessons for future planning. In addition, it occasionally leads to the somewhat embarrassing situation of a project encountering serious trouble while, according to past statements, most, if not all, performance, factors had been essentially "as anticipated."

It can rightfully be argued that factors affecting the performance of any single project will usually depend on unique circumstances which are not likely to recur. However, if aggregating the data shows that the same problems crop up in a wide range of products, then future planning must take these into account.

3. PREPARATION OF REPORT OVERALL CONCLUSIONS, REVISIONS AND RECOMMENDATIONS

This final and most important phase of the evaluation exercise consists of (*a*) stating overall conclusions (*b*) revising the project design, as necessary (*c*) deciding on actions to be undertaken or recommendations to be made (continuing projects), and (*d*) identifying the lessons learned from terminating or completed projects.

3.1 Overall conclusions (all projects)

On the basis of the analysis of project progress provide a concise narrative evaluation statement.

3.2 Project revisions (continuing projects only)

In the light of the analysis of project progress, identify any necessary or desirable changes in the project design. These revisions should be reflected in the responses to the questions. (The revised objectives, indicators, outputs, etc. will form the basis of any subsequent evaluation exercise).

3.3 Decisions/recommendations (continuing projects)

Most decisions or recommendations will be the direct result of the tests to which the project is subjected. Even the casualty test, which is intended primarily for long-range purposes, may serve to identify actions to be taken; for example, any factor rated important which is also rated negative presumably demands management's urgent attention.

Action identified as being necessary or desirable will need to be shown in evaluation report form. Some decisions may require action or approval by the funding agency, etc., while others presumably can be made and implemented locally by the review participants. The decisions and recommendations should show who will be responsible for the necessary action or approval and when it is required.

While the evaluation report is expected to record the action/decisions taken or proposed, it is not designed to serve as a means of requesting or initiating such action. If any action either need to be undertaken or authorized by parties not directly involved in the review government and funding agency not participating in the evaluation, etc., normally operating procedures and regular channels of communication should be followed.

3.4 Lessons learned (terminating and completed projects)

In the case of terminating and completed projects, the evaluation team will normally not propose new actions as a result of its work, unless there is to be some follow-up activity. Here, project management has the opportunity to identify, at the time of project completion, any lessons learned which might be applicable to other projects, as well as to make recommendations regarding appropriate timing for a follow-up evaluation. This sort of information is important in any event, but imperative if there is any possibility of another project along similar lines being undertaken at a later date, by which time the original staff members may no longer be available.

4. DISTRIBUTION OF THE EVALUATION REPORT

The description of the evaluation report needs to be limited to encourage candid comments; at the same time, reports must be available to those with a legitimate need. In the effect this means that only those directly involved in the funding, supervision, implementation and backstopping of a project should have regular access to evaluation reports.

A copy of the completed evaluation report should be dispatched within 15 days of the conclusion of the evaluation to each of the following:

- Funding agency
- Regional officer of the funding agency

- District or state level government department concern

It may also be desirable to provide a copy to each participant of the evaluation, if different from the above.

5. THE PROJECT EVALUATION REPORT FORMAT

The following evaluation report form may be used for all routine evaluations carried out by the project management. For a detailed discussion of each of the categories, a typical evaluation report of ILO's form is detailed as follows:

<table>
<tr><td>Project No:</td><td rowspan="3">Project Title:</td></tr>
<tr><td>Type of Projects: ☐ Inter-regional
☐ National ☐ Research
☐ Regional ☐ Other - specify</td></tr>
<tr><td>Areas Covered by Project:</td></tr>
</table>

<table>
<tr><td>Technical Field:</td><td>International Financing Agency(ies)</td><td>Total international Contribution (US$) or Rs.:
Total government contribution (US$) or Rs.:</td></tr>
<tr><td>Date Project Document signed:</td><td>Project Duration</td><td>Participating Executing Agency</td></tr>
<tr><td colspan="2" rowspan="3">Participants in evaluation:</td><td>Date of present evaluation:</td></tr>
<tr><td>Period covered by evaluation:</td></tr>
<tr><td>From:....................................
To:..................................</td></tr>
<tr><td colspan="3">I. EVALUATION RESULTS (continuing projects only)
1. Action/Decision required or recommended as a result of this evaluation.</td></tr>
</table>

<table>
<tr><td>Unit/Agency Responsible</td><td>Action/Decision Required or Recommended</td><td>Action/ Decision Deadline</td></tr>
<tr><td colspan="3">2. Issues resolved, decisions taken locally as a result of this evaluation and not reflected in 1:</td></tr>
</table>

II. PERFORMANCE ANALYSIS (CAUSAL FACTORS)		***Performance Vs. Expectations***			
	Not applicable	***Negative***	***As anticipated***	***Superior***	***Check, if important***
A. TECHNICAL ASPECTS 1. personnel a. UN/ILO job descriptions appropriate to project/local needs					
b. UN/ILO experts qualifications compared to job descriptions					
c. Adequacy of UN/ILO expertise to project/local needs					
d. Ability of UN/ILO staff to communicate expertise to local staff					
e. Assimilation of expertise by national staff					
f. Availability of technically qualified local personnel					
g. UN/ILO man-years available					
H. Government man-years available					
Other Factors and/or comments: 2. Strategy a. Adequacy of UN/ILO funding					
b. Adequacy of government funding					
c. Application of new techniques of country/region					
d. Strategy appropriate to local needs					
e. Strategy appropriate to local cultural/technological conditions					
f. Dissemination/multiplier effect of expertise provided					
g. Complementarity with other expertise existing/provided					
h. Adequacy of national counterpart institution					
i. Availability of reliable data/statistics					
Other factors and/or comments:					

		Performance Vs. Expectations			
	Not applicable	*Negative*	*As anticipated*	*Superior*	*Check, if important*
3. Equipment a. Quality of equipment procured with international resources					
b. Local capability to maintain/repair project equipment					
c. Quality of equipment procured/available from Govt. resources					
d. Adequacy of equipment to local technological needs					
e. Timeliness of receipt of necessary equipment					
f. Installation/use of equipment					
g. Complementarity between equipment and training					
h. Complementarity between equipment and expertise					
Other factors and/or comments: 4. Training (on-the-job and fellowship) a. Suitability of training to trainees' background					
b. Suitability of training to trainees' assigned position					
c. Suitability of training to local needs					
d. Suitability of training to local cultural/technological conditions					
e. Length of training					
f. Suitability of training institution (fellowship training only)					
g. Opportunity of trainees to apply new knowledge					
h. Suitability of manuals/teaching materials					
i. Complementarity between training and expertise					
j. Turnover of trainees (on-the-job)					
k. Turnover of fellowship recipients					
l. Availability of qualified trainees/fellowship applicants					
m. Return of fellowship recipients to project-related positions					
Other factors and/or comments:					

		Performance Vs. Expectations			
	Not applicable	*Negative*	*As anticipated*	*Superior*	*Check, if important*
B. PERSONNEL 11. ILO/International Personnel a. Awareness/agreement on project objectives					
b. Awareness/agreement on strategies/plans					
c. Adherence to programme/schedules					
d. Provision/continuity of project leadership					
e. Willingness to work outside duty station					
f. Adequacy of allowances					
Other factors and/or comments: 2. Government Personnel a. Awareness/agreement on project objectives					
b. Awareness/agreement on strategies/plans					
c. Adherence to programme/schedules					
d. Availability/continuity of project leadership					
e. Willingness to work outside duty station					
f. Adequacy of salaries and allowances					
g. Qualified personnel remaining in project positions					
Other factors and/or comments: C. MANAGEMENT/ADMINISTRATIVE SUPPORT 1. UNDP (UNDP-funded projects only) a. Support in preparing project documents/revisions					
b. Clarity/appropriateness of procedural guidelines					
c. Timely provision of project funds					
d. Response to requests for assistance					

		Performance Vs. Expectations			
	Not applicable	*Negative*	*As anticipated*	*Superior*	*Check, if important*
e. Guidance on local procedural formalities					
f. Support in recruitment of local staff					
g. Support in selection of local consultants					
h. Support in obtaining supplies					
i. Support in letting sub-contracts					
j. Payment of salaries/allowances/expenses					
k. Guidance on local political/institutional situation					
l. Co-ordination with related projects					
Other factors and/or comments: 2. ILO headquarters a. Support in preparing technical parts of draft project document					
b. Support in developing technical strategy					
c. Overall adequacy of technical backstopping					
d. Support in preparing project documents/revisions					
e. Guidance/assistance on design/evaluation methodology					
f. Clarity/appropriateness of procedural guidelines					
g. Timely provision of project funds					
h. Response to requests for assistance					
i. Support in obtaining supplies					
j. Support in letting sub-contracts					
k. Payment of salaries/allowances/expenses					
l. Guidance on local political/institutional situation					
m. Coordination with related projects					
n. Timely recruitment of international staff					

	Not applicable	Performance Vs. Expectations: Negative	As anticipated	Superior	Check, if important
o. Timely procurement of equipment					
p. Timely placement of fellows					
q. Coordination within ILO Headquarters					
r. Timely reply to administrative consultations					
s. Usefulness of replies to consultation					
t. Guidance on policies and procedures					
u. Clear assignment of project authority/responsibility					
Other factors and/or comments: 3. Other Participating agencies a. Timely recruitment of staff					
b. Timely purchase/provision of equipment					
c. Timely placement of fellows					
d. Timely replies to administrative queries					
f. Usefulness of replies to queries					
Other factors and/or comments: D. EXTERNAL FACTORS a. Government receptiveness to change					
b. Continuity in economic/social policy					
c. Enforcement of relevant legislation					
d. Support by employers' organizations					
e. Support by workers' organizations.					
f. Coordination among government agencies					
Other factors and/or comments:					

6. OVERALL CONCLUSIONS, REVISIONS AND RECOMMENDATIONS

1. Overall conclusions (all projects)

On the basis of the analysis of project progress and any other factors deemed appropriate, provide a concise narrative evaluation statement.

2. Project revisions (continuing projects)

In the light of the findings resulting from the analysis of the project progress, identify any necessary or desirable changes in the project design.

(a) Development and immediate objectives

(*i*) In the light of the current circumstances, do the development and immediate objectives remain fully appropriate? If no, state objectives.

(*ii*) If any indicators or targets are no longer appropriate because of changed objective(s), or for any other reason, show previous and revised indicators.

(b) Outputs

If any outputs are no longer appropriate in view of changed objectives, experience to date or other circumstances, show previous and revised outputs.

(c) Activities

If any activities are no longer appropriate or feasible in view of changed outputs, inputs or other circumstances, show preview and revised activities.

(d) Inputs

If any inputs are no longer necessary or obtainable in view of changed circumstances or plans, show previous and revised inputs.

(e) Assumptions

If any assumptions on any of the above levels are no longer valid, how is this likely to affect the achievement of the next level? Are new assumptions to be added?

3. Actions/decisions (continuing projects)

Actions or decisions required or recommended as a result of this evaluation should be shown on the cover page, while issues resolved or decisions taken and not reflected should be noted.

4. Lessons learned (terminating or completed projects)

Provide the following information for terminating or completed projects:

(a) Project planning

Given the benefit of handsight, was it appropriate to undertake the project in the first place? On the basis of what is known now, should the project have been planned differently? If not, why not?

(b) Project objectives

Comparing final project accomplishments with initial objectives, to what extent have the latter been actually achieved? Have the objectives remained basically the same throughout the project? If not, why?

(c) Project strategy

(*i*) Have there been major changes in the strategy followed during the Project? If so, why?

(*ii*) Are there any recommendations of a general nature regarding the strategy to be followed in similar projects in the future?

(d) Management

What, if any, have been the primary management problems encountered in the course of the project? What recommendations can be made to improve management of future projects?

(e) Administrative support and backstopping

(*i*) What, if any, have been the primary administrative support and backstopping problems encountered in the course of the project?

(*ii*) What recommendations are made to donor area/regional offices, other agencies or government to improve support and backstopping of future projects?

(f) External conditions

(*i*) Have expected events favoured or delayed achievement of objectives? Were these events unique or might they have been anticipated?

(*ii*) What particular conditions or events should be specifically considered in planning future projects of the same type or in the same area?

(g) General comments

On the basis of the experience gained with the project, what factors are not covered above should be kept in mind in planning future projects of this type or in the same area?

(h) Follow-up

Is any follow-up action or evaluation recommended? If so, what, how and when?

(i) Evaluation

From the project point of view, how do you assess the evaluation requirements? In retrospect, do they appear through or perfunctory? If an interim evaluation was carried out, did if contribute to the further development of the project?

INTERIM, TERMINAL AND EX-POST EVALUATIONS

In terms of timing, there are three categories of evaluation.

(*a*) interim (or on-going) evaluation looks at project outputs, likely effects and impact while the project is being implemented; it provides management and decision makers with the analytical data necessary to assess, and if necessary adjust, policies, objectives, institutional arrangements and resources. The results of interim evaluations may also provide useful information for the planning of new projects;

(*b*) Terminal evaluation is the analysis, at the end of a project or a distinct phase of an undertaking; it provides decision makers and planners with information for future planning and programme evaluations.

(*c*) Ex-post evaluation refers to a retrospective examination of a project at sometime after its completion.

EVALUATION VS. MONITORING

Monitoring and evaluation are basically different, though complementary. Evaluation analyses objective achievement in order to maximize the impact of continuing projects and to provide guidance for the planning of new ones. By contrast, monitoring primarily oversees the physical implementation process to verify that inputs are made available on time and properly utilized. Monitoring concerns itself largely with the transformation of inputs to outputs; it is expected to alert management to (primarily physical) implementation problems, while evaluation is more concerned with immediate and development objective, i.e. effect and impact. To summarize:

Monitoring	*Evaluation*
Keeps track of daily activities on a continuous basis	Periodically examines project effect/ impact (long-range view)
Accepts policies, rules	Questions pertinence of policies, procedures
Looks at production of outputs	Examines progress towards objective achievement and asks if objectives appropriate/adequate.
Focuses on transformation inputs to outputs	Focuses on transformation outputs to objectives
Concentrates on planned project elements	Assesses planned elements and looks for unplanned change searches for causes, challenges assumptions
Reports on implementation progress	Checks on progress and seeks to identify lessons learned.

Obviously this approach to design and evaluation is not the only possible one that could be advanced. However, it has the distinct advantage of providing the organization with a unified system (and set of instructions) applicable to most donor technical cooperation projects and acceptable to most donors.

PROJECT ABANDONMENT

A project may be required to be abandoned even before its completion. Such a situation may arise under the following circumstances:

- When the project has lost its strategic importance both in terms of long term and short term strategies.
- When the resources required for implementing the project have become scare and their availability has become restricted.
- When the progress of project implementation always lags behind continuously and also substantially and when steps taken to improve the phase of project implementation do not yield favourable results.
- When completing the project has become infeasible due to the changed circumstances.

Under the above circumstances, it will wise to abandon the project. Abandoning the project under such circumstances will avoid mis-utilization of resources and will minimize the seepage of resources. The decision to abandon the project should be taken after an objective analysis without giving room for any personal basis and without any consideration for the cost already incurred in the project.

The Lucknow Municipal Corporation has abandoned the Rs. 839 million municipal solid waste treatment plant due to reasons like insufficient supply of organic waste. Hailed as national demonstration project, the power plant was built by Chennai based Asia Bio Energy Limited. The plant was under contract with Lucknow Municipality Corporation, Non-conventional Energy Development Agency NEDA and ABEL. The plant was installed to generate 5 MW of electricity using municipal waste mainly bio-degradable and production of organic manure for the use of farmers of nearby villages.

REASONS FOR FAILURE OF PROJECTS

- Real problems of beneficiaries not addressed.
- Socio-cultural values of the people not respected.
- Less involvement of 'stakeholders' in the design of the project.
- Objectives not clearly and realistically defined.
- No distinction between specific objectives and the means to arrive at those objectives.
- Insufficient analysis of project ideas before deciding to move to the feasibility phase.
- Projects not embedded in a rational 'supporting' framework.
- Use of inappropriate technologies.
- Local management knowledge not taken into account.
- Risks no anticipated.
- Economic and financial aspects of projects not elaborated.
- Lack of adequate information and effective monitoring.
- Too many 'managers' in different places responsible for the same project cycle.
- Insufficient clarity regarding the division of responsibilities.
- Application of rules and procedures rather than managing projects.

WHAT CONTRIBUTES TO SUCCESS?

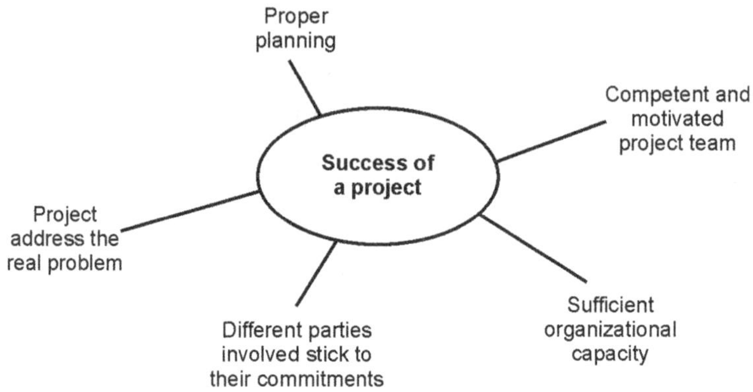

PURPOSE AND RELEVANCE OF EVALUATION

Alnor Ebrahim in his article "Accountability Mopia" has written the non-profit organization (NPO) utilize various kinds of evaluation, including performance and impact assessment. Donors commonly conduct external evaluations of NGO work near the end of a grant or program phase, and are increasingly employing midterm assessments as well. Such evaluations typically aim to access whether and to what extent programme goals and objectives have been achieved and are pivotal to determining future funding to NGOs'. These appraisals tend to focus on short-term results of organizational intervention (i.e., "outputs" or "activities") such as training programmes offered or housing units built. Increasingly, however, evaluations are being used to examine medium and long-tem results (i.e., "impacts" or "outcomes") such as improvements in client income, health, and natural resource base (Buckmaster, 1999; Roche, 1999, p. 22; United Way to America, 2002). Internal evaluations are also common in which NGO staff gauge their own progress, either toward and objectives of externally funded programs or toward internal goals and missions. Hybrid internal and external evaluations are not uncommon, with NGO staff working jointly with external evaluators.

Before examining the links between evaluation and accountability, it is helpful to explore why and for whom nonprofits engage in evaluation. In a study of 140 U.S. nonprofit agencies that had recently completed programme evaluations, Fine, Thayer and Coghlan (2000) found that the most commonly cited reason for conducting an evaluation was to measure program outcomes or impact, with about 56% designed for this purpose. From the same pool of organizations, less than one tenth reported other purposes, such as for informing strategic planning, assessing implementation, assessing quality of operations, and measuring client satisfaction. The audiences for these evaluations were primarily funders (69%), followed by programme staff (61%), board members (56%), potential funders (44%), government agencies (28%), clients or participants (24%), and other NPOs (9%). Somewhat similar findings were reported by Hoefer (2000, p. 171) in a study of 91 human service nonprofit agencies in the Dallas, Texas metropolitan area. He found that over half of the organizations conducted evaluations "to make sure that the program complies with proper procedures" and "to see how the programme is doing." Nearly 40% of the organizations conducted evaluations to satisfy funders, either to show them "how good the program is" or because a funder demanded an evaluation.

This pattern also appears relevant in the developing world – the global South – were NGOs typically engage in evaluations at the request of donors, usually midway through a project or programme and at its conclusion. In his review of a report on evaluations commissioned by 10 bilateral donors throughout the 1980s and 1990s, Riddel (1999) observed that the donor-initiated evaluations tended to emphasize cost-effectiveness and measurable benefits. In contrast, NGOs' own evaluations tended to allow for the use of more participatory method and placed a greater exphasis on evaluation as a means of providing feedback for enhancing future interventions. In their in-dept study of nine very successful development NGOs in South Asia, Smillie and Hailey (2001, p.84) have noted that it is not always clear whether evaluations are used for purposes of policing performance and financial expenditure or whether they shape future behaviour. They do suggest, however, that it is more common among older and more established organizations to treat evaluation as a positive process that can generate useful insights and learning. Smaller and younger organizations do not always have the experience or leverage with donors to shape evaluations to be more useful for learning.

Most evaluations, including those described above, tend to focus on specific programmes or projects, and they are often interchangeably described as assessment of "impact" or "performance" or "effectiveness." The universe of evaluations, however, is multidimensional and extends beyond specific programmes or projects. A useful model for framing evaluations is provided by Tassie, Murray, and Cutt (1998), who outline three dimensions along which evaluations may be conducted: (*a*) a "scope" dimension that identified who is being evaluated, be it a single project, a programme, an organization, or a system; (*b*) a "focus" dimension that refers to what is being evaluated, be it short-term outputs or activities, long-term outcomes or results, or the process by which activities are carried out and services are delivered; and (*c*) a "method" dimension that indicates how an evaluation is done, using formalized methods that aim at some degree of objectivity or non-formal methods that rely on conversation, impression, and reputation. The evaluations contained in the two U.S. studies cited above, for example, all appear to involve a scope at the programme level, but have a focus that varies from outputs to outcomes to process.

What this means for practical purposes is that one can come to different conclusions about an organization's "effectiveness" depending on how an evaluation is framed. Tassie and his colleagues argue precisely this point, showing how three funding organizations in Canada came to somewhat different conclusions about the same two non-profits as a result of how they framed their evaluations the multiple combinations of scope, method, and focus (12 in all) suggest that "inconsistencies can easily arise between evaluators, as they can have differing bases for their evaluations" (Tassie et al., 1998, p.63). Organizational effectiveness, as such, can be viewed as highly malleable.

This problem is particularly apparent in conflicts among NGOs and funders over whether they should be assessing processes such as "participation and "empowerment" or whether they should measure more tangible products such as the numbers of schools built and children graduated, or numbers of trees planted and land area reforested. For the most part, appraisals by funders tend to focus on products – they are short-term and emphasize easily measurable and quantifiable results over more ambiguous and less tangible change in social and political processes. Such measurement often operationalized through a method known as "logical framework analysis" has important implications for accountability. Edwards and Hulme (1996) suggest that the wide use of logical frameworks and their derivatives may "distort accountability by overemphasizing short-term quantitative targets and favouring hierarchical management structures" (p. 968).

Evaluations, especially those that build on logical frameworks, are typically premised on a goal-attainment model of assessment. That is, they are based on an assumptions that the goals, services, and products offered by the NGO can easily be measured. However, D' Aunno (1992) suggests that it might make more sense to vary assessments with the context of an organization. In cases where an organization's work is indeed fairly easy to measure (e.g., a nonprofit that aim to serve meals to the poor) and performance criteria are likely to be shared across different stakeholder groups, a rational or goal-attainment approach is sensible. However, in cases where performance criteria vary among stakeholders, it would make more sense to adopt a multi-constituency model that gauges organizational performance in relation to the preferences of different groups. This is likely to be more useful among organizations whose goals are more process oriented (such as participation or gender equity) and where there may be conflicting goals among constituents. In other cases, attainment of organizational goals may be even more difficult to measure, such as in the case of policy advocacy or empowerment. Such organizations may be better assessed by an institutional-theory model, that is, by measuring their conformity to what society expects of them. For example, if one were to measure the progress of a human rights organization based on the number of national policies it is able to change, its progress is likely to look slow and limited. However, an institutional-theory approach might instead assess the organization on its ability to garner resources from the public as a result of behaving how we expect it to – by fighting for a set of espoused rights and doing so through socially legitimated structures and processes such as courts, even if it takes decades to achieve those rights.

This brings us to a broader concern about the purpose and relevance of evaluation. It is natural to assume that evaluations serve a clear and objectively verifiable purpose: to access performance or effectiveness. There are at least three significant problems with this view. First, as already discussed, the results of an evaluation are dependent on how it is framed. A social constructivist perspective on organizational effectiveness opens the door to evaluations being conducted for purposes of social legitimating. Particularly in cases where a single NPO is subject to conflicting demands imposed by multiple funders or constituents, evaluations can be used as instruments which signal that an organization "appears to conform with social norms, values, and expectations" (Tassie et al., 1998, p. 77). As such, the information emerging from evaluations and impact studies is not simply utilitarian in its relevance (i.e., for assessing effectiveness or performance), but it also serves a symbolic function critical to conferring legitimacy. It is by no means unusual or uncommon for organizations to engage in such ceremonial activities, some of which may involve a decoupling of information from decisions (Feldman & March, 1988; Meyer & Rowan, 1977).

A second set of problem concerns NGO perspectives on the relevance of evaluation. Riddel (1999) lists several reasons why NGOs are skeptical about the need for the purpose of evaluation. On one side, NGO culture tends to emphasize action over analysis. NGO staffs are, by and large, "doers" that gain more legitimacy by helping the poor than by conducting time-consuming and costly evaluations. In addition, the tendency of donor evaluations to focus on discrete projects limits their relevance in examining longer-term processes. A reasonable donor response to such skepticism is, of course, that evaluations can help NGO staff become better doers by uncovering weaknesses in project planning or by developing more strategic interventions, and that evaluations can be designed to access longer-term process and outcomes rather than simply short-term outputs.

It is more difficult, however, to respond to NGO concerns that performance assessments give funders the arsenal to base funding on "successful" projects, thereby rewarding NGOs that stick to discrete and proven product-based approaches to development while punishing those that attempt to develop and test more innovative and risky process-based approaches (Riddel, 1999, p. 225-226). An additional crucial concern raised by small NGOs is that their limited staff and recourses are stretched too thin by evaluation and reporting requests of funders. Donors sometimes fail to recognize that complex evaluation requirements can overwhelm small organizations (and even large ones at times), and that NGO size and capacity should be key factors in determining the scale of appraisal. Onerous data requirements can lead NGOs to develop monitoring and evaluation system that although satisfying donor needs for information are viewed as irrelevant for internal NGO decision making. For example, a large European Commission grant to two of India's most highly reputed NGOs involved the creation of an elaborate monitoring system using 89 indicators. Although these data are used to legitimate the work of the two NGOs, they are rarely systematically analyzed for purposes of informing decision making (Ebrahim, 2002).

The third problem concerning the purpose of evaluation is more explicitly normative. Although it makes rational sense to conduct evaluations in order to access progress toward objectives, should this be the sole, or even the primary purpose of evaluation? For the most part, performance assessments tend to focus attention on projects or programmes while overlooking the organization itself (Fowler, 1996). Arguably, evaluations have the potential to be more than snapshots of impacts or performance, and they can be used proactively for facilitating broader organizational change, particularly through capacity building and organizational learning. In his study of Dallas nonprofits, Hoefer (2000) notes that "Almost all of the organizations (96 percent) have used or plan to use the results to make improvements in the programmes operations" (p. 173). But although these organizations may intend to use the collected data for informing decision making, this is likely to be ad-hoc if there are no protocols in place for systematically integrating new information into a decision process.

In practice, the mere collection of information does not necessarily lead to its use in improving performance, as is evidenced by the collection of dusty studies that sit on the shelves of many organizations. It is for this reason that Riddell (1999, p.237), in his study of a number of donor and NGO experiences with evaluation, concludes that "donor funds would probably be better spent in helping NGOs develop and experiment with different methods of assessment than in undertaking large number of impact studies based on methods used to date." This observation points to the potential use of evaluation as a tool for learning, rather than simply for impact and performance assessment.

There are three general insights about the use of evaluations in NPOs. First, evaluations are conducted not only to assess impact or effectiveness but also to satisfy funders. They are important for the symbolic purpose of legitimating organizational practices and thus for enabling continued funding. Second, one can come to different conclusions about an organization's effectiveness depending on how an evaluation is framed. In other words, organizational effectiveness is a malleable construct. And third, organizations that conduct evaluations do not necessarily know how to use their findings to change behaviour. If evaluations are to be useful for guiding deliberate change in organizations, they will require a link to organizational learning. There are indeed approaches to evaluation that are more compatible with multiple accountabilities and organizational learning.

Evaluations can be divided into three very general categories: those that provide a snapshot of progress to date, those that feed back into organizational decision making, and, those that involve multiple constituencies. The former type is likely to affect NGO decisions and actions only where it turns up results poor enough to threaten external sources of funding. Its value is punitive, and it functions as a mechanism of upward accountability. The second category of evaluation – in which evaluation results are designed, to guide NGO decision making – is really a means toward organizational learning. The third type is an extension of the second, as it provides feedback from different stakeholders for long-term learning purposes, but it also improves downward accountability. Such learning is a process that can be designed to help achieve (and rethink) organizational mission. In other words, whether evaluation is seen as enabling upward accountability or organizational learning depends on for what purpose and for whom it is used. In cases where donors are focused on short-term goals and demonstrations of funds well spent, one might expect evaluations to be used largely for purposes of upward accountability. But in cases where NGOs and their donors are more attentive to long-term goals and the difficulties of social change, one might anticipate an orientation toward organizational learning as well as downward accountability.

Observers of the international development funding context, and particularly of bilateral funders, suggest that the former situation is the norm – in which donors tend to emphasize short-term quantitative targets for purposes of control and justification rather than as part of a system directed towards complex learning and long-term change (Edwards & Hulme, 1996; Riddell, 1999; Smillie, 1996). This is one kind of accountability myopia, characterized by a short-term vision of accountability as rule-following behaviour rather than as a means to longer-term social change.

A second kind of myopia involves a tendency to see accountability as a set of binary and unconnected relations rather than as a broader system of relations. In their study of several of the world's most established NGOs involved in international emergency relief work, Lindenberg and Bryant (2001) offer a link between accountability and system of relations, which they argue is contingent and multidirectional in nature:

'One of the implications of multiple and competing audience pulls is that different kinds of information and feedback are needed for different audiences. Therefore accountability is necessarily contingent upon both the demander and the context of the demand. For example, donor often require formal evaluation reports, while other contributors expect some summary financial reports and annual mailings; beneficiaries, on the other hand, need results – though their own interpretation of favorable results can differ from the interpretations imposed by donors'.

The subtext of the above observation concerns power, although the authors do not describe it as such. Indeed, very little of the literature on accountability makes explicit reference to this concept. An organization's ability to control a resource is a form of power, with power being defined as "the ability to influence outcomes, changing what might have been in the absence of the use of power" (Preffer & Salancik, 1974, p. 148). Arguably, accountability mechanisms such as evaluations that focus on short-term and quantifiable results strengthen the hand of donors whose own reputations rely on measuring results and demonstrating success over annual budget cycles, while weakening the hands of communities where effective social change may result only over longer time frames.

It is analytically significant that power, like accountability, is relational: It inheres in the relationships between people and organizations. Lindenberg and Bryant's (2001) view that accountability is multidirectional is consistent with this perspective, for it suggests that there can be competing accountabilities among donors and NGO constituents. The asymmetries in these relationships are products of power. In practical terms, an analysis of power thus requires an examination of both for what and for whom resources such as money or information affect outcomes or behaviour, and the roles played by mechanisms such as evaluation. Donors, for example, use funds as a means of leveraging demonstrated results from NGOs (through evaluation and reporting), thus enabling them to build a reputation for funding "Success". Similarly, NGOs use evaluations and the information they provide to donors as a vehicle for accessing money. Information may thus be seen as a form of symbolic power that by conferring legitimacy can be used by individuals, organizations, or social groups to leverage other resources (Bourdieu, 1977, p. 178-179) Evaluations and other reports prepared for the benefit of donors serve as a means through which the organization conveys its activities to the outside world.

Research on the social psychology of accountability (e.g., Lerner & Tetlock, 1999; Markman & Tetlock, 2000, Tetlock, Skitka, & Boettger, 1989) appears to support this view and suggests that accountability relations are even more complex than discussed. For example, Lerner and Tetlock (1999) argue that individuals respond to accountability rules differently based on knowledge about their audience (i.e., those to whom they are accountable) such that (a) they conform to the views of their audience in cases where the interests of that audience are known; (b) they engage in preemptive self-criticism in order to appear objective and to anticipate reasonable objections in cases where the audience is unknown; and (c) they engage in defensive bolstering to justify decisions when they are already committed to a decision or course of action. For NGOs, this literature suggests that accountability is likely to be biased in favour of funders, and that self-critical evaluations oriented to organizational learning are only likely under circumstance where funders' wishes are uncertain.

In summary, if accountability is about relationships between organizational actors, then accountability mechanisms (such as evaluations) cannot be properly understood without some consideration of for whom and for what purpose they are employed. A central challenge for NPOs, as such, is to find a balance or a mix between mechanisms that respond to the upward accountability concerns of donors and those that meet the needs of staff and communities (i.e., internal and downward accountability), while also leading to positive changes in organizational behaviour. For many NGOs, finding this balance will require a reorientation toward learning processes and accountability to mission in order to place upward-driven evaluation reporting in proper perspective. It will also require the use of both short-term and long-term assessments. The key point is that accountability, like power, is a relational concept, and the effects of its mechanisms can thus only be understood when placed in context. In cases where funders share a long-term perspective with NGOs, this balancing can be expected to occur with less difficulty, but in cases where donor priorities emphasize short-term results at the expense of long-term learning, this mismatch can lead to conflicting accountabilities.

OUTLINING M & E DURING INITIAL PROJECT DESIGN

How initial project design influences M & E

Unintentionally, M & E is often set up to fail during initial project design. How? For example, there is lack of adequate budget for M & E, insufficient time and expertise have been allocated to M & E during the start-up phase, or there is insufficient flexibility in the project design to enable the M & E system to influence the project strategy during implementation. Initial project design influences M & E through:

1. The relationships and commitment established with partners and local people, particularly the intended primary stakeholders;
2. The logic and feasibility of the project strategy;
3. The resources allocated to M & E (funding, time, expertise);

4. The degree of inbuilt flexibility;
5. The operational guidelines for M & E.

Let's consider each point:

First, during project implementation, the effectiveness of M & E will be greatly influenced by the attitudes and commitment of local people and partners involved in the project and how they relate and communicate with each other. Individuals or organizations that have been active in the design phase are more likely to know if the project is genuinely in their interests and to understand the objectives. They are more likely to take an interest in monitoring the progress and achievements of the project. Alternatively, if people have been disillusioned, frustrated by or left out of the design process, then they are less likely to be interested in the commitment to M & E activities.

In practice, projects experience considerable delays between design and start-up and related changes regarding who is involved. Nevertheless, the experience and legitimacy of the design process will have lasting consequences for implementation. The definition of clear responsibilities may also require the formation of new institutions or groups/units within institutions to undertake them.

A weak basis for effective M & E

In many projects M & E department was not part of the project-management organizational structure. Instead, it fell under and was directly responsible to a government agency with a long-established M & E unit of its own based on national guidelines. Similarly the project director was also directly responsible to the chairman of the agency. This structure meant that the M & E unit had no direct access to resources and relied on minimal government funding. So no M & E reporting was undertaken. M & E activities required approval via a complex hierarchy of top-level managers. As the M & E department was responsible to the agency, relationships with project management were sensitive. This further affected the M & E budget, project incentives for M & E and adoption of M & E recommendations by the project. To make matters worse, project M & E was based on the existing government system without necessarily holding relevance to project specificities. This was compounded by the fact that project M & E staff were also responsible for M & E activities of other projects under the auspices of the government agency.

The second design fault is when a project lacks logic in its strategy or has unrealistic objectives, making good M & E almost impossible. This is because the evaluation equations and indicators often become quite meaningless and will not produce useful information. Furthermore, if you don't know clearly where you are heading then you will not know how best to use any information that might be produced. A good M & E system can help put a poorly designed project back on tract, but this created considerable extra work during start-up and implementation.

The third is when the design team does not allocate enough resources to the M & E system. Critical resources include: funding for information management, participatory monitoring activities, field visits, etc.; time for a start-up phase that is long enough to establish the M & E system, do a participatory baseline, train staff and partners, include primary stakeholders in M & E and monitor and reflect; and expertise, such as a consultant to support M & E development. As the design team, you must negotiate the level and extent of M & E that is possible for a given budget. Then you can make a detailed M & E budget.

The fourth factor is critical if M & E systems are to generate the learning that helps a group of project partners continually improve implementation and strategy. The more rigid a project design is, the more difficulty the project team will have in adjusting it as a result of changes in the context and understanding of interim impacts. As the design team, identify how flexible you feel the project design needs to be and what the boundaries of and processed for design adoption should be. A project with inbuilt flexibility provides an important rationale for the M & E system.

Fifth, it is important that during design, the broad framework of the M & E system is established. Then everyone's expectations about his or her responsibilities and information rights can be clear. The next sub-section indicates what could be included in the documentation that described the M & E system in the project appraisal report.

Documenting M & E in the project appraisal report

The last M & E related step for the design team is writing down the suggested M & E framework in appraisal report. How this is done can strongly affect the start-up of the project.

Implications of how the M & E system is documented at appraisal

Below table outlines what to include in the appraisal report as related to the M & E framework. This can serve to guide the writing process. As management functions relate to project M & E and implementation, so the M & E component of the appraisal report may either be included as a separate section or be integrated into a section on project organization and administration and/or management. The main point is that the more the M & E component is integrated into the management system, the more useful and effective it may be.

Suggested contents lists for the M & E component in a project appraisal report

Section Heading	*Description*
Introduction	Overview of purpose of this section of the appraisal report plus a summary of key innovations and potential obstacles for the project implementers to consider.
1. Specific project/context features that affect M & E	Features affecting the resources required for the M & E unit to remain viable, including, for example, geographic coverage and level of in-country communication systems; other contextual features: the range of project components and the project organizational hierarchy.
2. M & E purpose and scope	Broadly defined purpose and scope of M & E in the project context, including the project M & E needs and the information to be generated.
3. Key performance questions, indicators, information-gathering requirements and implications for the M & E system.	List of possible key questions and indicators for the goal, purpose and output levels, plus generally described information gathering and organizing methods to enable resource allocation.

4. Internal self-evaluation processes (input/output monitoring, ongoing evaluation and impact evaluation)	General outline of key processes, task and events.
5. External evaluation (ongoing and impact evaluation)	The frequency of external evaluations and how the project will be integrated into this evaluation process, including special evaluation studies or thematic studies that might be needed at key moments in the project.
6. Intended primary stakeholder and partner participation in M & E	Including the early identification of stakeholders for their involvement in M & E planning at start-up.
7. Structures and staffing for M & E	Approximately staffing levels and types, roles and responsibilities related to activities, and a clear description of the organizational structure of M & E and its interaction with other project sectors, particularly with project management.
8. Capacity-building for M & E	Types of support needed to create sufficient and appropriate M & E capacity among project stakeholders.
9. Information management	Any specific information management systems that are recommended for the project context.
10. Process for detailed planning of M & E during start-up.	Including draft timeframe for development of the M & E system
11. Communicating strategy	Broad description of key audiences and types of information that should be communicated to them.
12. Budget	Approximate budget for key items (staff time, materials, evaluation and training events, publication/ documentation, consultants).
Appendices	
M & E Responsibilities of project Management	
Terms of Reference for those responsible for M & E and for consultants providing M & E support.	
Detailed M & E budget	

Social Cost-Benefits Analysis

Chapter 10

An organization, investing in a project wish to earn return from project. The return may be of commercial in nature i.e. maximization of profit or reduction in cost and it may give social benefits like employment opportunities etc. Rural projects may not offer attractive returns as far as commercial profitability is concerned, but still such projects are undertaken since they have social implications. An irrigation or infrastructural project plays significant role in socio-economic development rather than commercial profitability.

An organization involved in imparting training may analyze its per capita expenditure and the expected outcome out of the training. The project investment gives result in the form of training, a social benefit. Government of India has been allowing foreign collaboration in the fields of high priority and in the areas where import of foreign technology is considered necessary. Foreign collaborations have led to improvement in technology but at the same time, certain practices and effects of multinational corporations have given rise to wide concerns and anxiety in many quarters. Now many multinational companies are undertaking social development and welfare projects in the rural areas. The projects being undertaken imposes certain costs to the nation and produces certain benefits to the nation. These costs and benefits may be direct costs and direct benefits and indirect costs and indirect benefits.

A dam project has its direct costs viz. financial investment and indirect costs viz. displacement of the community or environmental degradation and direct benefits viz. irrigation facilitation or power generation and indirect benefits like employment to local youths. The social cost-benefit analysis takes into account the 'real cost' of direct costs and 'real benefit' of direct benefits. The social cost-benefit analysis takes into account the real cost of inputs, the cost of inputs not subsidized. Accordingly, the required adjustments to direct costs of inputs are made for social-cost-benefit analysis. Similarly, cost adjustments may also be required for the benefits. For example, the output may be a product whose price is controlled by government like Petrol and Diesel. The commercial profitability analysis will take into account the controlled price (the price fixed by Ministry of Petroleum) while its actual benefit to the nation may be more or less than the controlled price.

If we talk about the commercial profitability analysis only direct cost and direct benefits are considered. The country, state or area bears the indirect costs and indirect benefits to the nation. Immunization programmes and social marketing programmes of the government had been criticized on various arguments leading to social-cost-benefit analysis.

Cost-Benefit Analysis (CBA) is a framework for evaluation of the social costs and benefits of an investment project.

This involves identifying, measuring and comparing the private costs and negative externalities of a scheme with its private benefits and positive externalities, using money as a measure of value.

Step 1: Identify all costs and benefits using the principle of opportunity cost.

Step 2: Measure the benefits and costs using money as unit of account.

Step 3: Consider the likelihood of the cost or benefit occurring (i.e. sensitivity analysis)

Step 4: Take account of the timing of the cost and benefit (i.e. discounting). A Rs. 10,00,000 benefit now is worth more than Rs. 10,00,000 benefit in 10 years time.

(A) IDENTIFY ALL COSTS AND BENEFITS

A firm deciding on an investment project will only take account of its own private costs and benefits e.g. total cost and total revenue. Firms ignore externalities. SCBA will take account of both private and external costs and benefits.

Consider a project to build a bridge over a river

- Private costs e.g. construction costs, operating costs and maintenance costs.
- External costs i.e. costs incurred by non user (*a*) monetary e.g. loss of profits to competitors e.g. to ferry owner and (*b*) non monetary e.g. noise, loss to countryside, inconvenience.
- Private benefits (*a*) direct the amount consumers are prepared to pay e.g. the tolls paid (*b*) indirect i.e. consumer surplus.
- External benefits i.e. benefits to non user e.g. consumer surplus of users; time savings for travelers and fewer accidents.

(B) MEASURE THE BENEFITS AND COSTS

Height can be measured using feet and inches. Benefits and costs can be valued using money. Private costs and benefits are relatively easy to measure in monetary terms.

Total costs and total benefits

Private costs

(*i*) To build the bridge: Rs. 25 crores

(*ii*) To operate it: Rs. 2 crores a year

(*iii*) To repair and maintenance: Rs. 1 crore a year

Private benefits

1,00,00,000 users each paying Rs. 10 each = Rs. 10,00,00,000

Externalities are more difficult to measure

- Noise or loss of countryside: What value do people place on these? By how much do those who suffer need to be, compensated. Ask them using a questionnaire! If 2000 affected people value the annual loss of countryside at Rs. 500 then cost Rs. 1,00,000.

- Time Saving: What value do people place on work time saved or leisure time saved? Is the time saved worth the same to everyone? If 1,00,000 hours are saved and valued at Rs. 4 per hour, benefit = Rs. 4,00,000.
- Fewer accidents: Economists value human life using money, so with insurance companies; one life = Rs. 75,000. If the bridge saves one life a year, annual benefit is Rs. 75,000.

(C) LIKELIHOOD OF THE COST OR BENEFIT

If there is a 50% chance that a life will be saved then the benefit is Rs. 75,000 × 0.5 = Rs. 37,500.

(D) THE TIMING OF THE COST AND BENEFIT

The major costs of the project occurs straight away. The benefits occur over the life of the project. The bridge may cost Rs. 25 crore to build but consumers benefit by Rs. 1 crore a year. If the expected life of the bridge is 35 years then how do we value now Rs. 1 crore of benefit in 35 years time? Economists discount the future benefits to identify the present value.

(E) IS A PROJECT WORTH UNDERTAKING?

Yes, if discounted benefits outweigh discounted costs. If the government has to choose between completing projects then the ones with highest positive net present value should be undertaken.

We invest in educating our children, sometimes it involves higher costs. These costs sometimes cause pain to others, but in the last, the cost and investment give good results when these children utilize education in employment, business, service or in any other occupation and become good citizen. This result may be called as benefit out of the investment. A question arise here that what is the ratio of this cost and benefit in terms of social goods. This analysis may be called social cost-benefit analysis (SCBA).

Objective of the SCBA is to appraise the total impact of a project on society, economy, environment and other segments. It also analyze the contribution of the project to improve the benefits to the poorer sections of the society and to reduce the regional imbalance. It provide justification of the use of scarce resources of the project to realize good benefits. Many projects have negative impact on the society, SCBA appraise the contribution of the project in the community development, environment protection and improvement as well employment generation.

Social desirability of a project

Social desirability depends upon the features of the area specially on availability of resources, community, climatic conditions, geographic location and other factors. Many times we have seen the insurgent opposition by the community of a project specially mineral based industries where large-scale rehabilitation is required. Hence the opposition reflects towards the social undesirability of a project.

Social-cost-benefit analysis of social labeling programme

Due to crusade against the employment of child labour in the carpet manufacturing by humanitarian organizations, NGOs and the German importers and American Senator Tom Harkins, the Indian carpet industry faced unexpected challenges in the export of Carpets and Dhurries. In a strategic intervention

'Rugmark Foundation' was established and the 'Rugmark label' was introduced. It is a social label because it is related with a social cause nad has social benefits in terms of elimination and rehabilitation of child labour.

NGO "South Asian Coalition for Child Servitude" led by Kailash Satyarthi and "Bachpan Bachao Andolan" led by Swami Swami Agnivesh did every successful efforts for the popularization of employment of child labour in carpet industry. Government announced and implemented various programme like IPEC for the elimination and rehabilitation of child labour in the carpet industry. Due to repeated propaganda, carpet industry was bound to take healthy initiative which later on resulted in the initiative like social labeling with the cooperation of exporters and importers. Arpana Ravi in article "Combating child labour with labels" had emphasized various dimensions of labeling programme of Rugmark Foundation in Bachdohi-Mirzapur carpet belt.

The large-scale use of labour in the hand knotted carpet industry in Uttar Pradesh in Northern India is not a new phenomenon. However, the issue has, in recent years, aroused much concern in India as well as the west, and led to new and promising initiatives to conduct it. One such initiative that has attracted much interest is Rugmark, a product-labeling scheme that is based on the desire of western consumers for goods produced under normally acceptable working conditions. By February 2000, over 1.5 million hand-knotted carpets exported from India had carried a 'Rugmark' label, which indicated that they had not been made by children below the age of 15. The Rugmark labeling initiative was founded in 1994 by humanitarian organizations in Germany and India with the support of carpet importers and the German government. It attempts to eliminate child labour in the Indian carpet industry by harnessing the desire of consumers in the two leading carpet importing countries., Germany and the US, for child-labour-free carpets. Carpet manufacturers who register with Rugmark commit not to employ child labour in production processes and allow the Rugmark Foundation to conduct unannounced inspections of their looms. The Rugmark Foundation then attaches labels to their carpets, thereby selectively promoting the export of carpets made without the use of child labour.

The emergence of labeling programmes like Rugmark is emblematic of global trends. The last decade has witnessed an increased awareness and concern for child labourers in different parts of the world as globalization has brought goods produced by children to the hands of consumers in industrialized countries.

ECONOMICS OF LABELING SCHEMES

Before looking at the achievements and limitation of Rugmark, it is necessary to examine the rationale behind using market initiatives such as labeling schemes to combat child labour. Richard Freeman., a professor of economics at Harvard University, believes that these programmes are based on the free market principle.

He wrote, "The consumer who cares about labour standards consumes not only physical goods but also the work conditions associated with them. He is in principle willing to pay higher prices for the goods produced under better working conditions, which provides a financial margin for improving conditions or increasing wages in less developed countries. Since consumers want this outcome, producing under humane conditions in those countries would improve the economy overall" (Freeman 1998).

To demonstrate that consumers are in fact concerned about working conditions, Freeman cited a survey done by Marymount University's Centre for Ethical Concerns, which asked a sample of Americans whether they would stop shopping at a particular garment store if they knew that those garments have been produced in sweatshops (Freeman 1996:6). Seventy-eight per cent of the respondents said they would, and 84 per cent said that they would be willing to pay an extra dollar for a $ 20 garment if they knew it had been produced under acceptable conditions. While admitting that there might be some discrepancy between how consumers say they will behave and how they act in practice. Freeman believes this evidence strongly suggests that consumers are willing to pay more for goods that they know have been produced at a legitimate shop.

The problem, according to Freeman, is not that consumers do not act in the way they say they will but rather a problem of information. The consumer is often ignorant of the circumstances under which the goods they purchase are produced, and this is especially so for goods produced in low-income countries. The cost of obtaining this information for an individual consumer is too high in terms of time and effort, and for exceeds that of buying 5 goods produced under poor working conditions (Freeman 1998:6). Thus, some other source needs to provide this information to consumers in order to help them make informed decisions. Product labeling schemes serve this purpose. In the case of labeling schemes that target child labour, the level informs the consumer that the particular good has not been made by children, and that by purchasing it instead of a similar but unlabelled product, he would not be contributing to an exploitative practice.

Labelling programmes attempt to reduce child labour by providing manufacturers with a disincentive to employ children. They try to remove children from the labour force of a particular industry by starting from the consumer and moving back in the marketing chain to affect the production process (Hilowitz 1997). The founders of labeling schemes hope that if consumers demand only those goods whose label indicates that they have been produced without the use of child labour, manufacturers will be forced to change their labour practices. Labelling initiatives also seek to combat child labour through an economic component by contributing to improvements in the situation of child labourers and their families in the region. A part of the fees that importers and exporters pay upon registering with a labeling programme as well as the additional costs that consumers are willing to pay for child-free products go into funding schools and rehabilitation facilities for former child labourers in the industry.

ESTABLISHMENT OF RUGMARK

The prevalence of child labour in the carpet industry and its export-oriented nature made it an ideal target for a labelling scheme. The original idea of labeling carpets came from a Delhi based NGO, the South Asian Coalition on Child Servitude (SACCS) and a German Foundation, Bread for the World. In 1991, these two organizations began to harness support for a labeling programme from carpet importers, international agencies such as the UNICEF, the German government, consumer groups and other humanitarian organizations in the west. After much debate among these groups, the Rugmark labeling initiative was finally established in 1994. the history of Rugmark reveals that the creation of the labeling scheme was based on a careful balancing of the economic interests of the Indian carpet industry with the moral concern of eliminating child labour and providing educational opportunities for former child labourers. Rugmark was established as much with the goal of protecting the market for Indian carpets in the west as with the goal of combating child labour in the industry.

The Rugmark initiative has three stated purpose: to organize individuals and companies in the carpet industry to stop using child labour; to establish an independent, professional and internationally credible monitoring and certification system for carpets manufactured without child labour, and to provide social welfare and education facilities for former child labourers in the carpet industry (The Rugmark Foundation 1999:2). The organizations that operate the labeling programme are the Rugmark Foundations in the two carpet producing countries, India and Nepal, and the two major carpet importing countries, the US and Germany. The Rugmark Foundation in India is a non-profit private sector company that operates the labelling initiative in the carpet-weaving region in Uttar Pradesh and attaches labels to carpets before they are exported. Registration with Rugmark is voluntary for carpet importers as well as for manufactures and exporters. Carpet importers who register with Rugmark Commit to purchase only labeled carpets. Manufacturers and exporters make a legally binding commitment not to use child labour and to pay labourers fair wages. In addition, they are required to provide list of all the looms where their carpets are produced, and permit surprise inspections of their loom-sheds by Rugmark's inspectors as well as by local NGOs. This last provision is required even though the looms often do not belong to the manufacturer, but to independent loom owners and contractors. Every loom registered with Rugmark is given a number and so is every carpet at the time when its weaving process begins. These are recorded in a computerized database allowing the Rugmark Foundation to be able to trace any carpet back to the actual loom in which it was woven. At the time of export, each carpet is given a Rugmark label identifying the location of the loom in which it was woven, its maker and exporter.

Apart from monitoring and affixing labels to carpets, Rugmark runs some social welfare and rehabilitation programmes. Upon registration carpet manufactures pay Rugmark 0.25 per cent of the export value of their carpets, and importers contribute 1 per cent of the import value. Rugmark uses these funds to carry out its inspections and to run schools and rehabilitation centres for former child labourers. Balashraya is a rehabilitation centre run by Rugmark that provides formal and non-formal education to formerly bonded and migrant child labourers. Rugmark also runs four elementary schools for children of poor carpet weavers and for those rescued from the looms. The four schools and the rehabilitation centre together provide education to nearly 1,000 children in the carpet-weaving zone (Rugmark Foundation India 1997:3).

In addition to the suspicion that accompanies any foreign initiative, NGOs in the region, government officials and exporters pointed to problems with the programme's implementation. The most criticized aspect of Rugmark has been its method of monitoring the participating looms to ensure that the loom owners are not using child labour. Shamshad Khan, the director of CREDA, said that while the idea of Rugmark was appealing in theory the programme was impossible to implement given the nature of the carpet industry. He believed that the loopholes in the inspection process made it difficult to establish with certainty that child labour had not been involved in the production of a particular carpet.

The carpet industry in Mirzapur and Bhadohi districts (the main carpet concentration region) is largely rural, household based and unorganized (informal)in nature. Independent household loom-owners spread over hundreds of thousand villages in the larger Poorvanchal region manufacture carpets of many kinds, but mainly hand-knotted ones. The largest concentration area in Poorvanchal region consists of about ten districts of which villages in Mirzapur, Bhadohi and Varanasi are the main production centres spread over 1500 villages in an area of 10,000 square kilometers. The weaving and knotting work is carried almost in more than 1,00,000 household based looms.

Poorvanchal region has both large and small-scale, traditional and modern carpet industries with annual exports nearing about US $ 340.87 million in 1999. There are six leading carpet suppliers in the word market e.g. Iran, China, India, Pakistan, Nepal and Turkey. Iran ranks number one followed by China. India ranks number three in terms of value and number one in terms of volume. The total share of Indian carpet exports has been increasing in absolute terms i.e. Rs. 2013.94 crores (in 1998-99), Rs. 2136.03 crores 9 (in 1999-2000), Rs. 2315.15 crores (in 2000-01), Rs. 2436.13 crores (2001-02) and Rs. 2590.26 crores (in 2002-03). Although share of national export of carpets for this region (Poorvanchal in general and Mirzapur in particular) has been declining over the last few years. Its share at present is believed to be about 65% only.

In this largely unorganized carpet sector, of entire Poorvanchal region, which is mainly, agrarian (rural and household-based) employs about 3 million people (an estimate for the year 2003). It is also believed that 1.5 to 3% of the total carpet based labour force in Pooranchal region is child labour, which over the last few years has been declining. Children are still employed on a large-scale in the weaving and production of hand-knotted carpets although their employment is banned under Child Labour (Prohibition and Regulation) Act. Earlier, according to Neera Burra (1995), children constituted 75 per cent of the labour force in carpet making. Both the carpet export and Promotion Council (CEPC) of India and the Government of India consider Neera Bura's estimate as too highly exaggerated. In a detailed sample survey of entire Indian carpet industry in 1993, Harvey and Riggin (1994) estimated child labour to be about 22 per cent of total 6,00,000 carpet weavers/workers. In absolute terms, according to Harvey and Riggin, there were about 1,30,000 children working on carpet.

The figures given by Harvey and Riggin also appear to be high. Nevertheless, the figure is now too old to be accepted in 2003. According to David Rangpal who runs "Project Mala' schools for the carpet working children in this region, 'much of the confusion about child labour was caused by a failure to differentiate between bonded, or slave labour; children working for wages on looms near their homes and children who helped their families to weave carpets.'

Production in the carpet industry is traditionally organized on a three-tier basis. At the top is the importer/exporter/manufacturer. In the middle are several intermediaries/contractors/small manufactures/loom owners. At the bottom of the ladder are master weavers/weavers/trainees. At the bottom are also these vulnerable child weavers. The trainees or the common weavers and master weavers work for the individual loom-owner on piece-rate wage basis. Sometimes the individual owner himself may also be the master weaver. These individually owned looms are small in size (generally 6 x 8 feet area) under a hut (cottage), dimly lit sheds, without proper ventilation and other facilities. The sheds are extremely susceptible to fires and other mishaps. Long hours of weaving related works make it a very depressing environment. If the loom-owner is not the master weaver, then he would give five percent extra commission to the master-weaver in addition to his piece-rate wage, for supervising the work of other weavers and for providing training to new weavers.

The loom-owners generally make carpets for specific exporters, small or big in lieu of advances taken from them. In many cases use of the words 'carpet manufacturer' can be misleading. Many of them are mainly exporters, who do not directly involve themselves in weaving or manufacturing. They generally process export orders, get designs made, procure raw materials and get woolen yarns dyed and then finally give it to some middlemen/intermediary or the contractor for weaving of carpets by master weavers. The loom owner or the contractor may sometimes only act as a link between the exporter and the master/common weaver. The loom owner or the contractor gets some commission, which are generally about 25% of the initial transaction. The contractor or the individual loom owner procures raw materials from the exporter, supplies them to the weavers, and supervises the quality and schedule of the production. He is mainly responsible for getting the carpet produced and return it to the exporter. There are also other artisans or workers (both adults and children) at the lower level, who are involved in clipping, washing, repairs and finishing jobs for the carpet on piece-rate wage basis. They also work under the close supervision of the individual loom owners or the contractors.

Some of the exporters/manufacturers have done away with the middle-tier of contractors. Either they have their own large-scale factory based looms (e.g. in house production units) or purchase carpets of a particular specification from various loom owners/master weavers. The manufacturer/exporter deals directly with the loom owners spread out all over the carpet weaving villages. In this system, there is a direct contract between the loom owner and the manufacturer. Their staff can make periodical visits to the loom owner's establishment but again because of the huge area where such weaving is done, these visits for practical reasons, cannot be more than once a month at best and hence less accountable to warrant employment of child labour.

Under the more traditional pattern of contract system, the manufacturer/exporter used to give his raw material, designs and order specifications to a completely independent entrepreneur, who was known as the 'contractor'. The contractor would generally find loom owners or master weavers to produce woven unfinished carpets, which he should finally give them back to the exporters/manufacturers. Here the contractors are given their commission or share of the transaction in monetary terms. The control of the industry is only by male manufacturers/exporters, male contractors, individual male loom owners and male master-weavers. Women and girl children do participate in the job of carpet weaving but only at the lower levels. Since it is a household-based industry, usually there are no fixed hours of working. Generally, there are also no written agreements between any two transactions or assigned work except for loans and raw materials taken and returned as finished/semi finished products. Rainy season is bad for carpet production; otherwise the work goes on through out the year.

The other unintended development has been the emergence of multiple labeling schemes. Care and Fair, a German labeling initiative, was established by German importers and retailers with the aim of improving the lives of children and their families in carpet producing regions. It also provided assistance to organizations like Jwala Hospital with a mobile medical van. In 1995, STEP, a small Swiss Foundation, was formed to improve the working conditions in carpet production. Unlike Rugmark, STEP and Care and Fair provide labels to entire retail establishments rather than to individual carpets. In 1995, the Carpet Export Promotion Council, a body of Ministry of Textiles introduced a label called 'Kaleen'. Exporters can obtain the Kaleen label by committing themselves to a code of conduct that includes not using child labour, and contributing a certain percentage of the export price to welfare measures.

Being a voluntary organization, registration with Rugmark is voluntary for importers and exporters. That is why multiple labeling schemes emerged. Rugmark's achievements demonstrate that the programme has not been harmful to the cause of eliminating child labour in the industry. Rugmark created widespread awareness in combating child labour. Rugmark Foundation receive fixed percentage of turnover which is being invested in the education, rehabilitation and welfare of child labour and former child labour. Under the social cost-benefit analysis, the benefit perceived was the elimination of child labour practice in the carpet manufacturing process and to make carpet free from this social evil. The labeling ensured importers that the said carpet has not been manufactured with the help of child labourers and henceforth ensured consumers about the initiative that the extra charges being paid by them is being utilized to get social benefits like health, education, training and other need based interventions.

SOCIAL COST-BENEFIT ANALYSIS OF HEPATITIS-B IMMUNIZATION

Hepatitis-B is caused by the hepatitis-B virus that infects the liver. It is transmitted through body fluids and most prevalent among blood donors, homosexuals, drug abusers and medical personnel. There is no curative medicine for hepatitis-B yet, and the efficacy of the interferon is still being tasted and debated.

While vaccination may be an effective tool for disease prevention, it is important to recognize that this logic need not necessarily be valid for all diseases and all people in all countries at all times. Issues such as disease prevalence, incidence pattern (uniform/endemic) and cost-benefit analysis become particularly relevant when decisions regarding selective vaccination versus universal vaccination in public health policies involve public money and public interest. Y. Madhavi has done cost benefit analysis of hepatitis-B immunization, the analysis critically examines the prevalence of disease in the population, cost-effectiveness etc.

Other diseases caused by Hepatitis-B

According to the Office of Registrar General of India (1991), jaundice was about 1 per cent of all causes of death, and deaths due to chronic liver cancer was 0.76 per cent including hepatitis B and C. The absence of regular monitoring of the disease and lack of unambiguous incidence data tends to complicate the cost-benefit analysis of universal vaccination against hepatitis B.

Cost-efficacy of vaccination

Unlike in western countries, extensive cost-benefit analysis (CBA) studies on vaccines were not conducted earlier in India before introducing them in immunization programmes (Madhavi 2001). At the most, the estimated costs were compared with the resource availability. The heavy cost of hepatitis B vaccine compared with other vaccines, and the controversial tendency to include every new vaccine under UIP has prompted detailed cost-efficacy studies on hepatitis B vaccination for the first time in the Indian vaccine scenario. A Delhi-based study estimated that selective vaccination would prevent only 40 per cent and 20 per cent HBeAg+ve and HBsAg+ve newborns respectively, whereas UIP would prevent all newborn carriers (Nayak et al. 1987). The conclusion of Aggarwal and Naik that the use of hepatitis B vaccine in UIP is cost-effective was based on a study in Delhi. This study of 8,575 infants in Safdarjung Hospital and the All-India Institute of Medical Sciences, concluded that universal immunization (UI) of all newborns in India is more cost-efficacious in reducing the HBV carrier pool (Aggarwal and Naik 1996).

However, Kale and Phadke (2000) were critical of these cost efficacy estimates, as their incidence data were based on the HBsAg pool and not the HBeAg pool. They were also critical of the cost assumptions ($ 0.75 per dose) especially the claim that selective immunization doubles the cost ($ 4.50 for three doses per infant) as against $ 2.25 for UIP, since economies of scale are not possible for SI. Kale and Phadke (2000) argued that the drug manufacturers offer prices as low as $ 0.55 per dose of hepatitis B vaccine for large orders, and economies of scale are not significantly affected by SI or Selective Immunisation (UI). Selective immunization of 93 million infants based on Aggarwal and Naik's estimate of HBV prevalence would require 2.79 million doses annually, which is a large enough order for economies of scale to function. Vaccine administration costs in SI are reduced considerably since the HBsAg+ mother would be identified during routine antenatal check-ups. The cost of the kit for HBsAg was around Rs. 25 (about $ 0.5) per test in May 2000, and with the orders running into million of kits the cost would reduce drastically.

Therefore, Kale and Phadke (2000) suggested that selective immunization of identifying and vaccinating all the newborns of HBeAg+ve mothers was more cost-effective than UI, as infants born to HBeAg+ve mothers were far more likely to be HBeAg+ve. According to them, identifying and vaccinating the newborns of all HBeAg+ve mothers (constituting 0.5 per cent of all newborns) in the first year would protect about 40 per cent of newborns from the risk of HBV infection. Such a selective immunization would be one-sixth the cost of UI of all the newborns. From the second year onwards, newborns would be tested and only the HBeAg+ve ones would be vaccinated along with vaccinating all the subsequent newborns of the cohort of HBeAg+ve mothers identified during the screening in the first year. This would bring down the target group for vaccination gradually, reducing costs further, though it does not lead to total eradication of the disease. However, they claim that total eradication of hepatitis B is neither warranted nor possible in the next 50 years even with universal vaccination, considering the reality and logistic of immunization in India.

Table: Cost of hepatitis B Vaccination Compared with other Diseases (cost in Rs.)

Cost of all EPI vaccines per child in 1992	17
Estimated cost at present	30
Current cost of hepatitis B vaccine per child	100
Number of newborns per year (approx)	25 Million
Annual cost of vaccine for newborns	2,500 Million
Number of children of the age group 0 – 4	110,4 Million
Cost of vaccine for 0 – 4 age group	11,040 Million
Annual cost for 0 – 4 age group, if covered over 3 years	3,700 Million
No of children of the age group 5 – 14	196 Million
Cost of vaccine for 5 – 14 age group	19,600 Million
Annual cost for 0 – 14 age group, if covered over 3 years	6,530 Million
Total vaccine cost pa for newborns + 0 – 4 age group	6,200 Million
Total vaccine cost pa for newborns + 0 – 14 age group	12,730 Million
Year's (2000) budget on malaria control programme	2,240 Million
Year's (2000) budget on TB control programme	1,050 million

Source: Complied from Kale and Phadke (2000).

Phadke and Kale (2000) compared the costs of hepatitis B vaccination with the cost of measles vaccination from hypothetical cohorts of 1 million people for each of the age groups 0-1, 1-5, 5-15, 15-45, 45-70, who would suffer from and die due to hepatitis B infection. The cost-efficacy of universal hepatitis B vaccination ranged from Rs. 1,767 to Rs. 5,890 per life saved for different age groups, compared with Rs. 292 for measles vaccination in infants. They reiterated that the universal hepatitis B vaccination of infants was neither a priority programme nor cost-effective in India as of today.

Dasgupta and Ritu Priya (2002) estimated the number of pediatric doses of hepatitis B vaccine required annually to fully cover the infant population (62.7 – 79.5 million), which worked out to around Rs. 5,790.5 – 7,353.75 million/year, assuming zero wastage for the years 2002-2006. The total cost of mass vaccination of hepatitis B Vaccine alone was equivalent to the total budget for health and family welfare (Rs. 58,530 million during 2000-01). Therefore, they suggested selective incidence zone-based strategic planning for hepatitis B vaccination.

But all these cost-benefit studies were done on the basis of incidence data. A major drawback of the Indian studies is the absence of reliable epidemiological data on the actual disease burden. But this is becoming increasingly true for all diseases, due to a virtual collapse of the health information system, as pointed out by many studies (e..g., Raghuram 1996).

Therefore, if hepatitis B were to be covered under UIP, the vaccine cost alone would be six times more than the entire budget for (all aspects of) the malaria control programme, and over 12 times the budget for TB control programme.

Table : Hepatitis B Vaccines in Indian market

Brand Name	*Year of Introduction*	*Manufacturer*	*Year Established*	*Price*	
				Adult Dose (Rs.)	*Child Dose (Rs.)*
Shanvac-b	1997	Shanta Biotech, Hyderabad	1993	192	140
Revac-b	2000	Bharat Biotech International, Hyderabad (markets Eli Lilly's vaccine)	1988	120	90
Energix-b	1987	SmithKline Beecham, Belgium		485	272
Enivac-B	1990	Cuban vaccine, marketed by Bharat Serums and Vaccines, Mumbai	1964	100	—
Gene Vac-B	2002	Serum Institute of India, Pune	1970s		55
Enivac-B	2000	Panacea Biotech, Delhi (Cuban vaccine)	1997	Not yet fixed	

Source: Compiled from various newspaper reports.

WHO sponsored a study by the National Institute of Communicable Diseases (NICD) by supplying the vaccine procured from SKB free of cost (www.delhihealth.com, Kalshian 1996). The study attracted media criticism on the grounds of alleged secrecy that the hepatitis B vaccination was being pushed without critically assessing the overall risk of HBV infection in the country (Menon 1997, The Times of India, July 8, 2000 'Rs. 2,825 crore for hepatitis B vaccination drive is a scam'). Eventually, the union government allotted Rs. 2,825 crore for hepatitis B vaccination in the Ninth Five-Year Plan and subsequently included it under UIP in the Tenth Plan (The Hindu, June 10, 2002 'Vajpayee launches new initiative to vaccinate children against hepatitis B') While several ministers in the states and the centre supported UIP, the then Karnataka health minister, H.C. Mahadevappa, was skeptical about the urgency of its inclusion in UIP and sought an enquiry into the epidemiology of hepatitis B (Priyadarshni 1999).

The industry did its bit to promote hepatitis B vaccination through health camps, medical practitioners and distributors by supplying the vaccines at lower prices (Sharma 2000). For instance, Shanta biotech sold 4 lakh doses of the vaccine wroth Rs. 4.8 crore in an awareness campaign held in Bangalore in December 1998 (Priyadarshini 1999). Similar camps were held in of other cities and towns around the country. The organizers of these camps such as various trusts, clubs and societies were lured by free gifts or concessional prices offered by the companies (Sen 1999). It was pointed out that these campaigns were creating a fear psychosis among the populace (Deshpande 2000).

The above examples reveal how national immunization policies were often influenced by the industry, regardless of the extent of disease burden and the costs involved. However, the debate in western countries centred mainly on the safety aspects of the vaccine, right to information and the lack of informed consent among the public (Orient 1999).

In developing countries, industry pushes its agenda either directly or through international agencies such as WHO, UNICEF, World Bank or GAVI, to adopt their vaccines in the National Immunization Programmes. The Indian government launched hepatitis B vaccination drive in 1996, and the Ministry of Health and Family Welfare mooted its inclusion under UIP.

It seems that the government is going to launch a universal hepatitis B vaccination programme, which involves giving hepatitis B vaccine to all newborns. This decision is questionable on various counts. A ridiculous impression has been created that hepatitis B is a more serious problem than AIDS. Hepatitis B infection spreads in the same way as AIDS and much more rapidly and easily. But the similarly ends there.

Untreated HIV infection is 100% fatal, but in the case of hepatitis B, 90% of the adults who are infected with the virus eliminate it within six months. However, among infected infants, only 10% eliminate the virus. Even among chronic carriers – those who cannot eliminate the virus – the average fatality rate is around 5% and not 25% as has been claimed.

It would be sensible to give the hepatitis B vaccine to those who are specially prone to the infection. These include medical professionals who come in close contact with blood, patients in need of dialysis and repeated blood transfusion, persons exposed to unsafe sexual relations and newborns of hepatitis B-positive mothers. Giving the vaccine to all newborns, that too six weeks after birth, does nothing to prevent mother to child transmission.

Besides, this strategy is bad economics. The claim that 4.7% of the Indian population is chronically infected with hepatitis B virus is a gross overestimation based on a paper by SP Thyagarajan and others. The paper assumes that all those who are found to be positive for hepatitis B are chronic carriers of the infection. Using the same data correctly, the actual hepatitis B carrier rate works out to be only 1.42%. The World Health Organization (WHO) has recommended hepatitis B vaccination of all newborns only for countries where this carrier rate is more than 2%.

Newborns who get hepatitis B infection at birth from other B-positive mothers (about 2-3% of mothers are B-positive) are at highest risk of contracting the most dangerous variety of hepatitis B infection and becoming carriers. WHO and the American Academy of Pediatrics have recommended that for such newborns, the first dose of hepatitis B vaccine be given not later than 48 hours after birth.

In India, since 77% of the births take place at home, the first dose of the vaccine would not be given immediately after birth but six weeks later, with the first dose of the triple vaccine in the national programme. Therefore, in this programme 77% of the newborns will not be protected from mother to child transmission.

If we want to take up the hepatitis B vaccination programme, a selective vaccination strategy should be used as in other low prevalence countries like Japan, the UK and Netherlands. This strategy consists of identifying B-positive mothers through blood test during pregnancy and vaccination of newborns within 48 hours of birth.

In India, about 3% of pregnant women are found to be B-positive. Vaccinating only these 3% of the newborns would cost only a fourth of the universal strategy.

This cost-effective selective vaccination programme will not be effective unless the services for pregnant women substantially improve, from 65% to 90-100%. It will not eradicate hepatitis B infection. But even if all newborns are vaccinated in the universal vaccination programme, it will take at least 65 years to eradicate hepatitis B infection in India.

With 25 million babies being born every year in India, assuming the cost of hepatitis B vaccine per child in this programme to be only Rs. 50 (much less than the current price), it would cost Rs. 125 crore annually for the vaccine alone. This is equal to our budget for the TB-control programme (the number one killer of Indian adults), and almost equal to combined cost of six other vaccines given to infants.

The cost-efficacy of this programe in unfavourable in terms of cost of life per year saved.

The epidemiology of a disease and cost-effective analysis relative to other infectious diseases and available resources is an important determination of selecting the vaccination strategy (UIP or SI). In India, we do not have any factual incidence data at all (even for blood donors), and existing western or even Indian blood bank data cannot be extrapolated, as they are seriously flawed. Indian studies in support of hepatitis B vaccination are based on the prevalence data in small sample populations and undue reliance on HBsAg positivity rather than HBeAg positivity to identify the carriers of hepatitis B infection. The corrected HBsAg positivity data indicate very low incidence in the population. There is no consensus in the medical community on the epidemiology of HBV. The disease burden due to HBV in India is most likely to be several fold less than other diseases like diarrhea, TB, acute respiratory diseases, nutritional disorders, or cancer.

The cost-benefit studies on hepatitis B vaccine in India are as equivocal as the incidence estimates. But it is clear that the vaccine today costs more than three times that of the other entire six EPI vaccines put together. The cost of UI against hepatitis B alone would be equivalent to the total budget allocated for health and family welfare (2000-01 and 2001-02), or 6 times the combined budget of the national malaria eradication programme and kala-azar (Rs. 225 crore), national leprosy control programme (Rs. 75 crore), national AIDS control programme (Rs. 210 crore) and the national tuberculosis control programe (Rs. 136 crore). On the other hand, the budget for safe drinking water (Rs. 2,010 crore) and sanitation (Rs. 150 crore) was only about half of the expenditure on hepatitis B vaccination in financial year 2001-02. If Indian government can afford to spend so much on a single vaccine, it might as well spend it on clean drinking water and sanitation as a priority to eradicate/control most of the water borne diseases and even some vector transmitted diseases (polio, typhoid, hepatitis A and E, diarrhoea, tuberculosis). Otherwise, it creates the impression that universal vaccination is becoming the ideology of disease control, regardless of its incidence level, epidemiology, costs and logistics. Once hepatitis B vaccine sets such a precedence, many other hi-tech expensive vaccines would follow.

Ship-breaking: social cost-benefit

Being home to the world's largest ship breaking yard may add to the country's economic sinews, but it isn't a crown that India should wear with pride, as the human costs may be much more than its monetary gains, Greenpeace has warned.

The NGO said in the latest instance where a decommissioned French aircraft carrier Clemenceau was headed to India to be taken apart, thousands of kilograms of toxic wastes, from the ship's asbestos linings and liters of liquid non-biodegradable wastes could be hazardous to both environment and ship breakers. Shailendra Yashwant, campaign director, Greenpeace India, said, "Working conditions are pathetic. Unskilled workers are exposed to toxic wastes without any protective gear. And with phasing out of single hull tankers, we expect that about 1,500 ships will be ready to be scrapped in the next two years." About 15,000 people work in Alang in Gujarat, world's largest ship breaking yard, where 15 ships are currently being scrapped, he added.

Clemenceau was being sent to India once before earlier this year, but the sail was stalled due to court cases by French anti-asbestos activists. But the sail was authorized after French officials said that the carrier had been "de-contaminated". Greenpeace insists that claim is false.

The controversy was unraveled at a news conference by Greenpeace and CITU. The two groups released a chilling report of the ways in which hazardous wastes can adversely affect thousands of workers employed for the task.

Titled "End of Life Ships: The human cost of breading ships", the release coincided with a joint working group meeting of representatives of International Maritime Organization, the ILO and Basel Convention in Geneva. Workers exposed to asbestos and polycholorinated-biphenyles face the risk of cancer and lung diseases.

Chapter 11

Impact Assessment

Development aid agencies are involved in dealing with Environment Impact Assessment (EIA). This exercise is now almost mandatory as a method to identify project's problem and impact on the environment. Apart from this, an EIA exercise is undertaken in order to influence project design and choice of project alternatives.

Gender Impact Assessment (GIA) has also now become a part of development aid projects, precisely because experience in the field revealed that many development projects had an unintentional impact of discrimination against women. Thus, whether it is environmental impact or gender assessment, the main objective is to bring into focus any possible negative impact on either the environment or women at a relatively early stage in the planning process so that these impacts are either mitigated or avoided.

Here, impact assessment exercise is detailed considering the child labour problem. By sensitizing people to the issue of child labour, it is hoped that those concerned will put children in the same category as the environment and women, and will look carefully to see that in their areas of cooperation there is no direct or indirect use of child labour.

The idea of undertaking a child labour impact assessment on development projects has similar objectives. There are many instances when well-intended projects have led to an increase in child labour. The unexpected impact of projects can be divesting, and this is where a child labour impact assessment becomes critical. A donor agency wanted to fund a bilateral training programme, with a state government for providing entrepreneurship development training to women. It was decided that training in carpet weaving would be a good idea, as it had good marketing potential. The project document mentioned that the target group was to be young women/girls (obviously older girls). The head of the agency, once visiting the centre realized that the programme for young women had degenerated into a training programme for young girls who were actually being removed from school by their parents, for the stipend of Rs. 100 per month they were receiving. The training programme was closed down even though, legally, a state-run training programme is exempted from the purview of the Child Labour (Prohibition & Regulation) Act, 1986. (Dag Larsson, Child Labour Impact Assessment, NORAD, New Delhi).

The need, therefore, to have a child labour impact assessment of development aid projects becomes apparent. According to article 24 of the Constitution of India, "No child below the age of fourteen years shall be employed to work in hazardous employment." Unlike other impact assessments, the child labour impact assessment can focus on very limited project categories. This is because projects that assist with state-of-the-art technologies either in agriculture, animal husbandry, forestry, fisheries, aquaculture, industry, mining and so on are by virtue of their intervention, removing child labour. Some kinds of projects are likely to worsen the situation of child labour. For example, sericulture is a sector which has been given a lot of support by donor agencies. Training programmes have been supported in order to improve employment opportunities. Children can be expected to even leave school or work long hours after school either cutting leaves to feed to worms or collecting cocoons from the forest or taking care of the cocoons. This last may be the job of mother, but she, in turn, lets her children perform this task so that she can do some other work.

There are many development aid projects designed to improve the lot of self-employed women and female headed households. Typically, the home-based working woman operates on a piece-rate basis, where her remuneration bears a direct relationship to her productivity such as Beedi making industry offer exploitatively low rates and one consequence is usually the induction of girl children to assist their mother to increase their output. Projects that seek to improve the lot of such working women by offering credit or legal services or support to build them into organized groups often ignore that negative impact of such work upon girl children. If the girl child is denied an education, she is most likely to end up like her mother in a spiral of exploitation, poor skills, low wages and poverty.

A proposal sent to donor agency for humanizing child labour for instance, in the Beedi or carpet industry suggested that working condition would be improved and that children will be unionized to fight for their rights. While both are laudable objectives, neither of these two objectives will in fact lead to the elimination of child labour.

ASSESSMENT APPROACH

The child labour impact assessment should be done at the designing stage of the project in order to be sure that there are no negative consequences for the child, whereby either his/her work load will increase or he/she will be removed from school and put to work. It is also possible to do a child labour impact assessment for on-going assisted project. For example, if a project has already been sanctioned to manufacture and market housing material. It is worthwhile to add on more components in an addendum. Additional funds can be made available to the NGO for running crèches, health centres and non-formal education centres in order to ensure that children are not put into similarly, conditions and additional provisions can be added on to projects already funded after doing a review of the project. It is worthwhile to hold workshops for project staff to alert them to the possibilities of a negative impact on child labour.

Proposals concerning street children must be viewed in the light of experience. Institutionalization does not appear to be the solution. Street children are most vulnerable when they are ill or are picked up by the police; in addition, shelter against the elements and the predators of the urban jungle is one of their needs. Projects that envisage shelters for street children with a health and educational component deserve support to the extent they are community based and encourage networking amongst street children they are likely to have a more lasting impact. In projects covering street children provision must be made for facilitation of a continuing dialogue between NGOs, street children, civil and police bureaucracies.

There are two types of projects that need to be assessed for child labour impact. Large development projects particularly bilateral projects in certain sectors and small NGO projects ostensibly meant to lead the direct elimination of child labour. In the first category of aid assisted projects, care has to be taken that at no stage of the process, either directly or indirectly child labour would be employed. Often certain processes are sub contracted so many times that it is difficult to piece the link of the chain together. And the question that arises is: Who is ultimately responsible? A good example is a bilateral irrigation project where the state government's irrigation department may sub-contract the recruitment of labour to sub-contractors on job work. There may be a number of children working on the construction sites, but the irrigation department does not consider it their responsibility to see that the labourers are paid their dues or that children are not involved. Can the funding agency do anything about the use of child labour in this kind of project? The answer is yes. In its agreement with the implementing agency (whether an NGO or a government body) the donor agency can stipulate that the implementing agency will be responsible if child labour is used in the project in violation of the provisions of the Child Labour (Prohibition & Regulation) Act, 1986. The agreement can also specify that in case the donor agency discovers at any stage that child labour is being used in the project in violation of the agreement between the parties, the said donor agency would be entitled to forthwith withdraw from the project and/or seek legal redress against the implementing agency for violation of the terms of the contract. Periodic review missions can be asked specifically to assess whether child labour is to be found as part of their terms of references. It may also be possible to involve local NGO to both monitor the use of child labour as well as to run non-formal educational centres and creches for children of working couples.

CHECK-LIST FOR INITIAL SCREENING OF PROJECTS

The following check-list is designed to establish whether proposed project is likely to have negative impact on children. Child labour impact assessment requires the use of discretion in judging to what extent the use of child labour is significant or not. For example, in a bamboo board manufacturing project or a sericulture project, if the children help out after, there is clearly no harm in it. On the other hand, if children are withdrawn from school to help increase the quantum of work that parents are doing, then the project would definitely have on adverse impact. In order to ensure that this does not happen, it may be necessary to include questions regarding children (numbers, ages, whether in school or not, availability of school in the neighbourhood and whether they are involved in work in any form). This kind of initial survey information would give some indications of the kind and extent of work children are participating in.

NGO PROJECTS

Will the Project:

(*i*) Support the idea of children working in non-hazardous work?

(*ii*) Favour the humanizing of child Labour?

(*iii*) Justify child labour on the grounds that it is inescapable?

(*iv*) Lead to the removal of children from school?

(*v*) Lead to children working 8 to 10 hours a day?

OTHER DEVELOPMENT AID PROJECT

Example: Livestock holding

(*i*) Increase the work load of women

(*ii*) Lead to children, particularly girls, being taken out of school

(*iii*) Make children spend more time collecting fodder

(*iv*) Mean that child will spend more time grazing animals

(*v*) Create debts when animals do not survive

SURVEY ON CHILD LABOUR

Don't presume that child labour is a result of poverty. It may be that:

- Children are preferred by adults because they are cheap labour.
- Children have been recruited by middlemen.
- Parents died or fully handicapped.
- Unemployed parents.
- Children are better human resource.

Go to the field with an open mind. Do not prejudice the situation

Employees and workers are usually the worst source of information on child labour. Most employees will deny they use child labour or pretend they are doing a favour by employing children. People are willing to talk (even employers) if you want to know about the history and background of the industry. Get as much information as you can on the different processes in an industry. Ask about the chemicals used or raw materials used for making components. Only at the end of discussion with the officials or employer ask about why they employ children or why children are employed in the industry?

Do not raise the issue of child labour directly. People are aware of the law and tend to get defensive. Children should never be interviewed at the workplace because:

- If they say something out of place, they can be beaten up;
- If they are working, diverting their attention may lead to injury;
- Interviews should be relaxed, with respondents having enough time to tell you about things, he/she is concerned with, as well as to ask you about the purpose of your research.

Always ask open ended questions

Try to avoid taking an interview schedule and filling in questionnaires. It distracts the respondent. You need a free flowing conversation. It doesn't matter if you do not have information like the name, age, sex, caste, community, origin etc. about the child. You need to know in general what the parents of the child do, how many brothers/sisters he/she has and what they do. Questions about social relationships such as whom they trust, what their relationship is with other children of their own age or what their relationship is with officials don't necessarily need to be asked directly. If you give a child the opportunity to tell you why he left home and why he doesn't want to return home, this will answer most of the questions.

Do not ask too many questions. Give people a chance to talk. If you are an NGO functionary working with grassroots level organizations:

Involve the people you are working with to collect data. Make the survey as participatory as possible; ultimately your observations and analysis will be far more valuable than merely filling in questionnaires. Ask local people for solutions to their problems. Sometimes they may come with very simple solutions that policy makers or your organizations may never have thought of. There may be secondary source of information including doctors, students, shopkeepers, teachers and others.

Cumulative report

After the end of the project, implementing agency is required to submit cumulative report to funding agency or the consultant. This facilitates learning experiences of the positive impact to share with other partners and to overcome with the bottlenecks in the project management. A typical CRS cumulative report is detailed below for better understanding:

Cumulative report format

1. Title of the Project
2. Duration (Date the partnership started and ended)
3. Geographical Area (Define the location where the intended impact of the project has occurred including the number and name of villages)
4. Profile of beneficiaries

	Men and Women	SC/ST
Direct beneficiaries		
Indirect beneficiaries		
Advocacy beneficiaries		

5. Impact on the lives: (impact is about more than the immediate outputs of interventions and their direct effects. It concerns the lasting and/or significant changes in the lives of women, men, boys and girls that have occurred as a consequence. These may be planned or unplanned, positive or negative. Say whether more or less people are benefiting than planned).
6. Changes in the policies, practices, ideas and beliefs: (Consider what, and whose, policies, practices, ideas and beliefs have changed or are changing. Changes may be in the institutions of the household, community, state or market and occur at a local, national or international level. Some changes will have been planned but others may have occurred more opportunistically or through informal means).
7. **Progress towards gender equality**

   Progress may be seen in terms of:

   - More equitable participation in decision-making processes in personal, social and political spheres.
   - More equitable access to and control over economic and natural resources and basic social services.
   - Fewer women suffering gender-related violent.
   - Gender stereotypes and discriminatory attitudes towards women and girls being challenged.

8. **Role of beneficiaries in the project**

   Consider the level of beneficiary involvement:

   - Beneficiaries control the project.
   - Beneficiaries take charge of some activities.
   - Beneficiaries are actively involved in project activities.
   - Beneficiaries are now taking up post project follow-up activities.
   - Beneficiaries are being asked their opinions or only provide information.

For advocacy, campaigning, research and networking projects, think about beneficiaries level of engagement/control in planning and implementation, their involvement in lobbying and campaigning and whether space is being created for poor people to be involved in decision-making processes affecting their lives.

Where networks or alliances have been built or strengthened, consider whether this has contributed to poor people's involvement and influences.

9. **Sustainability**

   Sustainability means the main changes achieved are likely to last, that activities can be sustained where necessary and/or that beneficiaries and their organizations have gained significant new capacities for pursuing their own development objectives.

   Think about the following dimensions of sustainability: economic/financial; social/organizational; technological; environmental; political).

10. **Cost effectiveness**

    Judging the cost-effectiveness of a project involves looking at the relationship between all the costs incurred (i.e. financial and non-financial resources from all sources) and the results achieved. It involves making judgments about the following:

    - Do the results of the project warrant the resources invested in it.
    - Within this project, are their ways by which the same or greater results could have been achieved for a smaller investment?
    - Could the resources invested have achieved more if used in a different way i.e. rather than on this project?
    - Where it is possible to make comparisons, are there factors that have added to, or reduced, the costs of this project compared to similar ones?)

11. Cumulative quantitative data
12. Cumulative qualitative data
13. Case studies (including photographs)
14. Key learning's from the project
15. Suggestions for improvement in future
16. Success stories.

Chapter 12

Fund Raising for Projects

A sound and successful management of projects requires financial sustainability and sufficiency, studies reveal that many organizations have discontinued projects due to unavailability of finance. NGOs suffer with critical arguments that they adopt only those activities for which sufficient funding is available. Organizations like CRY and Action Aid have proved that financial sustainability can be ensured through fund raising.

FUND RAISING STRATEGIES

In a charity football match Diago Maradona played for the welfare of disabled. Audience were asked not only to pay ticket fee but also bring 1 kg. of perishable food grain. CRY once motivated through an advertisement showing a child trying to hide in corrugated sheet box in winter night and requested to donate used clothes for the distribution to needy, orphans, street children. If we analyze we find that various strategies have been adopted by different organizations. These are:

1. **Donation:** Donation has been the prime source of fund-raising. Organizations like NGOs, political associations, associations of corporate houses like FICCI, CII have raised funds through donations from corporates and individuals for social cause.
2. **Calamity donation:** After Tsunami calamity India needed $2.1 billion to spend on long-term rehabilitation, while total funds India secured worth $2.18 billion for long term recovery. Indian government's portion of these funds was $1.38 billion. International organizations, NGOs, political parties roped in to raise funds for the rehabilitation of community affected by Tsunami disaster. In an appeal, SOS Children's Villages of India appealed for donations, "The Tsunami disaster still continues to affect thousands of lives. Help us help them." SOS Children's Villages of India is a voluntary child-care organization, looking after about 2 lakh children in India through 37 SOS Children's Villages and 122 community projects. SOS India is a member of SOS-Kinderdorf International, operational in 132 countries.

   Bharatiya Janata party Established BJP-Calamity Relief Fund and requested to contribute generously to "Bring back their happiness, light up their lives." Oxfam India Trust issued an urgent appeal for emergency response due to the tidal waves that ruined coastal regions of southern Asia. The advertisement said, "Oxfam Trust appeals to you to make a donation to support our emergency response work and to help save lives."

   'Prayas' a registered non-profit national level voluntary organization directly supports 50,000 children through projects relating to education, vocational training, food, shelter, health and child protection. It established 'Crisis Management and Emergency Relief Fund' "Tsunami Prayas India" and appealed to contribute generously in cash (cheques/draft/ and/or in kind (clothing, medicines, tinned/ packed food.

3. **Cause related marketing:** Cause related marketing is a marketing strategy linking purchases of a product with fund raising for a worthwhile charity, product or cause, cause related marketing creates a mutually profitable outcome for the business and charity. Cause marketing can be a highly effective method that contributes to building a positive image for the business while helping a charity gain much needed visibility. First introduced by American Express in 1983 by donating a part of their customer's charge card to Statute of Liberty. Now ITC did it with its expressions card, Archie's did it for CRY, Brooke Bond did it for SOS Children's Villages of India to raise funds for social cause.

   Cause marketing requires an agreement between a non-profit and a for-profit. The deal is struck to maximize perceived benefits to each partner. Brooke Bond contributed Rs. 1 crore, through its programme "Smile in every heart", to SOS Children's Villages of India.

4. **Sale of products:** CRY is attempting to raise funds in more innovative ways than just selling stationery. The CRY shop in Mumbai is its latest initiative. Formed with the twin objectives of fund-raising and providing a retail presence to products made by other social welfare organizations. A lot of individual projects have felt the need for an avenue like this to sell their products, as they find it difficult to hold their own in commercially-run retail outlets, as these individuals can offer only very limited quantities, this makes it difficult to negotiate

margins with retailers. Women's India Trust also established its shop in South Mumbai to market the products produced by weaker section and disadvantaged women. Now, most of the organizations have established retail outlet. In Chitrakoot, Sadguru Seva Sangh Trust and Deen Dayal Research Institute, have established well maintained retail outlets of in-house products made by SHGs.

5. **Charity collections:** During my Hindalco days, we organized programmes for charity collections. Individuals and organizations donated generously clothes, food grains, magazines, books, used bags, tin, furniture etc. which was distributed to weaker community, disadvantaged and needy persons.

6. **Celebrity programmes:** Tata Salt sponsored a telethon with CRY on Sony Entertainment Television with stars like Shah Rukh Khan, Adesh Shrivastava, Javed Akhtar, Abhijeet, Sonu Nigam and others and raised Rs. 1 crore to change the lives of millions of children. Such programmes are organized to benefit disadvantaged groups with the cooperation of cinestars, sports personalities and others.
7. **Tax-exempted contributions:** This strategy gives added advantage to contributor (donor) i.e. a donation for social cause and tax exemption on donations. World Vision advertised that all contributions for relief work in coastal areas due to Tsunami disaster, to World Vision are tax deductible under section 80 G of the Income Tax Act, 1961. Donations have been prime source of fund raising, hence NGOs offer value addition to donors and offer tax exemption.

8. **Charity with open heart:** Fund-raising at Action Aid is being called as "Open Heart Charity" in which every rupee donated to Action, Aid, donor gets benefits many times. A donor can choose one out of four donation plans starting at Rs. 3000 and going up to Rs. 24000. A person with the donation of Rs. 3000 can get life insurance cover of Rs. 25,000, holiday package of 3 days 2 nights, music CDs work Rs. 500, Reliance handset worth Rs. 5000 and tax saving of Rs. 1500. Total received value will be Rs. 15000. This strategy gives donor many times receipts on his donations.

9. **Charity matches:** India and Pakistan played against the rest World's Hockey Team to raise funds for the welfare of earthquake victims. A charity match was also played in between India and Sri Lanka for relief operations after Tsunami disaster. The audience supported through ticket fee to support activities for particular social cause.

10. **Adoption programme:** K.C. Education Trust supported by Mahindra & Mahindra Ltd. Offered sponsorship programme through its 'Nanhi Kali' project. The donor will be called 'foster parent' of a little girl by giving Rs. 125 a month towards her education. Foster parents will receive regular reports about her progress. CRY, CCF, Action Aid have also such sponsorship programmes.

11. **Fund raising for special purposes:** Help Age India issued advertisements for donation for 'Gift of Sight' with a statement 'for every Rs. 300/- you send, another old person will be able to see again.' Cancer Aid Foundation offered contributions and donations for the treatment of a child suffering from Acute Lympholdastic Leukemia (a type of cancer). It also said, "If surplus amount is received, the same will be passed on to the next patient in queue". These donations are utilized in the treatment of ailments of needy persons.

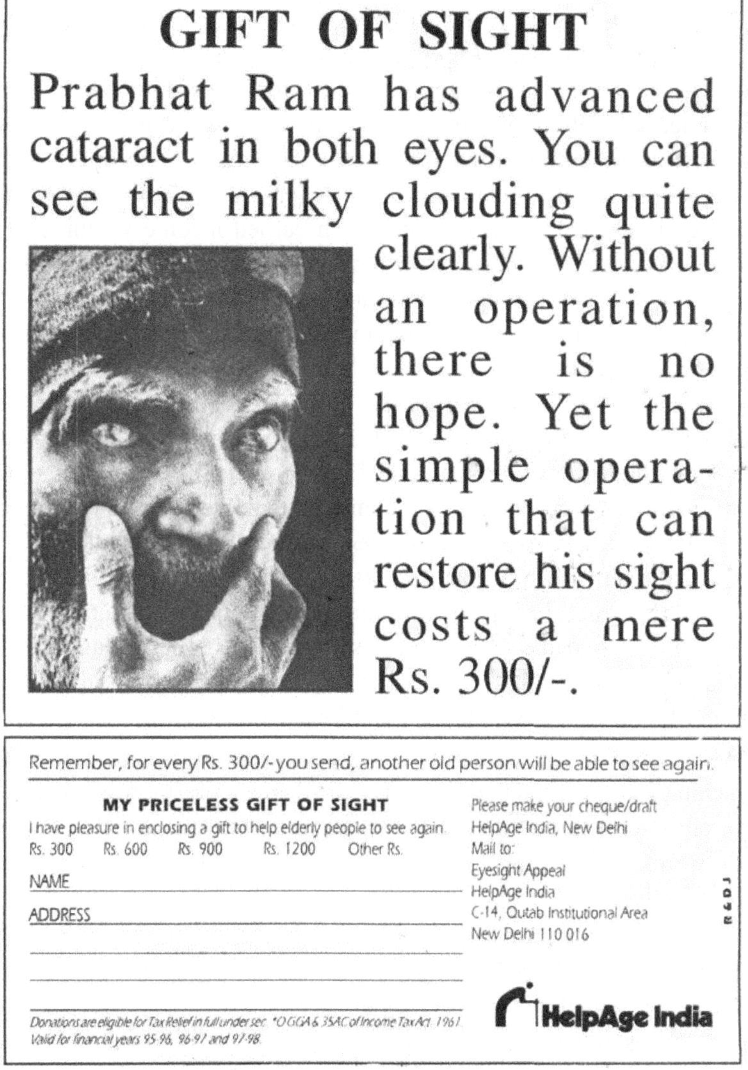

Non-profit Seeking Profits

Promoted in books and articles, conferences and courses, earned-income initiatives are becoming accepted – even expected – throughout the not-for-profit world. In 2003 Bridgespan Group Survey of U.S. non-profit's executives, half of the respondents said they believed earned income would play an important or extremely important role in bolstering their organization's revenue in the future. In India, many NGOs have issued advertisement for the selection of functionaries to make their organization financially independent and self-sufficient. Fund-raising skills are being given priority while selecting highly skilled and remunerative jobs. Purpose behind driving non-profits to pursue profits is as much social as economic.

NGOs and non-profit organizations are becoming social enterprise and social activists feel proud to be called as social entrepreneurs. William Foster and Jefffrey Bradach have written extensively on "Should non-profits seek profits?" in Harward Business Review. Managers of non-profits wants to be viewed as active entrepreneurs and social entrepreneurs rather than as passive bureaucrats, and launching a successful commercial venture is one direct route to that goal. Board members, many of whom are accomplished business leaders, often encourage and reinforce that desire. At the same time, many philanthropic foundations and other funders have been zealously urging nonprofits to become financially self-sufficient and have aggressively promoted earned income as a means to "sustainability". As a result, non-profits increasingly feel compelled to launch earned-income ventures, if only to appear more disciplined, innovative, and businesslike to their stakeholders. Burgeoning interest in earned income has generated a flood of publications, events, and experts. How-to-books with titles like Venture Fourth! The Essential Guide to Starting a Moneymaking Business in Your Non-profit Organization and selling social change (without selling out) have recently appeared. The Yale School of Management – The Goldman Sachs Foundation Partnership on Non-profit ventures sponsored a celebrated and rigorously judged business-plan competition for non-profits, in 2004, it garnered more than 500 entries. Even organizations that promote the broader topic of social entrepreneurship, such as the Social Enterprise Alliance, are often primarily focused on earned income. At that group's 2004 National Gathering for Social Entrepreneurs, attendance "flew past 600, a 50% growth rate that dramatically illustrated surging interest in the field of social enterprise, organizers reported. And Non-profit Business Solutions advertises that it can help "discover the earned-income opportunity you may have missed, for only $100." Indeed, the widespread enthusiasm for earned-income ventures has drowned out the handful of people, such as Greg Dees of Duke and Jed Emerson, a co-founder and former executive director of the Roberts Enterprise Development Fund, who have sounded cautionary notes.

It is clear that there has been a significant increase in the number of non-profits considering, investing in, and launching ventures, and the press has helped create the impression that these enterprises are contributing substantial profits. In late 2001, for example, the Chronicle of Philanthropy ran the headline "The Business of Charity: Non-profit Groups Reap Billions in Tax-Free Income Annually." The wide circulation of selected data reinforces the notion of a boom in earned income. From the impressive body of work published by johns Hopkin's Lester Salamon, one statistics mentioned with particular frequency. "Fees and charges accounted for nearly half of the growth in non-profit revenue between 1977 and 1997- more than any other sources."

In India, Action Aid established Partners in Change, which is working for the promotion of corporate philanthropy and fund raising. Indian Centre for Philanthropy and other agencies are working for the promotion of corporate giving. Most of the NGOs are working for increase in fund raising through donation, cause-related marketing, selling products and services of disadvantaged, weaker section, disabled, windows and others.

But out of context, such statistics can be misleading. Fees and charges grew no faster in that 20-year period than other sources of revenue; they represented nearly half of the sector's total revenue in 1997, just as they had in 1977. And the reason the fraction is so high is that educational and health care institutions, which extensively use fee-for-service income, account for nearly 70% of total non-profit revenue and thus dominate the data.

Two widely circulated surveys of earned-income ventures seem to suggest that our experience is anomalous. "Enterprising Non-profits: Revenue Generation in the Non-profit Sector" by the Yale

School of Management – The Goldman Sachs Foundation Partnership on Non-profit Ventures and "Powering Social Change: Lessons on Community Wealth Generation for Non-profit Sustainability " by Community Wealth Ventures (CWV) report that between half and two-thirds of the ventures these organizations examined were either profitable or breaking even.

The first concerns keeping in mind two caveats is the composition of the samples. Are they truly representative, or are they biased toward successful (and surviving) initiatives? The Yale-Goldman Sachs Foundation survey solicited research participants by highly publicizing the study through postings and advertisements. Such announcements are an efficient way to attract participants, but they amass a self-selected pool of research subjects, virtually guaranteeing a positive bias. Failing organizations are less likely to volunteer than successful ones-and ventures that have already closed their doors never do. The CWV study drew its initial sample form experts' suggestions and the research and researchers' personal contracts, this sample was then expanded through referrals from the initial group of non-profits. Here again, the probability of a positive bias is high, because successful ventures tend to have a much higher public profile than unsuccessful ones.

The second caveat involves the definition of "profitable." Are the Financial claims accurate? The results were self-reported, and our experience with non-profits reveals a tendency to overlook or undercount commercial ventures' operating costs (including management time, facilities costs, and other overhead expenses). In addition, the reported "profitability" may not adequately account for hefty start-up costs. This question is difficult to assess in the Yale – Goldman Sachs Foundation study, because the calculation of financial returns is not documented in detail.

In the CWV study's sample of 72 organizations, only four-just 5%-earned more than $50,000 in annual profit. In addition, the average time to profitability for most organizations was 2.5 years, and the average initial investment for all ventures was $200,000. Assuming a $200,000 start-up cost, two years of zero profit, and $25,000 in annual profit thereafter, a venture would take ten years to repay the initial investment, even without discounting the future profit for inflation. The ventures' intangible returns may be real, but from a purely economic perspective, the same return could be generated simply by hiding $200,000 under a mattress for ten years.

To better understand the odds of success, Bridgespan selected a random sample of non-profits that had received philanthropic funding for an earned-income venture in 2000 or 2001. This approach limited the pool to organizations of interest to philanthropy, but it tempered the likelihood of either a positive or negative sample bias.

LACK OF BUSINESS PERSPECTIVE

Because philanthropic contributions typically do not have significant operating costs associated with them, non-profits can easily misjudge the actual financial contribution that a venture will deliver. In particular, they tend to overlook the distinction between revenue and profit. If a non-profit receives an unrestricted charitable donation of Rs. 100,000 all Rs. 100,000 (expect for the comparatively small fund-raising costs) can be put to work in pursuit of the organization's mission. In this case, revenue is essentially the same as profit. However, if a non-profit generates Rs. 100,000 from a venture, such as a catering business, some of the funds must be used to cover expenses. Typically, what's left over is at best a small portion of total sales.

RELIANCE ON INDIRECT CUSTOMERS

In many earned-income ventures, the intended users can't afford the products or services. That's hardly surprising many non-profits work with society's most disadvantaged citizens. But it means that ventures must often rely on indirect customers for their revenues, making for complex and sometimes convoluted business models.

PHILANTHROPIC CAPITAL AND THE ESCALATION OF COMMITMENT

Even when non-profit managers realize that their ventures are facing financial problems, they rarely pull the plug. Instead, as is sometimes the case in the for-profit sector, they tend to throw good money after bad, hoping to turn the ventures around and avoid the embarrassment of failure.

The slope for deadly performing business is always slippery, regardless of which sector they belong to. But the problem of commitment escalation is made even more acute when philanthropic contributions provide the funding for an earned-income venture during its first few years. Because expenses during this period are covered, the risk of losing money seems less pressing to the non-profit. If (or, more likely, when) the philanthropic funding stops a few years later, what began as a well-funded earned-income ventures may become an unfortunate legacy.

A QUESTION OF MISSION

Non-profits that take a cold look at the disadvantages of launching a commercial business will probably conclude that the odds of it generating real financial returns are extremely low. That does not mean that all potential ventures should be abandoned. Rather, it means that executives of non-profits must ask a critical question: "Does this venture contribute to our organization's core mission?" If a venture furthers a non-profit's mission while allowing it to recoup some portion of the costs, the venture could well be attractive even if it never breaks even.

We have found examples of earned-income ventures that do support non-profits' missions, particularly in the area of job training. Rubicon Bakery, in Richmond, California, employs adults from a wide range of disadvantaged communities to produce premium cakes and tarts that it sells to retailers. Pedal Revolution, in San Francisco, employs homeless youths to repair and sell bicycles. These businessess operate primarily to fulfill the social goal of providing training to the poor, any money they earn in the process is a side benefit that helps them supplement their philanthropic funding. HMT Ltd. outsourced assembling of watches by the visually impaired youths of Amar Jyoti.

Sometimes, the pursuit of profit directly conflicts with the pursuit of social good. Take the case of one environmental organization that had unique database of statistics on important environmental issues. The broad dissemination of the information helped support the organization's causes, but the database was expensive to maintain. The organization decided, therefore, to begin charging users for access. But as soon as fees were imposed, the number of users plummeted and dissemination of the information was severely curtailed. The organization had reduced its environmental impact in its effort to generate revenue. That may be a trade-off worth making, but it highlights the complex interplay – and the managerial challenge – of balancing mission and income.

Even without such a direct conflict, an earned-income venture can impede a non-profit's pursuit of its mission. Launching and running a venture consumes scarce management recourses, diluting an organization's focus on its social programs. Consider what happened to an agency, we worked with, that provides training and support to the disabled. It opened a medical supplies store that proved to be chronically unprofitable – direct costs were routinely more than two times revenue. The store took up more and more of the agency's time and energy as the non-profit's management team made "figuring out this issue" one of its highest priorities. Yet the store was doing little to fulfill the organization's mission. Only a small percentage of the agency's targeted beneficiaries shopped there.

In cases where a clear mission fit is identified, fulfilling the mission's goals through the earned-income venture may be more difficult than envisioned. One job-training organization that focused on serving the homeless wanted to expand the types of training it provided. A major soft drink company offered it the opportunity to run a distribution venture. Enthusiastic about training its beneficiaries in truck driving and enchanted by a partnership with a major corporation, the non-profit jumped in with both feet. Unfortunately, few of its homeless clients had or could get driver's licenses. To this day, the organization has trouble hiring its target beneficiaries into the venture.

Putting Mission First

Given the low likelihood that earned income ventures will contribute significant funds and the substantial likelihood they will hamper pursuit of a social mission community urge non-profits to ask to themselves the following questions. Rather than start with financial potential, begin with its mission contribution. Ask:

1. What set of mission-focused activities should be our highest priorities?
2. If we had additional, unrestricted philanthropic rupees, would these activities still be our top priorities? In other words, have we made an impartial assessment of our mission priorities?
3. Do any of these activities have the potential to generate earned income? If so, which ones do and how would they do it?
4. Would generating earned income in this manner materially compromise our mission, perhaps by excluding some of our target beneficiaries from the goods or services we sell? How much management time and other resources would the venture probably consume? What's the worst-case scenario for the venture, and what would that scenario mean for our mission and finances?

   If, after these questions have been answered, the opportunity still seems promising, then ask:

5. Taking into account any constraints or disadvantages we would have in running a commercial enterprise, what is a preliminary but reasonable estimate of the financial potential for each activity (for example, "The venture might be able to cover half its costs")? Have we fully accounted for all direct and indirect costs in estimating profit (management salaries, facility costs, other overhead)?
6. What additional amount of philanthropic funding would be needed to fully finance the activity?
7. Given the estimated philanthropic requirements of each activity (full cost minus realistic earned-income contribution), which activities deliver the most mission-related impact per philanthropic dollar? (A mission-promoting activity that covers half its costs through earned income could have more impact per philanthropic rupee than a less mission-focused activity that covers three-quarters of its costs.)

8. Would other new or existing activities that don't earn income bring a greater impact per philanthropic dollar contributed?

A mission-first assessment of earned-income opportunities also returns the non-profits are non-profits is that the marketplace does not take adequate care of the needs they address. If the most promising mission-based programmes are able to generate some earned income, of course they should. For the vast majority of nonprofits, however, that is not a pathway to financial health or to mission accomplishment.

Non-profit organizations have acquired importance in Indian political thought in recent decades as reservoirs of public spirit and training grounds of democracy. Similarly, NGOs are in the forefront of efforts at economic advancement and the growth of political democracies in other developing countries. These organizations form a third sector often termed civil society, alongside the market and the government. William W. Clohesy has rightly explained Fund raising and the articulation of common goods in Non-profit and Voluntary Sector Quarterly journal.

Many free-for-service non-profits do not engage in fund-raising at all, relying wholly on fees and other payments. Numerous organizations are in competition with one another and even with for-profit firms for fee-for-service contracts. When non-profits provide services for fees, they often privatize the good they do as well as their attitude toward those receiving the good. In their fight to survive, however, many non-profits cannot do otherwise than perform like businesses; indeed, some were formed with such a commercial model in mind.

Notwithstanding fee-for-service organizations, the third sector has gained attention and respect in recent years because of its promise for enabling people to participate actively in their societies. It is important, in discussing the third sector, to be neither skeptical nor awestruck. Non-profits can indeed offer private citizens ways of taking direct action for public purposes, a fact that gains importance as government grows distant, impersonal, and inextricably intertwined with donors of campaign money who sap politicians' political will to act in matters offensive to wealthy contributors. At the same time, non-profit organizations are as liable to institutional hardening and bureaucratization as any other organizations. And, as noted, they can commercialize their services because they face the same economic pressures to survive as any business.

Fund-raising: Different Ways

Non-profit organizations have a number of sources of revenue: grants from foundations and the government, fees for services to the public contracted with the government, revenues from commercial enterprises, and fund-raising. Fund-raisers work as staff members of an organization or they are hired, or they volunteer, for a particular campaign. Their basic responsibility is to prospect for donors, "friends" of the organization who will not only make a donation but will become regular financial donors, volunteers, and spokespersons for the good the organization is doing. Typically, fund-raisers are viewed as doing work essentially external to the organization: necessary work, to be sure, but instrumental work that makes possible the organization's real mission-based work.

Albert Anderson (1996), in his book, Ethics for Fundraisers, sums up the fund-raiser's duties as "respect, beneficence, and trust." Donors are to be treated with respect: Their opinions should be heard, their privacy protected, and their money used as they intend. Donors, at the same time, should be reminded that the purpose of the donation is some beneficence, not just a tax break or public recognition for themselves. Finally, the fund-raiser needs to have trust in the organization's ability and perseverance to accomplish its stated goals; the fund-raiser needs to have trust in the word of the donor, and, above all, the donor needs to trust the word of both the fund-raiser and the organization.

The view of fund-raising that Anderson (1996) depicts gives pride of place to the donor. Because it is the donor's money, reputation, and time, the donor is given considerable say in how those resources are used. There is nothing wrong with this, to be sure. Donors can have great and well-informed ideas. In dealing with donors, however, the danger arises of what Philip Selznick (1957, cited in Wood & Hougland, 1990) terms "institutional surrender" (p. 118), the transformation of organization and its mission in order to protect itself by obtaining donors' fights. That is, there is a problem of donor dominance that is not addressed by Anderson. In fact, he insists that the interests of the donor should override all other considerations.

Donor dominance appears frequently in the literature in the guise of three metaphors: (*a*) Donors are spoken of as customers; (*b*) fund-raising is spoken of as marketing; and, alternatively, (*c*) donors are likened to stockholders, let us consider these metaphors in turn. When donors are likened to customers, fund-raising is frequently compared to marketing, although this comparison is not found prior to the 1970s. If donors are customers, then their donations are purchasing them something just as any other customer gets a private good in return for money. Yet, when a donor gives money to a non-profit, he or she is funding an organization that provides a common or collective good to whomever needs it. The prospective donor is introduced by the fund-raiser to an organization seeking to do some sort of common good; the customer is coaxed by the marketer to seek a private good for himself or herself in or through some business establishment.

The likening of a donor to a customer is deeply problematic; the comparison of fund-raising to marketing, although less so, requires careful qualification. In the first analogy, the distinction between public purpose and private satisfaction remains un-remarked. In the second, whether the fund-raiser attracts donors to a project through championing its purpose and promise or pressing its private rewards is unresolved. In both cases, the ultimate beneficiary of both the donor's generousity and the organization's efforts disappears altogether. Long ago, business marketing turned from educating consumers on the availability of products to creating needs where none existed. As fund-raising becomes more and more like marketing, the temptation will mount to produce appeals aimed at generating shallow, non-cognitive effects, such as a "warm glow" in donors. Fund-raisers should fight such temptations, because their profession is not about pulling in donors caught up in the latest fad. Fund-raisers should be informing would be donors about problems and possible solutions, as well as about need and the ability to satisfy it. It is too late to warn against using the term marketing to identify what fund-raisers do, but it is not too late to insist that the best form of marketing is the sharing of information, the expansion of people's vision, combined with the plea that, knowing what is at stake, people commit themselves to the realization of a solution or the attainment of a hope.

Likening donors to stockholders is the third troubling analogy. Stock-holders invest in a firm with the intention of making a profit on their investment. Once upon a time, stockholders took an active part in running a firm, but today that is no longer true. Most stockholders look at their investment purely in terms of buying low and selling high. If donors are like stockholders, then they are likely interested in little other than tax breaks, prestige, and "quick fixes" for social problems.

If business imagery must be used, certainly stakeholder theory would serve far better as a pattern for non-profit organizations. Stakeholder theory holds that rather than a device for generating profits for stockholders, the firm is a social institution making possible mutually beneficial relationships and activities uniting workers, customers, stockholders, suppliers, the local population, and others. To treat any one of these stakeholders as primary reduces the others to mere means for others' ends. Managers have an obligation to deal fairly with each stakeholder group as well as the encompassing duty of coordinating and maintaining the firm itself because it is vital for many. The purpose of the firm is not to make profits but to earn them through producing goods and providing services that benefit society. Through their investments of time, work, money, and other resources, the various groups of stakeholders interact within and around the firm for their mutual good.

Following stakeholder theory, rather than the triad of donor, fund-raiser, and organization with the donor dominant, we might think of the non-profit organization as establishing a social space in which various groups enter into dynamic relations with one another for some agreed-upon mission. Among these groups are the donors, fund-raisers, employees of the organization, its management, and the ultimate beneficiaries. All of these groups interact with, and affect, the well-being of the others; therefore, they should think of themselves in terms of their social roles and effects. There are many dimensions to these interactions that stand out as we take the position of each group of stakeholders, for that is what these groups are in comparison with a for-profit firm. The donor might appear primary from one perspective, but, from others, the donor might appear overbearing by forcing his or her interpretation of the organizations' mission on the others due to his or her financial leverage.

Two writers, Susan A. Ostrander and Paul G. Schervish (1990), proposed that the two best ways for fund-raisers to approach donors is through engaging donors in the work being done by an association and by making an honest case for needs the association requires to fulfill its mission. Philanthropy is not a one-way process of discovering need and satisfying it. Rather, philanthropy is a social relation between donors and recipients in which both sides give and get in return. There are numerous forms that the relationship between donors and recipients can take, although donor-directed forms tend to dominate by the simple fact of need and its resolution. However philanthropy is structured; it is value-laden; and, at its best, to bring people into productive relationships centered on those values. Fund-raisers, therefore, ought to have no hesitation in making their requests in moral terms. The donors are not asked only to give; they are asked to become engaged in an activity of great importance to specific people in their community or somewhere in the world. That is, the donors are invited to act publicly, to make a difference, and to enjoy the satisfaction that comes with public action on behalf of a worthwhile cause. Donors' public action can take many forms: simple giving, encouraging friends to join them in giving, establishing and participating in the work of donor-advised funds, and volunteering to work for an organization themselves.

Fund-raisers should place an emphasis on the recipients and their needs or on society and possibilities for its improvement. Donors can then become collaborators: They do not determine what good is pursued, but they are invited to participate with the others in articulating a good and traversing an effective course toward it. In the process of their engagement, " a set of conditions (is) set in motion that (has) the potential for transforming the very way donors and recipients think about and interact with each other, both individually and as social groups".

At many times donors have been acknowledged as Times of India acknowledged for generous support in rehabilitation works after Tsunami. Fund –raisers have a tougher job, on this strategy, for they must find collaborators willing to work with equals rather than merely donors who want recognition through their gift. Moreover, such fund-raising works best with the active participation by organization staff and their recipients in laying out their own needs, proposing structures of concerted action, and engaging donors with them; fund-raisers must be able to facilitate the flourishing of these intricate relationships. Competition for funds doubtless makes these strategies seem more visionary than they otherwise might, but through these strategies, an important function of the third sector is brought closer to realization: "If philanthropy is a form of public service, then ethical choices in philanthropy should enhance civic life and advance the values of democracy" (Boris & Odendahl, 1990, p. 196). By involving donors and beneficiaries in this way, the irreducible plurality of human opinion is preserved and used. Plurality of views is protected and integrated within the organization's activity through strategies of engagement and of presentation of needs.

Fund raising at Action Aid

For every rupee that you donate to Action Aid, these are the benefits that you stand to get...

Benefits	***Donation***			
	Rs. 3,000	***Rs. 6,000***	***Rs. 12,000***	***Rs. 24,000***
Life insurance (cover)	Rs. 25,000	Rs. 50,000	Rs. 100,000	Rs. 250,000
Holiday package	3 days-2 nights	5 days-4 nights	7 days-6 nights	9 days-8 nights
F & B coupon	—	Rs. 500	Rs. 2,000	Rs. 5,000
Music CDs	Rs. 500	Rs. 1,000	Rs. 2,000	Rs. 3,000
Reliance handset	Rs. 5,000	Rs. 5,000	Rs. 5,000	Rs. 5,000
Tax saving	Rs. 1,500	Rs. 3,000	Rs. 6,000	Rs. 12,000
Perceived value of returns	Rs. 15,000	Rs. 25,000	Rs. 40,000	Rs. 65,000

Action Aid India Society (AAIS) is a Bangalore-based NGO that helps downtrodden, disadvantaged communities come out of poverty. Removing poverty requires money and since there are so many poor AAIS wants to help, it needs a lot of money. By December 2004 AAIS hopes to raise Rs. 15 crore through 'Karm Mitra' – the 30-year old NGO's first serious fund-raising programme in India. This is really a lot of money because CRY, India's most successful NGO, needed almost 20 years to raise Rs. 23 crore in a year.

But getting people, caught as they are in the web of reality, to open their hearts is difficult. One of the reasons is that what you pack for the afterlife never shows up on this life's balance-sheet. AAIS' chief executive Jeroninio Almeida, has designed the fund-raising programme such that the donors gets benefits many times over what he donated in the first place. These privileges are expected to cost AAIS half of the total funds raised. Of this, a quarter will be spent on sales and other multi-level giving initiatives, another on marketing and administration costs and half on donor benefits. The remaining will be allocated to community welfare operations.

Jerry, as Jeroninio is called, and his team have devised a neat tariff plan (reminiscent of the cellular ones). A donor can choose one out of four donation plans starting at Rs. 3,000 and going up to Rs. 24,000. Jerry's got divine inspiration for this. Karm Mitra, or KM as the programme is called, is inspired from the theme at an ISKCON meeting, 'Mahamantra japo, holiday jeeto.' This unique style of marketing charity was launched in 2003 in Delhi after 10 months of research. In this programme, donors will be wooed through co-branded credit cards, music concert tickets, and events like a 'Madame Butterfly' supper theatre performance, Hollywood movie premiere, celebrity ball and live reporting.

But, before all this we must tell you about Bertrand Russell's turtles, which support the Earth from falling down giant cavities in space. Stacked one upon the other, the turtles lend stability to the order of things. AAIS is using its own turtle here: and the turtle is you. More precisely you, your friend, your friend's friend and so on – the gentle world of charity resting so tantalizingly on you all. To paraphrase Scott McNealy: "The network is the contributor". For every donor you introduce to the programme you get 6% of the donation made. Further, for every person the donor you introduced gets, you get 1%. This goes on. While it may not be Amway, it could be its distant cousin. (On the other hand, if you take the many afterlives over which this compounding will hold – Main Gott!).

By 2005, it is estimated that KM will have a presence in seven cities – Mumbai, Delhi, Hyderabad, Kolkata, Ahmedabad, Pune and Bangalore with 5,000 donors in each. AAIS expects 65% of the funds raised to come from the Rs. 3,000-donation plan. At the highest level it expects 750 couples from all cities combined. If we assume that the rest of the donors will give Rs. 6,000 each, the total funds raised amount to over Rs. 15 crore. This compares well with the Rs. 2.6 crore raised by AAIS internally in 2001-02 and the Rs. 10 crore in 2002-03.

What makes the AAIS offer compelling is that even corporations have been roped in a seemingly win-win situation. Not only has ICICI Bank committed to providing free credit cards to all KM members for the next three years, but also Rs. 300-plus to AAIS for every card distributed. Further, 0.05-0.3% of the 1% ICICI Bank earns on every purchase on a credit card will be donated to AAIS – the amount varying proportionately with the size of the spend. Normally, it costs the bank roughly Rs. 800 to acquire a new card user. Consequently, the bank ends up paying a minimum of Rs. 250 per card to AAIS, taking into consideration the card free (Rs. 750) forgone in the first year.

What's ICICI Bank angling for? Says R. Madhivanan, business head (cards): "Our biggest benefit comes from the fact that we enable the customer to fulfill the need for charity easily while at the same time ensuring the use of this card as the customers preferred credit card thus resulting in higher overall spends." Therefore, for ICICI Bank, the cost of acquiring a new customer reduces while consumer loyalty and spends increase.

Next life is fine, but what happens in this life. You want to bawl out: "I need protection for the physical apart from the metaphysical." Relax. Take a deep breath. Say "Om". Actually say: "Om Kotak". AAIS has also joined hands with OM Kotak Mahindra (OKM). The company has offered group term insurance for which the NGO is paying Rs. 2.5 for every Rs. 1,000 of insurance. The original cost involved being very low no substantial subsidy is involved but OKM is bearing a part of the programme's full advertising costs.

The gain to OKM in immediate revenues does not mean much but in terms of future customers is important. Usually group insurance is bought by companies in the employer-employee form. In the larger groups, the number of employees is in the range of a few thousands and the cover per employee in lakhs of rupees. What AAIS is offering is a huge future group of 35,000 members in the next year alone.

AAIS has also figured two other things out for you. One, that all this is just Maya. And you might want an escape. So it is throwing in holiday packages as well.

Holidays include free accommodation at one out of a list of 22 destinations offered by Heritage Holidays at a cost of Rs. 90 per package to AAIS. However, each donor must apply Rs. 800 for taxes, reservation, handling and courier charges at the Rs. 3,000 contribution level and four-fold at the Rs. 24,000 level. According to Sagar Arora, chief manager marketing and business development, Heritage Holidays, the economics of the proposition are based on the principle of realization just like in insurance.

And what good is a holiday if you cannot call office and talk to your stressed out collegues while sipping Daiquiri or Nariyal pani and feel indispensable. But what you need is not the hotel phone with a 100 mark-up. You need a low-cost solution. AAIS has a tie-up with reliance Infocomm, the details of which are as yet not available. However, the two more expensive donation plans offer coloured handsets as against white ones for the less costly plans. Other tie-ups, some existing and others in the pipeline, include those with Mantra Online, Times Foundation, BPL for CTVs at 60% discount, TVS Motor, Bharat Petroleum, Indiatimes and the Taj Group of Hotels for holidays over the course of the next one year.

On the downside, some questions need to be asked. First, is it really sound economics when the size of your welfare spend should equal your payout for benefits? After all, not only does CRY raise greater funds per year without such a grand marketing plan but it also spends the majority of those on cause-related operations courtesy its lower marketing spend. Further, is it necessary to feed-the-human-greed in order to inspire people to participate in charity when other NGOs seem to have survived so far without it?

But like Gordon Gekko said: "Greed is good. Greed cuts through. Greed clarifies". It clarifies that beneath that Maori warrior, look, there is nice man who just wants the good of mankind.

Making Charity Pay

For the last 2 years Action Aid has been using direct sales agents to rope in donors for its causes, which include helping every body from street children to sex workers and their children to dispossessed dalits. What led to the marketing brainwave? Soon after Almeida took over, he commissioned a comprehensive research on the charity habits of Indians. The findings were startling. The universe of donors was a mere two-lakh big, and 79 per cent of the donations went to religious causes. For the rest of the money, there were some 20,000 registered NGOs in the fray. In other words, there had to be strong incentive for the millions of others who were not into charity, to join the cause. Says Almeida: "Daan, or donation, has always been a part of the Indian culture, but it has always been mindless."

So instead of using poignant advertisements and mailers to solicit donations, Almeida decided to launch membership scheme called 'Karam Mitra'.

There are five categories of membership – Gold, Silver, Bronze, Copper and Black – that a donor can choose from. The basic proposition is simple: donate and get greater benefits, which are sponsored by respective companies exclusively for Action Aid. A Gold member, who needs to donate at least Rs. 24,000 to qualify as one, gets benefits worth Rs. 60,000. The benefits include tax savings on half the donation, life insurance from OM Kotak Mahindra, a co-branded credit card from ICICI and Action Aid, tickets to movies cassettes and CDs, and a copy of the Civil Society magazine (an NGO trade magazine), among others.

In April 2004, Almeida tied up with Hyderabad-based Smart Value, which already has got on board 40,000 donors for the education of street children. The UK government has promised to match in donations whatever amount Karm Mitra raises for the Commonwealth Education Fund, administered by Action Aid, Oxfam and Save the Children, UK. With ICICI Bank recently chipping in with Rs. 3.5 crore, the kitty for dispossessed children has swollen to Rs. 7 crore. What's also unique about Karm Mitra, says Almeida, is that it doesn't just give money to the unfortunate. Rather, it works like a venture capitalist, getting into a community, setting up a viable project, appoints a leader and then make its exit.

Karam Mitra apart, Action Aid runs its own version of multi-level marketing called multi-level giving (MLG), where ordinary folks such as housewives, students, retirees, even professionals network to raise funds for the NGO. At the same time, MLG is not unwieldy as the typical multi-level marketing scheme. It is three-tiered and it begins afresh after every set of three people to ensure transparency in the scheme. Almeida is exploring the possibility of replicating the Karm Mitra model by starting Karm Yuva for students and Karm Maitree, which will allow urban women to adopt female sex workers or impoverished women working in fisheries.

Fund Raising: Different Strategies

Even as non-government organizations begin to play more important role in the delivery of social service in the country. India is fast falling behind its neighbours in the ability to raise funds. "The objective is to find funds to do work at the grassroots", says Shanker Venkateshwaran, director of an umbrella NGO called the South Asia Fund Raising Group.

"It would be so much simpler if local NGOs, international NGOs and aid-giving agencies could talk to people who understood the issues on all sides of the table," says Usha Menon, the Singapore-based director of the International Fund Raising Group.

Both Venkateshwaran and Menon are pushing for specialized NGOs that can raise funds and monitor the work being done by grassroot organizations. Venkateshwaran, who has been working in Delhi-based NGO Partners in Change, should know. An alumnus of IIT Madras and IIM Calcutta, the 39-year-old former A.F. Ferguson consultant says that those doing grassroots work often lack the communications skills and strategies to attract funds even while some savvy NGOs swallow up large amounts without delivering the goods. Menon says that international donors are confused by the complexities of the local NGO set up and often prefer to give to well-known organizations.

Vijay Sardana, who heads the SPWD says: "We have to justify our fund giving to our principal donors. NGOs that can't present their point of view effectively and those that cannot understand the donors' perspectives lose funding." He points out that both Nepal and Bangladesh have made great strides in attracting international funding for NGOs by working on the interface with donors.

India desperately needs NGO work, Menon says, "If you were to shrink the globe into a single village of 100 houses, there would be 70 non-white households, yet six houses, all American, would control 50 per cent of the total wealth. Most of the non-whites would suffer from malnutrition and 80 of the houses would be substandard, she says. Within Asia, India and its neighbours are right at the bottom.

"With 22 per cent of the world's population, South Asia accounts for 40 per cent of the world's poor. More than 43 percent of the population of these countries live on daily wages of less than a dollar. South Asia is emerging as the poorest, the most illiterate, most malnourished, least gender-sensitive...indeed, the most deprived region in the world," says Mahbubul Karim, senior vice-president of the Bangladeshi NGO behemoth Proshika.

Menon says that while fund-collection has reached colossal proportions in the richer countries, poorer regions have not been able to do enough. She quotes her own experience with the Singapore Community Chest programme. Today more than 30 per cent of income earners in the city-state donate a monthly sum to the Community Chest, which in turn passes these on to NGOs doing grassroots work.

"Fund collection in the US, for example, is a finely honed business. More than 75 per cent of funding comes from individual contributions, while only 5 per cent comes from corporate donations. Here in India, 99 per cent of funding comes from either the government, bilateral agencies like USAID, and donor NGOs like Oxfam," says Venkateshwaran.

Even here India falls for behind... Nepal, for example. In 1962 that country had just 15 NGOs; by 1977 the number had grown to a mere 91 with a total income of Rs. 1.45 crore. Nepal then set up the Social Services National Coordination Council (SSNC) to facilitate NGO work. This was very successful. In 1990 NGO sector grew to Rs. 70.24 crore and in 1999 touched Rs. 900 crore, or the equivalent of 12 per cent of Nepal's national budget. There are now over 25,000 NGOs with about one million workers giving basic services in education, healthcare, and social infrastructure building.

Or take the case of Bangladesh. Today the NGO sector, according to some accounts, is a bigger social spender than the government itself. Bangladesh has been a large recipient of international aid. Since there are very few large industries and fewer industrial groups, NGOs have been involved in major industrial activities and operate out of large, multi-storey buildings in down-town Dhaka. NGOs in Bangladesh run the milk supply chain, dominate the market for poultry products, cellular telephony, and paging, and the small savings and rural banking sector.

By all accounts the Indian scene is quite bleak. According to Venkateshwaran there has been no enumeration of NGOs in the country and they have been listed under different heads in many cases. For example, those receiving foreign aid have to be registered with the home ministry and under the Foreign Contribution (Regulation) Act. Others, like trusts and schools, are listed with the income tax authorities. He estimates that there are somewhere between 25,000 and 40,000 NGOs active in India.

A study by the Charity Aid Foundation (CAF) found that less than 2 per cent of the Indian social welfare budget of Rs. 19,000 crore is channelled through the NGO sector. T.K. Mathew, chief executive of Deepalaya, an NGO, says foreign aid to Indian NGOs has increased a mere 21 per cent in the last five years. This compares badly with the more than tenfold increase in Nepal in same period.

Venkateshwaran suggests that more Indian NGOs specializing in raising funds are needed. There is a feeling that since the government's social welfare programmes are shambles, the NGO sector could help bridge the gap. He feels altruism, a business related focus, and a spirit of community involvement could help bring new funds into Indian NGOs. He says that once they also find some funds of their own, they would be able to present a better view to foreign donors. He holds out the example of organizations like Help Age, CRY, Concern, and the Spastics Societies.

NGO experts say this is important; since too little of Indian government funds are being channelled through the NGOs, their dependence on foreign funding is too high for their own comfort and that of the donors themselves.

There is a possibility that such involvement also brings benefits to the donors, as Citibank and Taj hotels found. Their staffs are now encouraged to be involved in such project since it gives them pride in what they are doing. It could be something simple, like bank staff helping NGOs develop financial monitoring systems or the Taj Pastry chefs teaching local bakers. Such programmes also carry the bonus of being showcase-able, which is important in attracting donors.

Specialized NGOs, which are willing to put in expensive skills in communication, marketing, advertising, financial management, and legal knowledge in a non-profit organization, would help the vast majority of NGOs that do not have the where-withal and exposure to handle issues outside their immediate environment.

FUND RAISING AT CRY

From an organisation that was started 20 years ago with Rs. 50, a dining table and a dream, CRY's support today touches the lives of eight lakh children through 162 projects. For the financial year ending March 1999, CRY generated a surplus of Rs. 11.5 crore, a 28 per cent growth over the previous year (Rs. 7.76 crore). Of this, Rs. 9.3 crore were deployed towards child development initiatives such as education and health of 314,000 children across the country (Rs. 1 crore in 1997-98). The total funds disbursed were Rs. 5.42 crore. For 1999-2000, CRY has set itself an ambitious target of reaching out to 100,000 children, in addition to the 812,000 children whose lives it has already touched in the last two decades. To achieve this, the organization is aiming at generating a surplus of Rs. 14.5 crore, or a turnover of Rs. 24 crore, this fiscal.. All NGOs, as a rule, reveal their financial results only to the Charity Commission. This is the first time that CRY has made its financial public.

"It is in keeping with building a transparent and open relationship with the public," explains Pervin Varma, director, CRY, "We are a public trust for children and, therefore, we are accountable to both the public who actually contribute, as well as the public who go out there and do the work. And the larger public itself", She adds. Besides, this is not altogether a newfound openness – CRY annual report is a public document, she adds, available to those who ask for it. Making accountability and transparency a cornerstone is a good way for CRY to endorse its credentials further and thus attract new contributors.

To the average person, the most visible face of CRY is the greeting cards they sell. But obviously there is more to CRY than that. In fact, the organization spans the entire spectrum of development activities – from working with children, to resource mobilization and developing effective systems of training as well as supporting networks from the grassroots to the regional and national level. It also plays an important role in enhancing development – related policies interacting closely with government officials. Notice cards business contributes 14 per cent of the organization's revenue. In fact, organizations from corporate houses to individuals contribute 50 per cent of the organization's resource. The approach is two pronged resource mobilization and building public awareness. CRY has 25 specialists in development issues which have an understanding of the grassroots.

For resource mobilization CRY has roped in marketing and communications strategies from corporates. CRY gauges the potential of streams of revenues viz. corporate's employees, families etc., then defines how a person wants to contribute; be it a card, donation for project funding. The role of corporates is usually by the way of direct project funding and the resources available from corporates are matched to the needs of child development initiatives. TNT worldwide, Hinduja Foundation, Cadbury Schweppes, Tata Salt, Archies Card, to name a few have been a part of this revenue. Corporate involvement in development by the way of project funding has been around 15 per cent of revenues.

CRY shop, which opened in Mumbai in 1998-99, was CRY's first experiment in setting up its own retail shop. While it stocks CRY products like cards, calendars, etc., the shop in an attempt to market the product of NGOs working with unprivileged communities, thus helping them to generate resources.

The turning point for CRY was in 1983, when it moved from being a run-by-well-wishers organization to acquiring its own space and incorporating specialized skills such as technology, systems, etc. What added weight to the organization was financial support from the Ford Foundation for three years (1989-1991). With this, the organization was able to rope in marketing, communication, finance, planning and technology specialists from the development sector as well those from corporates.

CRY measures its success by the number of projects that it helps initiate. The Dr. Shantha Sinha-run MV Foundation in Andhra Pradesh (AP) is one such project. Sinha wanted to eradicate child labour in state's agriculture sector, which has a history of bonded labour. She set out on the task almost a decade ago in the Ranga Reddy district. To begin with, she managed to convince a couple of families to let her teach their children. The fact that she succeeded was a major breakthrough. She started by teaching three children for three months. Sinha then took her efforts to other neighbouring districts like Shankarpally. Meanwhile, the Ranga Reddy district has seen an end to its history of child labour, becoming an internationally accepted model for eradication of child labour. Only one-tenth of MV Foundation is supported by CRY today, as they are also getting support from the government.

However, CRY hasn't limited its boundaries to India. An international cell was set up at Delhi in 1991 to involve NRI's in development work back home. Today, over 7,000 individuals contribute through the international cell, mostly, by way of donations. The US chapter of this cell, CRY Inc., essentially a volunteer-based organization, was started in 1998. Today, almost 600 volunteers work for CRY in America. CRY Inc. is a virtual organization on the Internet. For the first year, CRY Inc. reported $3,000 from card sales.

A NEW APPEAL

If cards and calendars are what come to mind when you think of CRY, its time you thought again. For Child Relief and You (CRY), the 18-years-old resource organization formed to help child-development projects around India, is attempting to raise funds in more innovative ways than just selling stationery. The CRY Shop in Mumbai is its latest initiative.

Formed with the twin objectives of fund-raising and providing a retail presence to products made by other social welfare projects, if offers a variety ranging from table linen, clocks and candle stands, children's educational toys, stationery, and even designer costume jwellary. With prices anywhere between Rs. 8 and Rs. 900, CRY has quite a range to offer.

Says Shaila Malik, a consultant with CRY for a decade, who has been associated with the setting up of the store since day on, "A lot of individual projects have felt the need for an avenue like this to sell their products, as they find it difficult to hold their own in commercially-run retail outlets." Often it's the absence of economies of scale which tends to drive costs upward. As these individuals can offer only very limited quantities, this makes it difficult to negotiate margins with retailers.

Further, unlike profit-driven companies which can cut expenses on areas like labour, a development project may invest substantially in upgrading the infrastructure of a village, and may hence need to build these costs into its pricing. Notes Vishal Kapoor, president of the Bombay Store, an up market gifts and lifestyle shop in South Mumbai, "In one instance, we were buying products form an NGO at the same price at which we were retailing the competitor's products. Obviously, we were forced to stop sourcing from the former." With shelf space at a premium, products with fatter margins get the best displays and typically move faster.

The consignment system is a dampener too. Typically, supplies do not get paid on making delivery of the goods to retailers, but have to wait for these sale to happen. Payments then have to be followed up relentlessly, which often means having one member of the staff dedicated to constant interaction with trade. With few employees and limited resources, this hardly remains a priority.

Take the example of paper works, an employment training project in Mumbai for street boys in the age-group of 16-30, which makes utilitarian products like candle stands and picture frames from recycled industrial waste paper. Says David, counselor, "One reason why we have not been proactive in the local market is that we are working with a group of people who demand a lot of personal attention and take up our time." Some of its products are now on display at Shop can be compared to the retail chain in Europe run by Oxfam, the international charity which stocks goods made by projects in developing countries. But the crucial difference is that the Oxfam shops also keep "used products".

One organization ahead of its time in establishing its own presence was the Women's India Trust (WIT). Within just a few years of its inception in 1968, its founders, Kamila Tyabji set up the first shop in Tardeo, a south Mumbai locality, where WIT also had its workshop for making linen and a kitchen for its popular jams and pickles. It has since grown to two more outlets in Mumbai.

Apart from its food products, WIT offers a wide array in linen, especially in block-prints for standard items like bedspreads and table linen, though it has a limited choice in ready-made garments. But watch out for creative novelties like laundry bags, oven gloves and baby quilts. All these items are made by women on a piece-rate basis and WIT loyalists swear by its down-to-earth prices and quality products.

Over the years, WIT has expanded sales through other channels as well exhibitions are held frequently in Mumbai and other places like Pune, Goa and Bangalore. Export is another thrust area.

Quality is the USP at WIT, too. Currently, sales from the three shops at Rs. 14 lakh a year form the largest chunk in WIT's annual Rs. 45 lakh turnover, Kotwal admits that shop sales may not have seen a spectacular rise in recent years, but it is still the "bread and butter business". But, competition from larger retailers like The Bombay Store has grown, who may be more expensive but can offer more by way of range of products and retailing ambience. "Constant creating inputs in our product range is what we really need", notes Kotwal.

One constraint for these shops is small space. Limited funds do not give much choice either. WIT is spread over 350 sq. ft., CRY is just 275 sq. ft. and the World Wide Fund for Nature (WWF) shop at Church gate in Mumbai is even smaller. Though located in the popular shopping area of Bhulabhai Desai Road, the CRY Shop does not face the road, and is nestled in a high-rise. Despite this, with its careful attention to design, it does not appear cramped. Nearby, WWF has managed to get space on subsidized rent from the Brahourne stadium, but the shop looks crowded if more than five people are present.

TYRANNY OF CHARITY

A recent survey has come up with some surprising criticism of the way Indian NGOs have been operating, compelling the need for mid-course correction in their approaches. Gallup-MBA, the market research agency, was approached early last year by well-known national NGO Child Relief and You

(CRY) to analyze and examine Indian NGOs and delineate areas of child development which CRY should concentrate on in the new millennium.

CRY specializes in raising funds and while it does not undertake projects itself, it partners other NGOs on children-related ventures. To that extent it is a funding agency. There are some 40,000 NGOs operating across the country today and Gallup-MBA noted some very keen competition for funding amongst most of them. The report was scathing in its observation of NGO modus operandi, observing: "In a lot of cases, NGO intervention is one-off, with no follow-up of the beneficiaries in 99 per cent of the cases; also, as soon as funding dries up, the NGO disappears." The survey deduces that the intervention hence becomes piece-meal and ineffective. Funding agencies tend to pay by fixed-tenure, fixed-objective projects rather than for a territorial franchise or a generic development agenda. They also tend to spread their money amongst maximum NGO projects, which are often one-off efforts.

The survey, therefore, suggests that major NGO funders coordinate their efforts at a national level in order to be effective. It highlights the need for an apex body comprising these major funders that can monitor the development efforts and help resolve some of the glaring lapses in NGO operations. But it stresses that such an effort must come from within the NGO community rather than from some government institution. CRY spokesperson says that the study has been circulated among its workers and project that are funded by it. It expects to incorporate the priorities set out in the study in its new programmes, beginning this financial year. He says the discussion process is long as there are hundreds of project partners involved and successful NGO work requires consensus-building among all stakeholders and constituents.

The survey also described NGO documentation as inadequate and poorly kept, rendering follow-up difficult with the beneficiaries for a rational evaluation of the project. With many NGOs inept in maintaining records, funding agencies are completely subjective in assessing their effectiveness, objectives, and methodology, the survey observes. Intervention in child development has to be a sustained effort.

Gallup-MBA suggests that CRY, as a major funding agency for child development, should build an organization that can identify and influence grass-roots-level NGO objectives. Justifying CRY's interference in those NGOs it funds, the market research agency feels this will allow more NGOs with varying core competences to function within the same area for a more broad based and sustainable development, "Funding agencies like CRY have to bring many NGOs together under its umbrella so that they can coordinate their activities more effectively," the report suggests, recommending "issue-based networks" for pooling experience and "task-based networks of different NGOs" for making intervention more effective.

CRY has clarified that there is no disgruntlement in its programming. The survey shows that maybe everybody has been missing the wood for the trees and that the survey, by questioning every aspect of how NGOs currently operate, has shown specific areas within the current scenario that need correction and change. Every body was perhaps doing it not so right and that a holistic approach to NGO operation shows that there is need for change.

Haphazard, even dishonest, NGO efforts in areas often spoil the case for good efforts that come subsequently. Beneficiaries tend to keep away from NGOs following such bad experiences. Intervention in child development has to be spread over a decade to be effective in a particular and NGOs have to find the means to make sure that they are there for the long haul.

FUND RAISING – CRITICAL ANALYSIS

When a charitable non-profit organization receives a grant from the government, contributions to charities could fall for two reasons. First, donors let their involuntary tax contributions substitute for their voluntary contributions and the second, that the strategic response of the charity will be to pull back on its fund-raising efforts after receiving a grant. James Andreoni and A. Abigail Payne in The American Economic Review (June 2003) examined using a rich panel data set of non-profit organizations for 15 years. When looking at the component parts of fund-raising expenses, they found that indeed there is strong evidence that government grants to non-profits are causing significant reductions in fund-raising efforts. This funding is important for two reasons. First, it means, that the behaviour of the non-profit organizations is consistent with the predictions of an economic model within a strategic environment. This suggests that more sophisticated models of fund-raising and competitions in 'charity markets' could bear fruit. Second, and more importantly, it adds an important new dimension to the policy discussions on the effectiveness of government grants to increase the services of charitable non-profit organizations charities are not passive receptacles of contributions, as they have so often been treated in the past, but are active players in the market for donations. When the government gives charities a grant, we should take into account the behavioural response of the charity itself, as well as the behavioural responses of the individual donors.

The social costs and benefits of fund raising must be analyzed. The fund raising expenditure should only be used towards the collection of private donations or funding unrelated to government grants. The reporting instructions to charities, however, define fund raising as "the total expenses incurred in soliciting contributions, gifts, grants, etc." Hence, a non-profit may include the costs associated with applying for government funding as a fund raising expenditure or, worse, the costs of reporting and complying with the conditions of the grants.

There are three main components of fund raising costs as reported by charities. First are "professional fund raising fees" which are payments to outside organizations for conducting fund raising or consulting on fund-raising. Second is the portion of officer's salaries allocated to fund raising. Third is the portion of overall salaries and wages allocated to fund raising. An issue concerns the fact that some government grants may be in the form of a matching grant, whereby the non-profit organization is expected to raise funding from other sources to qualify for the government funding (or vice versa).

If the services of an organization are in high demand, such as the SOS Children's Villages of India after Tsunami, we might expect demands for both private and public contributions to be high. And, naturally, if both demands are high, these organizations should increase their pursuit of both public grants and private donations. In other words, unmeasured influences may be increasing both government grants and fund raising.

Philanthropic foundations are important because of their collective ability to devote substantial resources to a selected set of issues and organizations through which they exert a great deal of influence on the non-profit sector and society at large. NGOs seeks to mobilize funding support to ensure the related goods of financial stability and survival, on one hand, and legitimacy, on the other. To understand the essential characteristics of philanthropic foundations and funding agencies, it is necessary to analyze the historical emergence. The early foundations were established in response to the growing societal awareness of problems that required holistic approach. It was made possible by the hitherto unprecedented concentration of wealth in the hands of very few individuals, such as Andrew Carnegie, John D. Rockefeller, who believed that philanthropy would be most efficient if it attacked the "root causes" of social problems by means of rational scientific inquiry.

Foundations, like other non-profits, do not operate under the conditions of market competition, and their goals such as the welfare of mankind. Foundation's professed commitment to social change raises the question of their support for social movement organizations generally seen as important agent of social change.

British Airways general manager South Asia, Kevin Steele was made responsible for improving the airline's yields. Steele's India stint will be remembered for the highly personal and innovation efforts, he put in to boost BA's involvement in community work. He raised some Rs. 16 lakhs from those who sponsored his weight loss programme. The funds were donated to CRY and used in projects for welfare of under privileged children in Mumbai.

FUND RAISING – FROM INTERNAL SOURCES

"I am feeling much better now, doctor." The speaker is 100-year-old Jairoh Devi, and her rasping voice brings a smile to the faces of those gathered around her: a sundry crowd of relatives, interested villagers and health workers. "Please don't let her die without seeing her great granddaughter's wedding," jokes one of her relatives. This could well be a scene from a Bollywood melodrama but it isn't. Jairoh Devi is for real, as is her recovery. She lives in Pratapgarh (pop: 700), a village in Haryana, one of the 30 in the state that serves as a setting for TeleDoc, a pilot project in rural healthcare that is the brainchild of the Faridabad-based Jiva Institute, a non-governmental organization. And for the record, the man responsible for Devi's cure, Sumeet Sagon, isn't a doctor at all.

TeleDoc is build around two strands that are a few thousand years apart: the ancient Indian medical system of Ayurveda and the as-recent-as-you-can-get phenomenon of mobile telephony. Every day, three TeleDoc workers, each armed with a Nokia 6800 phone, fan out to the 30 villages the project covers. At each village, villagers gather at a designated place to discuss their ailments with the teledocs. The teledoc transmits this information through the GPRS-enabled phone and a Java-based software to a team of five Ayurvedic doctors at Jiva's Faridabad clinic. The doctors analyse the symptoms and prescribe medication; medicines are compounded at the clinic itself and delivered the following day by the teledocs. The phone is a recent addition (October 2003). When the project started in September 2002 with a Rs. 23-lakh grant from New York-based Soros Foundation, the teledocs used handheld PCs, then simputers. Jiva's doctors could access patient information only when the teledocs returned.

"There are 3.1 lakh villages in India with a population of less than 500," says Rishi Pal Chauhan, President, Jiva Institute, "and 77,500 of these do not even have a shop." "Over one lakh have just once small shop that sells small things; none of these villages have proper medical facilities, so we decided to do something for them." Chauhan's target is what terms the bottom of the pyramid, people earning less than $1 (Rs. 46) a day. Yet, Jiva's TeleDoc project isn't about charity.

A cause with a business model

Teledoc isn't about a well-intentioned NGO working for the benefit of the less privileged; it is about a sustainable business model (why, Jiva even boasts an American exec – Steven Rudolph designated Director). Jiva's founders like to call their organizations " a social enterprise". Jiva charges its TeleDoc patients Rs. 70 a week. "Villagers pay when they see it works," says Rudolph. TeleDoc currently services 1,500 paying patients; that's some Rs. 100,000 in revenue every week. Encouraged by this response, Jiva proposes to take TeleDoc national by April 2004. "By April 2005 we will cover 5,000 villages and earn a profit of Rs. 8.42 lakh," claims Chauhan. "By April 2006, we will cover 10,000 villages and return profits of Rs. 2.5 corre."

A franchising model will facilitate reach, reckons Chauhan. And he expects that to come with its own path to profitability. "Large companies find the top of the pyramid saturated," he explains, referring to the fact that urban markets for most product categories have been exploited to the extent possible. "They want to target the bottom now but there's a problem: the cost of delivering something to a far-flung village is sometimes more than its cost itself." Teledocs, he reasons, can do as much, for a commission. The way Chauhan sees it, everyone wins: villages get access to low-cost healthcare and other products (at their doorstep); and companies gain access to villages at a viable cost.

Jiva has order revenue streams as well: a school that charges Rs. 500 a month; textbooks, up to Class V that Jiva has published, incorporating what it terms 'India's Curriculum of Tomorrow' (ICOT), which it sells to 500 schools across India; and ayurvedic website ayurvedic.org that sells Ayruvedic products; and an online Ayurveda college targeting oversees customers and offering courses in Ayurveda to anything between Rs. 1,600 and Rs. 68,000 a pop.: "The face of non-profit will change form NGOs to social enterprises in the next 10 years," gushes Rudolph, a wealthy American who came to India at Chauhan's instance and who believes that technology and innovation can create a rural economic boom in India.

Scaling it up

NGOs may go the way Rudolph expects them to, and become social enterprises. And they may not. However, Jiva's effort at providing distance health services to the poor has received some recognition, in the form of a World Summit Award. These awards are presented by the UN and the International Telecommunications Union (ITU) to organizations that use technology to bridge divides. Of the 40 awards presented this year, Jiva bagged one in the e-health category. The only other Indian entry to win an award was n-Logue Communications, a company promoted by IIT Madras' TeNet Group, which offers low-cost internet and telecommunications services in rural areas.

The award has brought Jiva and TeleDoc some attention: requests have come in from Sri Lanka and Indonesia to run pilot TeleDoc projects. And ITC and n-Logue have both expressed interest in taking TeleDoc to the villages where they are active.

Fund raising from internal sources through the sale of products by organizations and charge on the services is being done by most of the organizations. In Chitrakoot, Jankikund Hospital of Sadguru Seva Sangh Trust charged Re. 1 for the duration of 1 months prescription, it was increased to Rs. 5 for the duration of 15 days and again it is increased to Rs. 10 and period of the validity of prescription was reduced to 1 week. So, the fee for service on prescription for out door patients has been increased while the validity of prescription is reduced.

Fund raising in Tsunami

Tsunami calamity caused damages to human lives. NGOs, corporates, government and individuals joined hands in the rehabilitation and resettlement. Many NGOs, government, banks and others strove hard to raise funds for the socio-economic development.

Chapter 13

Managing Human Resources for Rural Projects

Rural Projects are being executed by project officer, programme manager or other officials. The staff is considered to be most effective resource for the success of a project. Douglas Mc. Greger developed theory X and Y on human behaviour. Theory X implies an autocratic approach to managing. It assumes that most people dislike work and will try to avoid it, if possible. They engage in various work restrictions, they have very little ambition and will avoid responsibility, they are self-centered, indifferent to organizational needs, and resistant to change. The common rewards given by organizations are not enough to overcome their dislike for work.

Theory Y implies a humanistic and supportive approach to managing people. If management will provide the proper environment to release their potential, work will become as natural to them as play or rest. Project management's role is to provide an environment in which the potential of people can be released at work.

Management of human resource is concerned with the growth and development of people toward higher levels of competency, creativity, and fulfillment, because people are the central resource in an organization. The human resources approach means that better people achieve better results. It is similar to Mc. Gregor's theory Y.

Nearly all-conscious behaviour is motivated. Project management's job is to identify and activate employee motives constructively toward task performance. Needs create tensions that are modified by one's culture to cause certain wants. A.H. Maslow classified needs into physiological needs, safety, security, esteem and self-actualization needs. When needs are conditioned by environment, the result is a set of employee wants.

Human resource for rural projects is slightly different from others. They are required to work in rural areas with weak infrastructure and facilities and even in remote areas. If a person is motivated to work in rural projects he may have high job satisfaction which led to high productivity. Lawler and Porter have developed a model that suggests that productivity lead to satisfaction. Performance leads to rewards; and if these are perceived to be equitable as explained by equity theory, employee satisfaction is the result. One feature of job satisfaction is that it is influenced by community conditions. What usually happens is that employees compare their job conditions with community conditions.Rural project worker also compare a job's "way of life" with the community's way of living and they are most satisfied when these two value systems come reasonably close together. A job in rural project allows independence, variability and a moderate pace.

Rajendra Singh opted to work in the remote areas of Rajasthan, this created in him a sense of belongingness and motivated for the well being of rural community. With this, he worked hard and

Magsaysay Award recognized his work. Arun Tyagi of Gram Sudhar Samiti is working in the rural areas of Sidhi district of M.P. Working in rural projects require motivation. Governments have warned doctors at many occassions to work for the service of rural community. Chhattisgarh government started three years medical course to prepare a cadre of human resource for rural medical services.

Institutions like IRMA, MGCG Gramodaya Vishwavidyalaya have been established to prepare rural development professionals. In rural development projects it is likely that personnel management function will be the direct responsibility of the project manager. An organization with projects dispersed across various districts and states assume national or state characteristics. One crucial factor that assists their operations is constant co-ordination and networking between employees of these geographically dispersed projects. Coordinating between scattered projects may not necessarily be an easy task. But with Human Resource Management taking charge of the situation, things tend to fall in place in a smooth and effective way.

Most of my students joined grassroot NGOs and worked in rural projects then having experienc they are working with international and funding agencies. Universities and institutions like IITs and IIMs rely heavily on alumni for funding and maintaining relationships with them has become a core skill. NGOs and non-profits are equally predisposed to capture value from their alumni. Many NGOs have been successful in launching broad alumni outreach efforts. These organizations always mention those alumnies who are working with international agencies and invite them to participate in annual meetings and other porgrammes. This helps in the orientation and training of new project staff, developing relationship with funding agencies and motivating present staff to excel in project management.

As head of the organisation or project manager, we have a core responsibility to help our subordinates realize their potential. But we also have limited time, energy and budget. So, how do you allocate these limited resources among employees to elicit the best performance from each person – and thus, deliver the best performance for your organization? Do you need the experts who maintain that star performers deserve the lion's share of your time and attention as well as the juiciest rewards? Or do you follow the advice of those who believe that differential treatment splinters a work force by alienating productive members of the rank and file who shoulder workloads far from the lime light. And if you do believe that some differential treatment among employees is required, how will you see that it manifests itself in a way that allows you to get the best results for your rural project or organization. A good performance appraisal system will ensure good reward mechanism in rural project. Appraisal plan should be applied on each functionary without any rejoice.

Human resource is rated high enough in well-managed organizations. It is at par with every other strategic or financial division in an organization. Human resource audits are an exercise in SWOT assessment, it suggest ways for companies to fine tune personnel management functions. Audits help organizations shape a vision for the future, channel their resources into their people more effectively, and help the organization sail smoothly through testing times of change. Human resource audits may be conducted internally or externally. If it is a self-audit, the directors must appoint a fair and competent team whose experience, skill and qualifications can never be called into question; otherwise, the credibility in the process will be lost. The process of audit itself is a relatively free of complications. After agreeing on the scope, methods, recourses and time-frame of the report, and based on what the organisation expect to glean from the audit, the audit group draws up an action plan. The audit team then goes through the required documents (claims and compensation-related records, salary systems, records of grievances etc.) and interviews staff member of rural projects. There are those who say that audits are unnecessary, or that they cause needless deviations from the normal scheme of things as for as human resource is concerned. But there is proof enough from research to dispel any such notion. Human resource audit not only tells you volumes about the state of health of human resource department of a rural project, it also shows you how to remain strategic for the future. It is evident that money, as a means of rewarding employees, is important to employees for a number of reasons. Certainly money is valuable because of the goods and services that it will purchase. Salary does have status value, it shows the hierarchy in rural projects. Expectation theory states that Valence × Expectancy = Motivation. Valence refers to strength of preference for an outcome compared with others, and expectancy refers to strength of belief that a particular act will be followed by particular outcomes. This means that money is to act as a motivator, an employee must want more of it (valence) and also believe that the reward will follow better performance (expectancy). With regard to expectancy, the employee response tends to be less evident. Promotions, increments and upgradation of scales should be framed in such a way that employees of a rural project consider that additional performance will lead to additional money. There should be justice to those employees who deliver high performance. Expectancy is an area where management has much opportunity for positive action, because it can substantially change the connection between increased performance and reward.

A rural development project may have project based appointment, as usually funding agencies provide assistance for fixed duration. Organizations involved in the management of such projects must do the job analysis. Job analysis involves developing a detailed description of the tasks involved in a job, determining the relationship of a given job to other jobs, and ascertaining the knowledge skills, and abilities necessary for an employee to successfully perform the job. For example, a project on watershed management may require a person qualified in rural management with relevant experience. A mobile healthcare project may require a person with suitable qualifications viz., MBBS, BAMS, BHMS etc. The organization must have a job description and job specification statement. Job description is a written statement of what a jobholder does how it is done, and why it is done. It should accurately portray job content, environment, and conditions of employment. The job specification states the minimum acceptable qualification that an employee must possess to perform a given job successfully. It identifies the knowledge, skills and abilities needed to do the job effectively. So, job descriptions identify characteristics of the job, while job specifications identify characteristics of the successful job incumbent. The job description and specification are important documents for guiding the selection process. The job description can be used to describe the job to potential candidates. The job specification keeps the attention of those doing the selection on the list of qualifications necessary for an incumbent to perform a job and assist in determining whether or not candidates are qualified.

For the successful implementation and management of rural projects an honest, transparent and quality recruitment and selection procedure should be adopted. The post should be advertised with full details in local media and special supplements like Times Ascent in Times of India, Power Jobs in the Hindustan Times. Few websites like ruralnaukri.com and devnetjobs.com have been established to advertise for rural jobs. These sites may be helpful in attracting youths because youths are most visitors to these sites. After receiving the application a proper screening of applications will ensure quality and reduction in interviews calls. A panel of qualified and experienced persons must be formed and letter of interest to participate as an expert should be sent with a telephonic consent. All the candidates with requisite qualifications and experience should be called. After the selection the organization involved in the management of rural project should follow following requirements for successful management of human resource.

(*a*) Induction at the Project

It is always good practice to meet newly appointed staff at their point of arrival prior to joining the project. This may be at the nearest railway station for someone coming from another district within the country. This should help to establish good relationship and enable the person to settle down as quickly as possible.

There are many activities, which might be carried out, in the initial phase, from providing information throughout to giving supplementary training:

(*i*) **Records**

One of the first formalities should be to record on each personal file, in addition to the personal history (*Curriculum vitae*), the name, telephone number and address of the person(s) to be notified in an emergency.

(*ii*) **Training**

The senior project staff will presumably have been selected because they are trained, qualified, and experienced to carry out their job requirements. Senior staff may not necessarily, so for, be the junior staff who may need some supplementary training to enable them to carry out their work in the way require this.

Virtually all staff should attend induction courses given by the project manager, to acquaint them with the brief history of the project, the development and immediate objectives, and outline of the various activities of the project as set out in the project document work plan. This should help new staff to see where they fit into the project team, and the objectives they are all working for.

(*iii*) **Conditions of service**

Before actually commencing work it may be desirable to clarify some of the basic personnel information such as:

Hours of work: the number of hours a day, which may be between fixed hours, a 'flexi-time' which stipulates certain items of the day when all should be on duty and then leaves it to each person whether he wished to start and/or finish either early or late. This information would also clarify the days to be worked in the week.

Holidays: these will include national holidays and vacation time, which is arranged for each individual. The system of requesting vacation time and how this is dealt with to ensure that all the project staff do not decide to go on vacation at the same time or critical times, must be clearly explained.

Discretion of the project manager: many rural development field staff work more hours and longer working weeks than their formal requirements, and this is sometimes without receiving or expecting any extra payment. In these circumstances the project manager usually has discretion to grant some free time during normal working hours.

(*b*) Wages and Salaries

(*i*) **Job evaluation**

This has been defined as 'the process of analyzing and assessing the content of jobs, in order to place them in an acceptable rank order, which can then be used for a remuneration system'.

Job evaluation can rank by broad pay classes and may go further to consider the factor by which each job is to be rated, e.g. skill, effort, responsibility and conditions of work. Despite the contribution job evaluation can make, the project manager may still be faced with problems, such as reconciling the likely difference between the payment to be made to the man recruited from the private sector open market, and the fixed wages and salaries of government staff.

(*ii*) Special incentive payments over and above wages and salaries are not normally payable to rural project staff but considering the performance it may be given to deserving staff.

(*c*) Incentives

(*i*) An appraisal of staff should be made on a regular basis, perhaps every six months. The project manager and his sub-managers will have private meetings with each of the staff who are directly responsible to them. In these personal discussions a joint review should be made of past performance based upon fact, and the junior staff member should have the opportunity to explain his problems and to make any complaints.

In addition to those who may be recommended for promotion to a more demanding job and higher payments there may be others who are recommended for transfer to another job at the same payment, and some to be transferred in the project. The project staff generally welcomes this personal appraisal, which can result in rewards for good work.

(*ii*) Career development is an important incentive and often underestimated. Although many rural development workers are prepared to tolerate either moving their family to the rural area, or to keep up two homes and commute perhaps monthly, and to live with inferior facilities such as rural schools, hospitals, water supplies, electricity, housing and entertainment, they are not prepared to waste precious years of their career life out of sight of the 'corridors of power' in the capital city. For this reason the project manager must be prepared to recommend for promotion to those who deserve it, even if the project will loss their services.

(*iii*) Management by objectives is an approach developed for business as an aid to practical management. The approach can be utilized for the needs of rural development projects, in particularly large projects, a continued process of:

- Reviewing critically, and restating the project's strategic and tactical plans
- Clarifying with each sub-manager the key results and performance standards he must achieve in line with the development and immediate objectives, and gaining his contribution and commitment to these.
- Agreeing with each sub-manager a job improvement plan, which makes a measurable and realistic contribution to the project's plans for better performance.
- Providing conditions in which it is possible to achieve the key results and improvement plans, notably: an organization structure which gives a sub-manager maximum freedom and flexibility in operation; management control information in a form, and at a frequency, which makes for more effective self-control and better and quick decisions.
- Using systematic performance review to measure and discuss progress towards results, and potential review to identify men with potential for advancement.

- Developing management training plans to help each sub-manager to overcome his weaknesses, to build on his strengths, and to accept a responsibility for self-development
- Strengthening a manager's motivation by effective selection, salary and succession plans.

(*iv*) Morale is probably more important in an isolated rural development project than in many other working groups of men. In addition to morale in the working project, it is also important to consider the lives of project staff who may still have to live close together even in non-working hours.

Chapter 14

Financial Assistance to NGOs for Rural Projects

NATIONAL AGENCIES

1. Society for Rural, Urban and Tribal Initiative (SRUTI)

SRUTI is registered under the Societies Registration Act, 1860 by founder members like Ela Bhatt, Pumam Mutreja, Bunker Roy and others. It provides assistance to *NGOs* for non-formal education, training, saving programme and environment. *SRUTI* fellowship is given to an individual for short duration. Interested *NGOs* or individuals may contact to:

Executive Director,
SRUTI
Q 1, Hauz Khas, Enclave
New Delhi - 110 016

2. National Foundation for India (NFI)

NFI provides financial assistance to *NGOs* for rural development work on women empowerment, natural resource management and other development issues. Interested *NGOs* may apply to:

Executive Director
NFI
India Habitat Centre
Lodhi Road
New Delhi.

3. Help Age India

Help Age India provides financial assistance to *NGOs* for the welfare programmes for aged old under following schemes:

1. Old age home.
2. Income generation activities.
3. Micro-finance for aged old.
4. Mobile health clinic for aged old.
5. Adoption scheme.

Interested *NGOs* working in the field of aged old welfare may contact:

Help Age India
C-14, Qutub Institutional Area
New Delhi - 110 016
Email: helpage@nde.vsnl.net.in
Website: ww.helpageindia.com

4. Rashtriya Gramin Vikash Nidhi (RGVN)

The organization, registered under the Societies Registration Act, 1860 is established in 1990. It provides assistance to *NGOs* to undertake programmes for the welfare of Tribal Women and Children and Poor Community. *IFCI, IDBI* and *NABARD* are the promoters to this fund which are the members in the Governing Board. The schemes are:

1. *NGO* Support Programme
2. Support Services
3. Credit and Savings Programme
4. Primary Education Project
5. Prabhav Dutt Fellowship
6. *RGVN* Fellowship
7. *RGVN* Ford Fellowship

Interested *NGOs* may contact for assistance to:

Headquarter:
'Hina Three' Kannachal
Silpurvari, Guvahati - 781 003
Email: rgvnho@gwl.vsl.net.in
Regional Office:
Regional Coordinator
RGVN
65 'A' Shahid Nagar
Bhubaneshwar 751 007 (Orrissa)

5. National Backward Classes Finance & Development Corporation (NBCFDC)

NBCFDC is an autonomous organization under the Ministry of Social Justice & Empowerment and provide assistance to NGOs under following schemes:

1. Micro Credit Scheme
2. Training

Interested *NGOs* may contact to:

NBCFDC
Vth Floor, NCVI Building, 3, Siri Institutional Area
August Kranti Marg, New Delhi 110 016

INTERNATIONAL FUNDING AGENCIES

1. Ford Foundation

The foundation provide financial assistance to *NGOs* registered under *FCRA* and working in the field, under following schemes:

1. Capacity Building and Community Development
2. Management of Water Resources
3. Reproductive Health
4. Human Rights and Social Justice
5. Education, Media and Culture

Interested *NGOs* may write a concept paper for assistance to:

The Ford Foundation
55, Lodi Estate
New Delhi - 110 003
Email: ford_delhi@fordfound.org

2. Paul Hamlin Foundation

The foundation is established in 1987 and provide assistance to *NGOs* in India to undertake following activities:

1. Education
2. Publication

Interested *NGOs* may contact to:

Paul Hamlin Foundation
18, Queen Ane Gate
London S.W., 1 H 9AA, U.K.
Email: information@phf.org.uk

3. Cooperative for Assistance and Relief Everywhere (CARE)

CARE started its work in India in 1950, now provide assistance to work as partner under following programmes:

1. Nutrition and Health
2. Reproductive Health
3. Small Economic Activities Development (*SEAD*)
4. Education of Girl Child
5. Urban Development
6. Sustainable Tribal Empowerment Project (*STEP*)

Interested *NGOs* may contact to:

CARE-India
27, Hauz Khas Village
New Delhi - 110 016
Email: cbox@careinida.org

Or
CARE-UP
B-718, Sector-C, Mahanagar
Lucknow - 226 006
Email: careup@careindia.org
Or
CARE-MP
Nishat Manjil
Shamla Hills
Bhopal - 462 013
Email: caremp@careindia.org

4. Asha

A group of responsible *NRIs* in *USA* established trust to support down-trodden community in India. It provide assistance to *NGOs* for the welfare of disadvantaged children and educational programmes.

Interested *NGOs* may write for assistance to:

Sri Sandeep
A-893, Indira nagar
Lucknow - 226 016
Ph: 0522-2238333
Email: ashain@lwl.vsnl.net.in
Or
Ms. Lata Iyer
100 Pine AV, 136
Red Land, CA 92373 USA
Email: lata_iyer@esri.com; asha_wide@egroups.com

5. Charity Aid Fund (CAF)

Established in 1921, *CAF* works with Chambers of Commerce and Industry Associations using charity cards for tax exemption on donations and provide assistance to *NGOs*. Interested *NGOs* may contact to:

Shri Mathew Charian
CAF-India
25, Naujeevan Vihar
In front of Geetanjali Enclave
New Delhi - 110 017
Email: cafinida@caf.charitynet.org

6. Hifer Project International (HPI)

HPI started its work in India in 1955, is now a pioneer organization in livestock development and management. It works for the participatory development and rural transformation and optimum utilization of resources. It provides assistance to *NGOs* for the programmes related to livestock. Interested *NGOs* may contact:

Country Director
Hifer Project International
Po.Box.- 4244, Greater Kailash
New Delhi - 110 048
Or
S-472, Greater Kailash-II
New Delhi - 110 048
Email: hpi.hpinida@gems.vsnl.net.in

7. T.D.H.

TDH, stands for "Tere Des Homes", is working in many countries including India for the sustainable development and child development. *TDH* assists *NGOs* on human rights movement, welfare of marginalized groups and innovative programmes. Interested *NGOs* may contact with:

Programme Coordinator
TDH
Rezzi House, P. Ramabai Road
Pune - 411 002

8. HIVOS

HIVOS is an international development organization of Netherlands. It works primarily on sustainable development, gender development, poverty alleviation etc. interested *NGOs* may contact to:

Director
HIVOS
Flat No. - 402, Eden Park
No. 20, Vitthal Malay Road
Bangalore - 560 001
Email: hivos@hivos_india.org

9. Functional Vocational Training Forum (FVTF)

FVTF assists *NGOs* to undertake training programme for the skill development of youths as a measure to alleviate poverty. It is established by 'Misereor' development organization of the Catholic Church of Germany. Interested *NGOs* may contact to:

FVTF
19, First Floor, 3rd Cross
Hupins Road, Look Town
Bangalore - 560 084
Email: futf@vsnl.com

10. National Education Group (NEG)

NEG works for the betterment of educational standards both in schools and community through innovative programmes, motivation and awareness. Interested *NGOs* may contact for assistance to:

Secretary
National Education Group
110 B, Gautam Nagar
New Delhi - 110 049

11. CARITAS India

Caritas India is established by *CBCI* in 1962 towards the sustainable development, welfare of disadvantaged groups and poverty alleviation. Interested NGOs may contact to:

Director
Caritas India
CBCI Centre, Ashok Place
New Delhi - 110 001

12. The Hunger Project

The Hunger Project started its work in 1984 in India. It provide support to *NGOs* for leadership development, empowerment for livelihood and local self-governance. Interested *NGOs* may contact:

The Hunger Project
3, Palam Marg, Vasant Vihar
New Delhi - 110 057

13. ACTION AID

Action Aid is established in *UK* under the Companies Act in 1971 for the integrated development of the backward areas. It has partnership with corporates in the social development. It provide assistance for the advocacy, participatory development, and poverty alleviation. It has commercial wings like Action Enterprises, *PRAXIS*, Partners in Change and others which are working on sectoral events. Interested *NGOs* may contact to:

Action Aid
Hamlyn House
MacDonald Road Archway
London - N 195 PG
Email: mail@actionaid.org.uk
Or
Action Aid
P.B No. 5406
3, Rest House road
Bangalore - 560 001
Email: coblr@actionaidindia.org
Or
Bhopal Regional Office
E/23, Basant Kunj
Area Colony
Bhopal - 642 016

14. Churches Auxiliary for Social Action (CASA)

CASA works for the sustainable social system under Peoples Action for Transformation (*PAT*) and other programmes. Interested NGOs may contact to:

CASA
Rachna Bhawan, 4th Floor, Rajendra Palace
Pusa Road, New Delhi - 110 008
Email: clare.casard@axcess.net.in

15. Canadian International Development Agency (CIDA) Gender Equality Fund (GEF)

GEF assist *NGOs* to undertake programmes for the women empowerment, gender development, networking and advocacy.

16. Canada Fund for Local Initiatives (CFLI)

CIDA provide assistance under CFLI for the socio-economic development of community, reproductive health and employment generation. Interested NGOs may contact to:

Director
India Canada Cooperation Office
86 West Road, Vasant Vihar
New Delhi - 110 057

17. Plan International

Foster Parent Plan International, established in 1937, is working in 42 countries including India. It is caring, collaborating institution which provides assistance for the welfare of vulnerable Children, sustainable development and resource management. Interested *NGOs* may contact to:

Plan International
C - 6/6 Safdarganj Development Area
New Delhi - 110 016
Email: bradenr@plan.geis.com

18. CBR Forum

CBR Forum is working in India for the welfare of handicapped through community based rehabilitation. Forum provide assistance to *NGOs* to work in backward areas. Interested *NGOs* may contact to:

CBR Forum
38, 11th Main. 100 ft. Road.
BTM Lay Out, 1 Stage, Bangalore - 29
Email: cbrforum@blr.vsnl.net.in

19. Catholic Relief Services (CRS)

Established in 1943, *CRS* works, now in 86 countries, on people's development through empowerment, peace and reconciliation and natural resource management through *NGOs* in India. *CRS* also provide assistance on children's education, watershed development and livelihood. Interested NGOs may contact to:

Director
CRS
5 Community Centre, Jamrudpur
Kailash Colony Extension
New Delhi - 110 048
Or
CRS (headquarter)
209, West Fatate Street
Baltimore, Meriland 21201, USA

20. Save the Children (U.K.)

Established in 1919, Save the Children works now in 50 countries. It provide support to NGOs for projects on quality education, child labour, handicapped welfare, gender development etc. Interested NGOs may contact to:

Save the Children (U.K.)
IInd Floor, A-20 Kailash colony
New Delhi - 110 048
Or
Zonal Director
Save the Children
20 Kiran Path, Suraj Nagar
Civil Lines, Jaipur - 302 006

21. Christian Children's Fund (CCF)

CCF works with *NGOs* on the integrated development of children in Inida. Interested may Contact to:

CCF
22, Museum Road,
Bangalore - 560 001
Or
CCF
5th Floor, Padma Palace
86, Nehru Place
New Delhi - 110 019
Email: cfinida@blr.vsnl.net.in

22. Catholic Fund for Overseas Development (CAFOD)

2, Romero Close
Stockwell Road
GB - London SW 99TY
U.K.
Email: reception@cafod.org.uk

23. Comite Contre La Faim ET Pour Le Development (CCFD)

4 Rue Jean Lantier
F - 75001 Paris

24. Fastenopper Der Schwfizer Kotholiken

Habsburgerstrasse 44
Postfach 2856
CH – 6002 LUZERN
SWITZERLAND
Email: mail@fastenopfer.ch

25. Intraide Et Fraternite

Ne du Government Provisoire, 32
B-1000 Brussels, Belgium

26. KOORD/DKA - Austria

Wilheminerstrasse 91/11F
A-1160 Viena, Austria

27. Concern India Foundation

14, Birbal Road, 2nd Floor
Janpura Extension, New Delhi - 110 014

28. MISEREOR

Postfach 1450
Mozartstrasse 9
D-52015 AACHEN
GERMANY

29. TROCAIRE

169, Borterstown Avenue
Blackrock
El-Co Dublin
Ireland

30. Fredrich Ebert Stiftung

K-70 B, Hauz Khas Enclave, New Delhi 110 016
Email: fres@gias101.vsnl.net.in

31. Australian Agency for International Development (AUSAID)

GPO Box 887
Canberra ACT 2601, Australia
Website: http://www.ausaid.gov.au

32. DANIDA

2 Asiatisk Plads
DK - 1447 Copenhagen K,
Denmark

33. Swedish International Development Cooperation Agency (SIDA)

Seveavagen 20
S-105 25 Stockholm
SWEDEN

34. Deptt. For International Development (DFID)

94, Victoria Street
London SW IE 5 JL
Email: d_wright@dfid.gtnet.gov.uk

35. Norwegian Agency for Development (NORAD)

Tollbugata 31, Post Box 8034, Dep. N. 0030
Oslo, NORWAY
Email: parvez.kapoor@norad.no

36. Swiss Development Cooperation (SDC)

Eigerstrasse 73
CH-3003 Berne
SWITZERLAND
Email: Kathryn.imboden@deza.admin.ch

37. United States Agency for International Development (UVSAID)

1300 Pennisylvania Ave, NW
Washington, DC 20523 (USA)
Website: http://www.info.usaid.gov

38. Christian World Service (CWS)

P.O. Box: 22652, Christ Church 8,32
New Zealand
Email: cws@christianworldservice.org.nz

39. International Needs New Zealand

P.O. Box: 1165
Tauranga, New Zealand
Email: Iwainnz@intemet.co.nz

40. Habitat for Humanity

11 Marewa Road Greeniana
Auckland, New Zealand
Email: habitat.nz@clear.net.nz

41. World Vision of New Zealand

P.B. 92078, Auckland
New Zealand

42. The Evangelical Alliance Relief Fund (Tear Fund)

Auckland, New Zealand
Email: action@tearfund.org.nz
Website: http://www.tearfund/org.nz

43. Canadian Foundation for World Development (CFWD)

2441 Bayview Avenue
Walllowadale, Ontario MZ LIAS (CANADA)

44. Food for the Hungry International

7729 East Greenway Road, SuitZ.
Scottsdaly A285260, USA

45. Calmeaclow Charitable Foundation

95, Wellington Street
W. Suite 2000
Toronto (Ontario M5) 2W7 (CANADA)

46. Action on Disability and Development (ADD)

23, Lower Key Ford, From Somerset
BA 114 AP, UK

47. The Aga Khan Foundation

33 Thurloe Square, London SW 725D, UK

48. Christian Aid

A 15/18 Vasant Vihar
New Delhi 110 057
Website: www. Christian_aid.org.uk
Or
Christian Aid
P.B. 100, London Se17RT
UK

49. International Child Care Trust (ICCT)

D 16 Peabody Estate, Wild Street
London WC 2B4AG

50. The Karuna Trust

186 uwtey Road
Oxford Ox41UE

51. Brother to All Men

Ruede Londres 18
1050 Bruselles, Belgium

52. ADD-India Office

4005, 19th Cross, Banashan Kari, 2nd Stage
Bangalore - 560070, Karnataka

53. Homeless International (HI),

5 The Buffs
Covventry, CV13GH, UK

54. International Children's Trust

50, Willesden Avenue, Peterborough PE46EA

55. Water Aid

1 Queen Anne's Gate
SW1H9BT London (UK)

56. Centre for Development Aid with Liberty & Progress

Rue de Naples
391050, Brusells, BELGIUM

57. Vet Aid

CTVM, Easter Bush
Roslin, Mid Lothian EH 259RG

58. Helping Hands

Box: 9109, 58009 Linkoping
SWEDEN

59. World Vision India

Khaleelshirazi Estate 344
Pantheon Road, Chennai - 600 008

60. Aid for Children in Need

Zuglergasee 49, 107 Owien
Austria

61. Association Child

Box: 67, 66800 ED Sweden

62. Danish Association for International Cooperation

Borgergade 10-14, 1300 Kobenhavnk
DENMARK

63. Agency International Pourle Development

(AIDE) 32 run Traversiere 75012
Paris, France
India Office:
Aide ET Action 123
St. Action 123, St-peelers Road
Royapettah, Chennai - 600 086

64. Foundation De France

40 Avenue, Hoche 75008
Paris France

65. KNH

Dusseldorfer
Landstrasse 180 Poffacg 281143
4100, Duisburg 28 Germany

66. EZE

Mittelstrasse
D-53175 Bonn, Germany

67. Bread for the World

P.O. Box 101142 D 70010
Stutgart, Germany

68. International Organization for Cooperation in Health Care

Po.Box: 1547 6512 BM Njimegen
Netherlands

69. Asian Aid Organization

P.O. Box: 88 gatston
NSWR 159, Australia

70. Australian Catholic Relief (ACR)

19, Mackenzie Street, North Sydney 260
Australia

71. Iwatani Naoi Foundation

712TBR Building, 2-10-2 Nagata-cho chiyodo Tokyo - Ku
Tokyo

TRAINING INSTITUTIONS IN RURAL PROJECT MANAGEMENT

1. **Pria**
   42, Tughlakabad Institutional Area
   New Delhi - 110 062
   Email: info@pria.org
2. **Sahbhagi Shikshan Kendra**
   Sitapur Road, Near Police Fire Station
   Lucknow - 227 208
   Email: sahbhagi@pwl.vsnl.in
3. **Nav Jagriti Kendra**
   Amrit Nagar, PO. Korra
   Hazaribagh - 825 301
   Email: hbjkhzb@dte.vsnl.net.in
4. **Samarthan**
   E-7/81, Arera Colony
   Bhopal - 462 116

TERMS AND CONDITIONS OF GRANT-IN-AID FROM GOVERNMENT

To avail financial assistance from the Central/State Government, the organization has to follow the general terms and conditions of grants-in-aid, as mentioned below:

1. The grant receiving agency will be required to confirm in writing that the conditions laid down in the grant-in-aid rules are acceptable to it and will execute a bond in favour of the President of India to the effect that in the event of failure to abide by the same, it will refund the whole or such part of the grant as the Government of India may decide.
2. The organization in receipt of financial assistance shall be open to inspection by an officer of the concerned department/Ministry of the Government of India/Concerned State Department or a Nominee of these authorities.
3. The accounts shall be maintained properly and separately and submitted as and when required. They should be open to check by an officer deputed by the Government of India or the State Government and Comptroller and Auditor General of India at his discretion.

4. The audited accounts together with the utilization certificate in the prescribed form duly countersigned by the chartered accountant are required to be furnished within financial year.

FINANCIAL ASSISTANCE TO NGOs FROM MINISTRIES

1. Ministry of Culture and Tourism

1. Scheme for building and equipment grants to *NGOs* involved in cultural activities.
2. Scheme for promotion and dissemination of tribal art and culture
3. Scheme for research in cultural activities.

Application should be sent to:

Secretary
Department of Culture
Ministry of Culture & Tourism
New Delhi

2. Ministry of Agriculture

1. National Disaster Management Programme
2. Scheme for the establishment of Krishi Vigyan Kendra (*KVK*).
3. Scheme for development and use of bio-fertilizer.
4. Scheme for strengthening of agricultural extension services.

Application should be sent to:

Secretary
Ministry of Agriculture
Krishi Bhawan
Janapath, New Delhi

3. Ministry of Environment & Forests (Department of Environment, Forests and Wildlife)

1. Scheme for promotion of environmental research.
2. Scheme for ambulance service to animals in distress.
3. Scheme for provision of shelter houses.
4. Scheme for afforestation and eco-development.
5. Scheme for organizing seminars.
6. Scheme for Capacity Building.

Application should be sent to:

Secretary
Ministry of Environment & Forests
CGO Complex, Lodhi Road,
New Delhi - 110 003

4. Ministry of Human Resource Development, Department of Education

1. Scheme of National Literacy Mission.
2. Scheme for eradication of illiteracy
3. Scheme of Jan Shikshan Sansthans
4. Scheme for integrated education for disabled children.
5. Scheme for studies of intellectual property rights
6. Scheme for seminar and studies
7. Scheme for area intensive programme for educationally backward minorities.

Application should be sent to:

The Secretary
Department of Education
Ministry of Human Resource Development
Shastri Bhawan
New Delhi

5. Department of Women & Child Development

1. Scheme under Support to Training and Employment Programme for Women (*STEP*) programme.
2. Scheme of integrated programme for women's empowerment (*IWEP*), Swayam Sidha.
3. Scheme for the construction/expansion of hostel for working women.
4. Scheme for assistance to educational work for prevention of atrocities on women.
5. Scheme of organizational assistance to voluntary organization for women and child development.
6. Scheme on community based production of nutritious foods.
7. Scheme for early childhood education.

6. Ministry of Labour

1. Scheme for taking up action programmes/projects for the benefit of child and women labour.
2. Programme under Indus Child Labour Project for the education and vocational training of child labour.

Interested NGO functionaries should apply to:

Secretary
Ministry of Labour
Shram Shakti Bhawan
New Delhi

7. Ministry of Rural Development

Ministry of Rural Development provides financial assistance to NGOs to undertake rural development programmes through:

1. National Wasteland Development Board for the wasteland development, afforestation etc.
2. Council for Advancement of People's Action and Rural Technology (*CAPART*) through its schemes on people's cooperation, organization of beneficiaries, watershed development, rural technology and other scheme based support to *NGOs* to undertake rural development work.

   Interested NGO functionaries may apply to:

   Director General
   CAPART
   India Habitat Centre
   Lodhi Road
   New Delhi

8. Ministry of Health & Family Welfare

Ministry provides financial assistance to NGOs through:

1. Scheme of Community Health Centres.
2. Scheme of Community Based Distribution of Contraceptives through *NGOs*.
3. Scheme for Promotion of Voluntary Blood Donation Programmes.
4. Scheme of Special Health Scheme for Rural Areas

   Interested NGO functionaries should apply in prescribed proforma through CMO to:

   Director (NGO)
   Ministry of Health & Family Welfare
   Nirman Bhawan, New Delhi

Chapter 15

Foreign Contribution (Regulation) Act, 1976

Acceptance and utilization of foreign contribution by organizations is regulated by the *FCRA*, 1976. Any society, trust or organization desirous of receiving any foreign contribution in the form of financial assistance from a foreign source, is required to obtain registration under this Act. In order to obtain registration under the *FCRA*, the applicant association should preferably be incorporated as a legal entity. It must be registered under the Societies Registration Act, Indian Trusts Act or any other Act and should have been working for a period of atleast three years. The application for the permanent registration is to be made in from *FC*-8, alongwith the following documents:

1. The memorandum and article of association.
2. Copy of registration certificate
3. Annual report of the organization for last 3 years

The application, with above enclosures, duly signed by the authorized functionary of the organization should be sent to the Secretary, *FCRA* Division, Ministry of Home Affairs, Government of India, Lok Nayak Bhawan, New Delhi.

Procedure to obtain prior permission to receive foreign contribution:

To receive a specific project based amount from one or more agencies prior permission is required to be obtained by the organization. For this, the application in Form FC-1 should be sent to the above address.

Operation of bank account: A bank account should be maintained and operated exclusively for receipt of foreign contribution. No local contribution should be transacted through this bank account.

Filing of *FCRA* returns: Organizations in receipt of foreign contribution must furnish the *FCRA* return in *FC*-3 with balance sheet and other relevant documents.

FORM FC-1A

[See rule 3(aa)]

Form of application for seeking prior permission from the Central Government under the Foreign Contribution (Regulation) Act, 1976 (hereinafter referred to as the Act) for the acceptance of foreign contribution by an Association having a definite cultural, economic, educational, religious or social programme

No.................. Date.................

To,

The Secretary to the Government of India

Ministry of Home Affairs, Lok Nayak Bhavan, Khan Market

New Delhi - 110 003

Subject: Application for seeking the prior permission of the central Government under the Foreign Contribution (Regulation) Act, 1976 for acceptance of foreign contribution under provision to sub-section (1) of section 6 or under sub-section (1*A*) of that section or clause (*b*) of section 10 of the Act.

1. (*i*) Name of the Association and its complete postal address;

Name

Address

Town/City

State

District

Pin Code

(*ii*) If the Association is a registered trust or society please indicate its-

(*a*) registration number

(*b*) place of registration

(*c*) date of registration (certified copy of the registration certificate to be attached).

(*iii*) Nature of Association:

(*a*) religious (*b*) cultural (*c*) economic (*d*) educational (*e*) social

Note: If a religious association, then state whether:

(*a*) Hindu (*b*) Sikh (*c*) Muslim (*d*) Christian (*e*) Buddhist (*f*) Others

(*iv*) Please indicate the main aim(s) and object(s) of the Association (enclose copy of the Memorandum of Association and/or the Articles of Association, if applicable).

(*v*) Please furnish the name and address of the members of the Executive Committee/Governing Council etc. of the Association, including the Chief Functionary, in the following manner:

Sl.No.	*Name*	*Name of Father/ Husband*	*Nationality*	*Occupation*	*Office held in the Association, if any*	*Relation with other office-bearers, if any*	*Address*
(1)	(2)	(3)	(4)	(5)	(6)	(7)	(8)

2. Please indicate whether any member of the Executive Committee/Governing Council etc. of the Association, including the Chief Functionary has, in the discharge of his/her official functions-
   (*a*) been convicted by any court of law;
   (*b*) a prosecution for any offence pending against him/her;
   (*c*) been found guilty of diversion or mis-utilization of funds of the Association or any other association in the past.
3. Please indicate whether the applicant Association-
   (*a*) is a branch/unit/associate of foreign based organization or another association already registered under the Act. If so, name and address of the parent organization should be furnished;
   (*b*) has been directed by the Central Government in terms of the proviso to sub-section (1) of section 6 of the Act to seek prior permission. If so, the number and date of the relevant order should be furnished;
   (*c*) has been directed by the Central Government in terms of section 10 of the Act to seek prior permission. If so, the number and date of the relevant order should be furnished.
4. Please indicate-
   (*i*) whether the Association ever applied for registration under the Act in the past, if so,
   (*a*) the date of submission of application for registration;
   (*b*) the number and data of last reference, if any, received from the Ministry;
   (*c*) whether registration was refused;
   (*d*) whether the application for registration is still pending.

(*ii*) Whether the Association has close links with another association, or its unit or branch which has been-
   (*a*) refused registration under the Act.
   (*b*) Prohibited from accepting foreign contribution.

5. Please indicate-
   (*i*) whether the Association was-
   (*a*) granted prior permission to receive foreign contribution under the Act in the past. If so, the number and date of the letter granting prior permission should be furnished;
   (*b*) whether the account of the receipt and utilization of the foreign contribution received above was sent to the Central Government in the prescribed form. If so, the date of submission of the accounts should be furnished;
   (*c*) if the prior permission was granted in the current year, details of the foreign contribution received and utilized, purpose-wise, showing the unspent balance should be annexed.
   (*ii*) Whether the Association has received foreign contribution without the prior permission of the Central Government, in the past. If so,-
   (*a*) full particulars of the foreign contribution received, address of the branch of the bank and account number in which deposited should be furnished;

(*b*) whether the said violation has been condoned by the Central Government;

(*c*) whether the Association has been prohibited from accepting foreign contribution under the Act.

6. Please indicate whether the Association is owner/printer/publisher, editor of a publication which is a "registered newspaper" under the Press and Registration of Books Act, 1867.

7. Please furnish-

(*i*) Details of the activities of the Association during the past three-years;

(*ii*) copies of the audited statement of account of the association for the past three years.

8. (*i*) Please indicate-

(*a*) the nature and value of foreign contribution to be received (a copy of the latest commitment letter from the donor should be furnished);

(*b*) the purpose for which the foreign contribution is proposed to be received and utilized indicating also the geographical area(s) to be covered.

(*ii*) a copy of the proposal/project which has been approved by the foreign source for funding, including projected outlays/budget breakup, should be enclosed.

(*iii*) a copy of the proposal/project which has been approved for funding out of the foreign contribution should be enclosed. (This column applies only to subsequent recipients).

9. Please indicate-

(*i*) the name of the bank and address of the branch through which the foreign contribution is proposed to be received;

(*ii*) the account number in the said branch of the bank.

10. Please indicate the particulars of the foreign source or the sources* from which the foreign contribution* is proposed to be received-

(*a*) If an individual, his personal particulars including name, present address, permanent address, nationality, profession;

(*b*) If an organization/institution/association/trust/trade union, etc., full particulars thereof, including-

(*i*) Full name and complete address

(*ii*) Address of the Head Office/Principal Office

(*iii*) Particulars of Chief Functionary and important office bearers.

(*c*) Please indicate whether the foreign source is a Government of a foreign country or agency thereof.

[1][10A. Whether a recommendation certificate from the competent authority is attached (Yes/No)].

11. Any other information which the Association may like to furnish.

Yours faithfully,
Signature of the Applicant
[Name of the Chief Functionary or
authorized office bearer (with seal of the
Association)]

Declaration

I hereby declare that the above particulars furnished by me are true and correct.

Yours faithfully,
Signature of the Applicant
[Name of the Chief Functionary or
authorized office bearer (with seal of the
Association

Place:

Date:

*If the foreign contribution, whether currency or article is to be received from any person or association who has received the same as first, second or subsequent recipient, particulars of such person or association should be given against column 10 above.

Note:

1. An incomplete application i.e., without necessary documents/details/explanation is likely to be rejected summarily.
2. In case the space against any column is insufficient, separate annexure should be attached.
3. Please use *CAPITAL LETTERS*.
4. The application should be signed by the Chief Functionary or authorized office bearer of the Association.

[1]Certificate

(To be submitted along with the application)

This is to certify that the......................................

(name of the association) having its registered office at.................................. (Address) has been formed for undertaking activities in its chosen .... (economic, educational, cultural, religious and social*) field of activity. The antecedents of the organization have been verified and there is nothing adverse against them.

2. Its proposed project shall be undertaken in the .... (District) of .... (State), the said project will be beneficial to the people living in the area.
3. The grant of prior permission to the aforementioned association to accept foreign contribution amounting to .... (currency/amount) from .... (name and address of foreign donor) under the Foreign Contribution (Regulation) Act, 1976,for the said project is recommended.

(Recommending authority)**
(with seal)

* Strike out whichever is not applicable.

[1]Inserted by the Foreign Contribution (Regulation) (Amendment) Rules, 2000, w.e.f. 25.1.2000.

** Any concerned-

(1) Collector of District;

(2) Department of the State Government;

(3) Ministry/Department of the Government of India.

[2]Form FC-3

[See rule 4(a)]

Account of Foreign Contribution for the year ending on 31st March..........

1. Association's details-

   (*i*) Name and address (in capital letters)

   (*ii*) Registration number and date

   (under the Foreign Contribution (Regulation) Act, 1976).

   (*iii*) Prior permission number and date, if not registered

   (*iv*) Nature of association: (1) Cultural, (2) Economic (3) Educational (4) Religious (5) Social.

Denomination in case of religious associations: (*a*) Hindu, (*b*) Sikh, (*c*) Muslim, (*d*) Christian, (*e*) Buddhist, (*f*) Others.

1A. (*i*) Total amount of foreign contribution received during the year.

   (*ii*) Interest earned on the foreign contribution during the year.

   (*a*) In the designated bank account:

   (*b*) On investments made (Fixed Deposit Receipt etc.) during the year or in the preceding years:

2. Purpose(*s*) for which foreign contribution has been received and utilized:

(in Rupees)

Sl. No.	*Purpose*	*Previous Balance*		*Receipt during the year*				*Total*	*Utilized*		*Balance*	
		In cash	In kind (value)	As first recipient		As second/ subsequent recipient			In cash	In kind (value)	In cash	In kind (value)
				In cash	In kind (value)	In cash	In kind (value)					
(1)	(2)	(3)	(4)	(5)	(6)	(7)	(8)	(9) (5+6+7+8)	(10)	(11)	(12)	(13)

1. Celebration of national events (Independence/Republic day/festivals etc.).
2. Theatre/Films
3. Maintenance of places of historical and cultural importance.

[2]As substituted by GSR 557 (E) dated 6.7.2001.

4. Preservation of ancient/tribal art forms
5. Research.
6. Cultural shows.
7. Setting up and running handicraft centre/cottage and khadi industry/social forestry projects.
8. Animal husbandry projects.
9. Income generation projects/schemes.
10. Micro-finance projects, including setting up banking cooperatives and self-help groups.
11. Agricultural activity.
12. Rural Development.
13. Construction and maintenance of school/college.
14. Construction and running of hostel for poor students.
15. Grant of stipend/scholarship/assistance in cash and kind to poor/deserving children.
16. Purchase and supply of educational material-books, notebooks etc.
17. Conducting adult literacy programs.
18. Education/Schools for mentally challenged.
19. Non-formal education projects/coaching classes.
20. Construction/Repair/Maintenance of places of worship.
21. Religious Schools/education of priests and preachers.
22. Publication and distribution of religious literature.
23. Religious functions.
24. Maintenance of priests/preachers/other religious functionaries.
25. Construction/Running of hospital/dispensary/clinic
26. Construction of community halls etc.
27. Construction and Management of old age home.
28. Welfare of the aged/widows.
29. Construction and management of Orphanage.
30. Welfare of the orphans.
31. Construction and Management of dharamshala/shelter.
32. Holding of free medical/health/family welfare/immunization camps.
33. supply of free medicine, and medical aid, including hearing aids, visual aids, family planning aids etc.
34. Provision of aids such as Tricycles, calipers etc. to the handicapped.
35. Treatment/Rehabilitation of persons suffering from leprosy.
36. Treatment/Rehabilitation of drug addicts.
37. Welfare/Empowerment of women.
38. Welfare of Children.

39. Provision of free clothing/food to the poor, needy and destitute.
40. Relief/Rehabilitation of victims of natural calamities.
41. Help to the victims of riots/other disturbances.
42. Digging of bore wells.
43. Sanitation including community toilets, etc.
44. Vocational training - tailoring, motor repairs, computers etc.
45. Awareness Camp/Seminar/Workshop/Meeting/Conference.
46. Providing free legal aid/Running legal aid centre.
47. Holding sports meet.
48. Awareness about *AIDS*/Treatment and rehabilitation of persons affected by *AIDS*.
49. Welfare of the physically and mentally challenged.
50. Welfare of the Scheduled Castes.
51. Welfare of the Scheduled Tribes.
52. Welfare of the Other Backward Classes.
53. Environmental programs.
54. Survey for socio-economic and other welfare programmes.
55. Establishment expenses-
    (*i*) Asset building:
    (*a*) Establishment of Corpus Fund, and
    (*b*) Purchase of land
    (*ii*) Construction/Extension/Maintenance of office, administrative and other buildings
    (*iii*) Payment of salaries/honorarium
    (*iv*) Publication of newsletter/literature/books etc.
    (*v*) Other expenses
56. Activities other than those mentioned above (furnish details)

    TOTAL

CAUTION:- Submission of false information or concealment of material facts shall attract the relevant provisions of the Foreign Contribution (Regulation) Act, 1976 warranting appropriate action.

3. Name and address of the designated branch of the bank and account number (as specified in the application for registration/prior permission or permitted by the Central Government).

A/C No.....................

Bank........................

Branch.....................

Address:...................

..........PIN.............

4. Donor wise receipt of foreign contribution:

(in Rupees)

Sl. No.	*Institutional/Individual/ Other Donors*	*Name(s) and Address(es)*	*Purpose(s)*	*Date and Month of Receipt*	*Amount*
(1)	(2)	(3)	(4)	(5)	(6)
(i) (ii) (iii)	Institutional donors Individual donors above rupees one lakh Individual donors below rupees one lakh (Only Columns 4 and 6 need to be filled				
Total					

5. Country wise receipt of foreign contribution:

S. No.	*Name of the Country*	*Amount*
(1)	(2)	(3)
Total		

DECLARATION

I hereby declare that the above particulars furnished by me are true and correct. I also affirm that the foreign contribution has been utilized for purpose(s) for which the association has been registered/ prior permission obtained. To the best of my knowledge, I have not concealed or suppressed any fact.

Place...................... Date......................	Signature of the Chief Functionary(Name of the Chief Functionary and Seal of the Association)

Certificate to be given by Chartered Accountant

I/We have audited the account of........................(name of association and its full address including State, District and Pin Code, if registered society, its registration number and State of Registration), for the year ending 31st March,........... and examined all relevant books and vouchers and certify that according to the audited account:

(*i*) the brought forward foreign contribution at the beginning of the year was Rs.......... .

(*ii*) foreign contribution of/worth Rs......... was received by the Association during the year...........

(*iii*) the balance of unutilized foreign contribution with the Association at the end of the year.......... was Rs............

(*iv*) Certified that the Association has maintained the accounts of foreign contribution and records relating thereto in the manner specified in section 13 of the Foreign Contribution (Regulation) Act, 1976 read with sub-rule (1) of rule 8 of the Foreign Contribution (Regulation) Rules, 1976.

(*v*) The information in this certificate and in the enclosed Balance-Sheet and Statement of Receipt and Payment is correct as checked by me/us.

Place....................... Date......................	Signature of Chartered Accountant with seal, address and registration number

Form FC-6

[See rule 8(a)]

FOREIGN CONTRIBUTION (ARTICLE) ACCOUNTS

DESCRIPTION OF THE ARTICLE:

Receipt							*Date*	*Name and address of the person to whom issued, sold or otherwise transferred*	*Utilization/Disposal*						
									Quantity						
Date	*Name and address of the person from whom received*	*Mode of receipt*	*Purp-ose of rec-eipt*	*Quantity received*	*Approx. value of articles received*	*Date of intimation sent to the Central Gover nment*			*Purpose for which issued or other wise trans-ferred*	*Utilized by the organi-zation*	*Sold*	*Other wise trans ferred*	*If sold the amount for which sold*	*Reference to entry in the Foreign contribution (Currency Account)*	*Balance in stock*
(1)	(2)	(3)	(4)	(5)	(6)	(7)	(8)	(9)	(10)	(11)	(12)	(13)	(14)	(15)	(16)

DECLARATION

I hereby declare that the above particulars furnished by me are true and correct.

....

Signature

Form FC-7

[See rule 8(c)]

FOREIGN CONTRIBUTION (ARTICLE) ACCOUNTS

(1) Name of securities.

(2) Nominal value of each security

Date	*Name and address of the person from whom received*	*Distinguishing number of each security*	*Total of securities*	*Total nominal value of securities*	*Particulars of permission of the Reserve Bank of India to acquire or to hold foreign securities*	*Particulars of intimation sent to the Central Government*	*Date*	*Dividend or interest received*	*Date up to which dividend or interest has been received*
(1)	(2)	(3)	(4)	(5)	(6)	(7)	(8)	(9)	(10)

Details of Dividends/Interest Received

Reference to the credit entry in the Foreign Contribution (Currency) Account	*Date*	*Name and address of the person to whom sold/ tran-sferred*	*Total No. of securities sold/ transferred*	*Distinguishing number of each security transferred*	*Total amount for which sold/ transferred*	*Particulars of permission of the Reserve Bank of India to sell/transfer securities*	*Particulars of intimation sent to the Central Government*	*Reference to the entry in the Foreign Contribution (Currency) Account*
(11)	(12)	(13)	(14)	(15)	(16)	(17)	(18)	(19)

DECLARATION

I hereby declare that the above particulars furnished by me are true and correct.

....

Signature

FORM FC-8

[See rule 3A]

Form of application for seeking prior permission from the Central Government under the Foreign Contribution (Regulation) Act, 1976 (hereinafter referred to as the Act) for the acceptance of foreign contribution by an Association having a definite cultural, economic, educational, religious or social programme.

No.................. Date.................

To,

The Secretary to the Government of India
Ministry of Home Affairs, Lok Nayak Bhavan, Khan Market
New Delhi - 110 003

Subject: Application for registration under the Foreign Contribution (Regulation) Act, 1976 for acceptance of foreign contribution.

Sir,

I,.................................. on behalf of the Association named hereafter apply for registration of the Association under clause (*a*) of sub-section (1) of section 6 of the Act for the acceptance of foreign contribution.

1. (*i*) Name of the Association and its complete postal address;

    Name
    Address
    Town/City
    State
    District
    Pin Code

   (*ii*) If the Association is a registered trust or society please indicate its-

    (*a*) registration number
    (*b*) place of registration
    (*c*) date of registration (certified copy of the registration certificate to be attached).

   (*iii*) Nature of Association:

    (*a*) religious (*b*) cultural (*c*) economic (*d*) educational (*e*) social

    Note: If a religious Association, then state whether:

    (*a*) Hindu (*b*) Sikh (*c*) Muslim (*d*) Christian (*e*) Buddhist (*f*) Others

   (*iv*) Please indicate-

    (*a*) the main aim(*s*) and object(*s*) of the Association (enclose copy of the Memorandum of Association and/or the Articles of Association, if applicable).

    (*b*) the main object(*s*) and definite programmes(*s*) for which the foreign contribution is to be accepted/utilized.

(*v*) Please furnish the names and address of the members of the Executive Committee/Governing Council etc. of the Association, including the Chief Functionary, in the following manner:

Sl.No.	*Name*	*Name of Father/ Husband*	*Nationality*	*Occupation*	*Office held in the Association, if any*	*Relation with other office-bearers, if any*	*Address*

2. Please indicate whether any member of the Executive Committee/Governing Council etc. of the Association, including the Chief Functionary has, in the discharge of his/her official functions-
   (*a*) been convicted by any court of law;
   (*b*) a prosecution for any offence pending against him/her;
   (*c*) been found guilty of diversion or mis-utilization of funds of the Association or any other association in the past.
3. Please indicate whether the applicant Association is a branch/unit/associate of foreign based organization or another association already registered under the Act. If so, name and address of the parent organization should be furnished;
4. Please indicate-
   (*i*) whether the Association was-
   (*a*) granted prior permission to receive foreign contribution under the Act in the past. If so, the number and date of the letter granted for prior permission should be furnished;
   (*b*) Whether the account of the receipt and utilization of the foreign contribution received above was sent to the Central Government in the prescribed form. If so, the date of submission of the accounts should be furnished.
   (*ii*) Whether;
   (*a*) Association has received foreign contribution without the prior permission under Act in the past. If so, full particulars of the foreign contribution received along with complete address of the bank branch and bank account number in which deposited should be furnished.
   (*b*) said violation has been condoned by the Central Government;
   (*c*) Association has been prohibited from accepting foreign contribution under the Act.
5. Please indicate whether the Association is functioning as editor, owner, printer or publisher of a publication required to be registered as "newspaper" under the Press and Registration of Books Act, 1967. If so, the details thereof.

6. Please indicate-
   (*i*) whether the Association ever applied for registration under the Foreign Contribution (Regulation) Act, 1976, if so,-
   (*a*) the date of submission of application for registration;
   (*b*) the number and date of the last communication, if any, received from the Ministry;
   (*c*) whether registration was refused;
   (*d*) whether application for registration is still pending.
   (*ii*) Whether the Association has close links with another association, or its unit or branch which has been -
   (*a*) refused registration under the Act;
   (*b*) prohibited from accepting foreign contribution.
7. Please furnish-
   (*i*) Details of the activities of the Association during the past three-years;
   (*ii*) copies of the audited statement of account of the association for the past three years.
   (*iii*) details of the area(s) of operation.
8. Please indicate whether the Association has been specified as an organization of a political nature, not being a political party, under section 5 of the Act. If so, the details of the notification should be furnished.
9. Please indicate-
   (*i*) the name of the bank and address of the branch through which the foreign contribution is proposed to be received;
   (*ii*) the account number in the said branch of the bank.

[1][9A. Whether a recommendation certificate from the competent authority is attached (Yes/No)].

10. Any other information which the Association may like to furnish.

Yours faithfully,
Chief Functionary for and on behalf of
the Association
(Name of Association)

DECLARATION AND UNDERTAKING

The Association named here-in-above affirms that the information furnished above is correct and undertakes:-

(*i*) to inform the Central Government (Ministry of Home Affairs) within thirty days, if any, change takes place in regard to the name of the Association, its address, its registration, its nature, its aims and objects with documentary evidence effecting the change;

(*ii*) to obtain prior permission for change of office bearer(s), if, at any point of time such change causes replacement of 50% or more of the office bearers as were mentioned in the application for registration under the Foreign Contribution (Regulation) Act, 1976 and undertakes further not to accept any foreign contribution except with prior permission till the permission to replace the office bearer(s) has been granted;

(*iii*) not to change the bank or branch of the bank without prior permission of the Central Government. The reasons for changing of bank or branch of the bank shall have to be relevant and justifiable; and

(*iv*) Not to accept any foreign contribution unless it has obtained either the registration number, as applies for hereinabove, or prior permission of the Central Government under sub-section (1A) of section 6 of the Foreign Contribution (Regulation) Act. 1976.

Yours faithfully,
Chief Functionary for and on behalf of
the Association
(Name of Association)

Place:
Date:

Note

(*i*) The receipt of application for registration is not a commitment for grant of registration by the Central Government;

(*ii*) An incomplete application i.e., without necessary documents/details/explanation is likely to be rejected summarily; and

(*iii*) In case the space against any column is insufficient, separate annexure should be attached. Please use *CAPITAL LETTERS*.

[1][Certificate

(To be submitted along with the application)

This is to certify that the....................................... (name of the association) having its registered office at.................................. (Address) has been engaged in economic, educational, cultural, religious and social activities in the .... (district) .... (State) for the last...................... years.

2. It has undertaken welfare activities in the area and has incurred expenditure (excluding administrative expenditure) amounting to........... (amount in rupees) during the last three years on its chosen (economic, educational, cultural, religious and social) field of activity.
3. The antecedents of the organization have been verified and there is nothing adverse against them.
4. The grant of registration to the aforesaid association to accept foreign contribution under the Foreign Contribution (Regulation) Act, 1976,for the said project is recommended.

(Recommending authority)**
(with seal)

* Strike out whichever is not applicable.

** Any concerned-

(1) Collector of District;

(2) Department of the State Government;

(3) Ministry/Department of the Government of India.]

[1]Inserted by the Foreign Contribution (Regulation)_(Amendment) Rules, 2000, w.e.f. 25.1.2000.

CORRECTION FORM

I- Association Details

Registration Number under FC® Act, 1976:....................

Name:....................

Address:...............

Pin Code:................

Association Nature:

•	•	•	•	•
Religious	Cultural	Economic	Educational	Social

Religion (if having a religious nature):

O	O	O	O	O	O
Hindu	Sikh	Muslim	Christian	Buddhist	Others

Mark the relevant box

II- Bank Details

Name of Bank:..............................

Address:..........................

Account Number:...............

(CHIEF FUNCTIONARY)

To,

The Secretary to the Government of India
Ministry of Home Affairs, (Foreigners Division)
Lok Nayak Bhavan, Khan Market
New Delhi - 110 003.

LIST OF AGENCIES OF THE UNITED NATIONS, AND OTHER INTERNATIONAL AGENCIES AND ORGANIZATIONS NOTIFIED TO BE NOT COVERED UNDER FOREIGN SOURCE, UNDER SECTION 2(1) (E) (II) OF FCRA[1]

The United Nations System

I. Secretariat

Office of Internal Oversight Services, New York.

Office of Legal Affairs, New York.

Department of Political Affairs, New York

Department of Disarmament Affairs, New York

Department of Peacekeeping Operations, New York

Office for the Coordination of Humanitarian Affairs, New York.

Department of Economic and Social, Affairs, New York.

Department for General Assembly Affairs and Conference Services, New York.

Department of Public Information, New York.

Department of Management, New York.

United Nations Office at Geneva.

United Nations Office at Vienna.

United Nations Office at Nairobi.

II. Bodies of the United Nations

International Research and Training Institute for the Advancement of Women (*INSTRAW*), Santo Domingo, Dominican Republic.

Joint United Nations Programme on *HIV/AIDS* (*UNAIDS*) Geneva

Office of the *UN* High Commissioner for Human Rights (*OHCHR*), Geneva.

United Nations Capital Development Fund (*UNCDF*), New York

United Nations Conference on Trade and Development (*UNCTAD*), Geneva.

United Nations Development Fund for Women (*UNIFEM*), New York

United Nations Institute for Disarmament Research (*UNIDIR*), Geneva.

United Nations Institute for Training and Research (*UNITAR*), Geneva.

United Nations Interregional Crime and Justice Research Institute (*UNICRI*), Rome.

United Office for Project Services (*UNOPS*), New York.

United Nations Relief and Works Agency for Palestine Refugees in the Near East (*UNRWA*), Gaza and Amman.

United Nations Research Institute for Social Development (*UNRISD*), Geneva.

United Nations University (*UNU*), Tokyo.

United Nations Volunteers (*UNV*), Bonn.

---

[1]Vide Notification No. S.O. 1014(E), dt. 13.11.2000.

III. Funds and Programmes

United Nations Children's Fund (*UNICEF*), New York.

United Nations Development Programme (*UNDP*), New York.

United Nations Environment Programme (*UNEP*), Nairobi.

United Nations International Drug Control Program (*UNDCP*), Vienna.

United Nations Population Fund (*UNFPA*), New York.

World Food Programme (*WEP*), Rome.

IV. Regional Commissions

Economic Commission for Africa (*ECA*), Addis Ababa, Ethiopia.

Economic Commission for Asia and the Pacific (*ESCAP*), Bangkok, Thailand.

Economic Commission for Europe (*ECE*), Geneva.

Economic Commission for Latin America and the Caribbean (*ECLAC*), Santiago, Chile.

Economic Commission for Western Asia (*ESCWA*), Beirut, Lebanon.

V. Law of the Sea Treaty Bodies

International Seabed Authority, Kingston.

International Tribunal for the Law of the Sea, Hamburg.

Commission on the Limits of the Continental Shelf, United Nations Divisions for Ocean Affairs and the Law of the Sea, New York.

VI. Environmental Bodies

Secretariat of the United Nations Framework Convention on Climate Change (*UNFCCC*), Bonn.

Intergovernmental Panel on Climate Change (*IPCC*), Geneva.

Ozone Secretariat to the Vienna Convention for the Protection of the Ozone Layer and the Montreal Protocol on Substance that Deplete the Ozone Layer, Nairobi.

Secretariat of the Convention on Biological Diversity (*CBD*), Montreal.

Secretariat of the Convention on International Trade in Endangered Species of Wild Fauna and Flora (*CITES*), Geneva.

UNEP/CMS Secretariat of the Convention on the Conservation of Migratory Species of Wild Animals (*CMS* or Bonn Convention), Bonn.

Secretariat of the Basel Convention on the Control of Trans-boundary Movements of hazardous Wastes and their Disposal, Geneva.

Secretariat of the United Nations Convention to Combat Desertification in Countries Experiencing Serious Drought/or Desertification, especially in Africa (*CCD*), Bonn.

Global Environment Facility, Washington *D.C.*

Bureau (Secretariat) of the Convention on Wetlands (Ramsar), Gland, Switzerland.

VII. Specialized Agencies

International Labour Organization (*ILO*), Geneva.

Food and Agriculture Organization (*FAO*), Rome.

United Nations Educational, Scientific and Cultural Organization (*UNESCO*), Paris.

International Civil Aviation Organization (*ICAO*), Montreal.

World Health Organization, Geneva.

Universal Postal Union (*UPO*), Berne, Switzerland.

International Telecommunication Union (*ITU*), Geneva.

World Meteorological Organization (*WMO*), London.

World Intellectual Property Organization (*WIPO*), Geneva.

International Fund for Agricultural Development (*IFAD*), Rome.

United nations Industrial Development Organization (*UNIDO*), Vienna.

VIII. The World Bank Group

International Bank for Reconstruction and Development (*IBRD*), Washington *D.C.*

International Development Association (*IDA*), Washington *D.C.*

International Monetary Fund (IMF) Washington *D.C.*

International Finance Corporation (*IFC*), Washington *D.C.*

Associated Organizations of World Bank Group:

- International Centre for the Settlement of Investment Disputes (*ICSID*), Washington D.C.
- Multilateral Investment Guarantee Agency (*MIGA*), Washington D.C.
- Consultative Group on International Agricultural Research (CGIAR), Washington D.C. (IT has 16 Research centres).
- International Plant Genetic Resource Institute (*IPGRI*), Rome.
- International Wheat and Maize Improvement Centre (*CIMMYT*), Mexico.
- International Centre for Living Aquatic Resource Management (*OCLARM*), Philippines.
- International Irrigation Management Institute (*IIMI*), Colombo.
- International Food Policy Research Institute (*IFPRI*), Washington D.C.
- International Centre of Research in Agro-forestry (*ICRAF*), Nairobi.
- International Centre for Agricultural Research in Dry Areas (*ICARDA*), Syria.
- International Centre for Tropical Agriculture (*CIAT*), Columbia.
- International Livestock Research Institute (*ILRI*), Nairobi.
- West Africa Development Association (*WARDA*), Abidjan.
- International Service of National Agricultural Research (*ISNAR*), The Netherlands.
- International Crops Research Institute for the Semi-Arid Tropics (*ICRISAT*), Hyderabad.
- International Rice Research Institute, Manila, Philippines.
- International Potato Centre, Peru.

- Centre for International Forestry Research (*CIFOR*), Indonesia.
- International Institute of Tropical Agriculture (*IITA*), Nigeria.

IX. Regional Development Banks

African Development Bank (*ADB*), Abidjan.

Inter-American Development Bank (*IDB*), Washington *D.C.*

Asian Development Bank (*ADB*), Manila.

Caribbean Development Bank (*CDB*), St. Michael, Barbados.

X. Other Bodies Related to United Nations

International Atomic Energy Agency (*IAEA*), Vienna.

Organization for the Prohibition of Chemical Weapons (*OPCW*), The Hague.

Provisional Technical Secretariat (*PTS*) for the Comprehensive Nuclear Test Ban Treaty Organization (*CTBTO*), Vienna.

International Consultative Group on Food Irradiation (*ICGFI*), Vienna.

International narcotics Control Board (*INCB*), Vienna.

International Trade Centre *UNCTAD/WTO* (*ITC*), Geneva.

International Union for the Protection of New Varieties of Plants (*UPOV*), Geneva.

World Tourism Organization (*WTO/OMT*), Madrid.

World Food Council (*WFC*).

United Nations Social Defence Research Institute (*UNSDRI*).

United Nations Statistical Office (*UNSCO*)

XI. Other International Organizations

United Nations Outer Space Committee.

International Sugar Organisation, London.

Asian Productivity Organization, Tokyo.

Asian and Pacific Development Administration, Kuala Lumpur.

Asian African Legal Consultative Committee, New Delhi.

European Community (*EC*).

Asia/Pacific Cultural Centre for *UNESCO* (*ACCU*), Japan.

Commonwealth Secretariat, London.

Afro-Asian Rural Reconstruction Organization (*AARRO*), New Delhi.

Centre on Integrated Rural Development for Asia and the Pacific, (*CIRDAP*), Dhaka.

International Centre for Genetic Engineering and Biotechnology (*ICGEB*), New Delhi.

Asia and Pacific Centre of Transfer of Technology (*APCTT*), New Delhi.

Centre for Science and Technology of the Non-Aligned and Other Developing Countries (*NAM S* & *T* Centre), New Delhi.

Commonwealth Agricultural Bureaux International (*CABI*), UK.

The Asia Pacific Association of Agricultural Research Institute (*APAARI*), Bangkok.

The Regional Co-ordination centre for Research and Development of Coarse Grains, Pulses, Roots and Tuber crops in the Humid Tropics of Asia and the Pacific (*CGPRT* Centre) Indonesia.

The Regional Network for Agriculture Machinery (*RNAM*), Bangkok.

Commission on Genetic Resources for Food and Agriculture (*CGRFA*), Rome.

The International Seeds Testing Association (*ISTA*), Zurich.

International Water Management Institute (*IWMI*), Sri Lanka.

Management of Tax Exempted Donations

Chapter 16

Many organizations have received tax-exempted donations for welfare and development projects. The application for registration should be made to the Commissioner, Income Tax in Form No. 10A, 10B, and 10G, along with relevant documents. The income of an organization may include:

1. Subscriptions.
2. Donations and contributions.
3. Income form property held under the trust (including its business units).
4. Capital gains on property held under trust.
5. Income from organization's business.

Section 11 of the *I.T.* Act lays down that any income derived from property held for religious and charitable purpose shall not be included in the total income of the trust or institution. While section 11 and 12 deals with the tax exemptions available to charitable or religious institutions, donations made to charitable and religious institutions are eligible for tax exemption of the donors, under the provisions of section 80G of the *I.T.* Act. Organizations established in India for a charitable purpose, are required to obtain approval from the Commissioner, Income Tax and fulfill certain conditions laid down in section 80G (5) that the income of the organization shall be exempt under the provisions of sections 11 and 12 or 10 (23AA) or 10 (23C).

The applications for approval *U/S* 80G (5)(iv), is to be made in Form No. 10G in triplicate to commissioner Income Tax with relevant documents

Trusts and institutions formed for the promotion of research, education, khadi and village industries, or hospitals and notified charitable institutions are entitled for total exemption under clauses (21) to (23C) of section 10. The exemption available under various clauses of section 10, is separate from and in addition to the exemption granted under section 11.

The organization should maintain regular and proper book of accounts supported by receipt and vouchers. Any voluntary contribution received by the organization (other than those received towards the corpus of the organization) shall be deemed to be income derived from the property held under the organization. An organization, whose total income for a year exceeds Rs. 50,000 is required to get its accounts audited by Chartered Accountant and obtain the audit report in Form No. 10B.

FORM NO. 10

[See rule 17]

Notice to the Assessing Officer/Prescribed Authority under Section 11(2) of the Income Tax Act, 1961

To,

The Assessing Officer/Prescribed Authority

....

....

I, ..., on behalf of .... [name of the trust/institution/ association] hereby bring to your notice that it has been decided by a resolution passed by the trustees/ governing body, by whatever name called, on .... (copy enclosed) that, out of the income of the trust/institution/association for the previous year(s), relevant to the assessment year 20...- 20... and subsequent .... Previous year(s), and amount of Rs...................... per cent of the income of the trust/institution/association/such sum as is available at the end of the previous year(s) should be accumulated or set apart till the previous year(s) ending .... in order to enable the trustees/governing body by whatever name called, to accumulate sufficient funds for carrying out the following purposes of the trust/association/institution:-

(1) ....

(2) ....

2. Before expiry of six months commencing from the end of each previous year, the amount so accumulated or set apart has been/will be invested or deposited in any one or more of the forms or modes specified in sub-section (5) of Section 11.
3. Copies of the annual accounts of the trust/institution/association along with details of investment (including deposits) and utilization, if any, of the money so accumulated or set apart will be furnished to you before the expiry of six months commencing from the end of each relevant previous year.
4. It is requested that in view of our complying with the condition laid down in Section 11(2) of the Income-tax Act, 1961, the benefit of the section may be given in the assessments of the trusts/exempting the income in respect of the trust/institution /association in respect of the incomes accumulated or set apart as mentioned above.

Date:...........................

....
Signature

....
Designation

....
Address

Notes:

1. This notice should be signed by a trustee/principal officer.
2. Deleted the inappropriate words.

FORM NO. 10A

[See rule 17A]

Application for registration of charitable or religious trust or Institution under Section 12A(a) of the Income Tax Act, 1961

To,

The Chief Commissioner or Commissioner of Income-tax

....

....

Sir,

I, ..., on behalf of .... [name of the trust/institution/ association] hereby apply for the registration of the said trust/institute under section 12A of the Income Tax Act, 1961. The following particulars are furnished herewith:

1. Name of the trust/institution in full (in block letters)
2. Address
3. Name(*s*) and address(*es*) of author(*s*)/founder(*s*)
4. Date of creation of the trust or establishment of the institution
5. Name(*s*) and address(*es*) of trustee(*s*)/manager(*s*)

I also enclose the following documents:

1. (*a*) *Original/Certified copy of the instrument under which the trust/institution was created/ established, together with a copy thereof.
   (*b*) *Original/Certified copy of document evidencing the creation of the trust or the establishment of the institution, together with a copy thereof. (The originals, if enclosed, will be returned).
2. Two copies of the accounts of the *trust/institution for the latest *one/two/three years.

I undertake to communicate forthwith any alteration in the terms of the trust, or in the rules governing the institution, made at any time hereafter.

Date:............................ ....

Signature

....

Designation

....

Address

*Strike out whichever is not applicable.

FORM NO. 10B

[See rule 17B]

Audit report under Section 12A (*b*) of the Income Tax Act, 1961, in case of charitable or religious trusts or institutions

To,

The Assessing Officer/Prescribed Authority

....

....

*I/We, have examined the balance sheet of............................... as at .... (name of the trust or institution) and the profit and loss account for the year ended on that date which are in agreement with the books of account maintained by the said trust or institution.

*I/We have obtained all the information and explanations which to the best of *my/our knowledge and belief were necessary for the purposes of the audit. In *my/our opinion, proper books of account have been kept by the head office and the branches of the above named *trust/institution visited by *me/us so far as appears from *my/our examination of the books, and proper returns adequate for the purposes of audit have been received from branches not visited by *me/us, subject to the comments given below:

In *my/our opinion and to the best of *my/our information, and according to information given to *me/us, the said accounts give a true and fair view-

(*i*) in the case of the balance sheet, of the state of affairs of the above named *trust/institution as at........................ and

(*ii*) in the case of the profit and loss account, of the profit or loss of its accounting year ending on..................

The prescribed particular are annexed hereto.

Place........................ ....

Date......................

Signed

Accountant...

Notes:

1. *Strike out whichever is not applicable.
2. ...This report has to be given by-
   (*i*) a chartered accountant within the meaning of the Chartered Accountants Act, 1949 (38 of 1949); or
   (*ii*) any person who, in relation to any State, is, by virtue of the provisions of sub-section (2) of section 226 of the Companies Act, 1956 (1 of 1956), entitled to be appointed to act as an auditor of the company registered in that State.
3. Where any of the matters stated in this report is answered in the negative, or with a qualification, the report shall state the reasons for the same.

ANNEXURE

Statement of Particulars

I. APPLICATION OF INCOME FOR CHARITABLE OR RELIGIOUS PURPOSES

1. Amount of income of the previous year applied to charitable or religious purposes in India during that year ....
2. Whether the trust/institution *has exercised the option under clause (2) of the Explanation to section 11(1)? If so, the details of the amount of income deemed to have been applied to charitable or religious purposes in India during the previous year accumulated or set apart* ....
3. Amount of income........................ (finally set apart) for application to charitable or religious purposes, to the extent it does not exceed 25 per cent of the income derived from property held under wholly* trust........... (in part only) for such purposes. ....
4. Amount of income eligible for exemption under section 11(I)(*c*) (Give details) ....
5. Amount of income, in addition to the amount referred to in item 3 above, accumulated or set apart for specified purposes under section 11(2). ....
6. Whether the amount of income mentioned in item 5 above has been invested or deposited in the manner laid down in section 11(2)(b)? If so, the details thereof ....
7. Whether any part of the income in respect of which an option was exercised under clause (2) of the Explanation to section 11(1) in any earlier year is deemed to be income of the previous year under section 11 (1B)? If so, the details thereof ....
8. Whether, during the previous year, any part of income accumulated or set apart for specified purposes under section 11(2) in any earlier year- ....

   (*a*) has been applied for purposes other than charitable or religious purposes or has ceased to be accumulated or set apart for application thereto, or(*b*) has ceased to remain invested in any security referred to in section 11(2)(*b*)(*i*) or deposited in any account referred to in section 11(2)(*b*)(*ii*) or section 11(2)(*b*)(*iii*), or(*c*) has not been utilized for purposes for which it was accumulated or set apart during the period for which it was to be accumulated or set apart, or in the year immediately following the expiry thereof? If so, the details thereof. ....

II. APPLICATION FOR USE OF INCOME OR PROPERTY FOR THE BENEFIT OF PERSONS REFERRED TO IN SECTION 13 (3)

1. Whether any part of the income or property of the *trust/institution was lent, or continues to be lent, in the previous year to any person referred to in section 13(3) (hereinafter referred to in this Annexure as such person)? If so, give details of the amount, rate of interest charged and the nature of security, if any ....
2. Whether any land, building or other property of the *trust/institution was made, or continued to be made, available for the use of any such person during the previous

year? if so, give details of the property and the amount of rent or compensation charged, if any ....

3. Whether any payment was made to any such person during the previous year by way of salary, allowance or otherwise? If so, give details. ....
4. Whether the services of *trust/institution were made available to any such person during the previous year? If so, give details thereof together with remuneration or compensation received, if any ....
5. Whether any share, security or other property was purchased by or on behalf of the *trust/institution during the previous year from any such person? If so, give details thereof together with the consideration paid. ....
6. Whether any share, security of other property was sold by or on behalf of the *trust/ institution during the previous year to any such person? If so, give details thereof together with the consideration received. ....
7. Whether any income or property of the *trust/institution was diverted during the previous year in favour of any such person? If so, give details thereof together with the amount of income or value of property so diverted. ....
8. Whether the income or property of the *trust/institution was used or applied during the previous year for the benefit of any such person in any other manner? If so, give details. ....

*Strike out whichever is not applicable.

III. INVESTMETS HELD AT ANY TIME DURING THE PREVIOUS YEAR(S) IN CONCERNS IN WHICH PERSONS REFERRED TO IN SECTION 13(3) HAVE A SUBSTANTIAL INTEREST

Sl. No.	*Name and address of the concern*	*Where the concern is a company, number and class of shares held*	*Nominal value of the investment*	*Income from the investment*	*Whether the amount in col. 4 exceeded 5 per cent of the capital of the concern during the previous year-say, Yes/No*
(1)	(2)	(3)	(4)	(5)	(6)
Total					

Place.................. ....

Date.................. Signed

Accountant

FORM NO. 10G

[See rule 11AA]

Application for grant of approval or continuance thereof to institution or fund under Section 80G (5)(*vi*) of the Income Tax Act, 1961

1. Name of the institution/fund in full (in block letters)
2. Address of the registered office of the institution/fund
3. Legal status [please specify whether the institution/fund is-(*i*) constituted as public charitable trust;(*ii*) registered under the Societies Registration Act, 1860 (21 of 1860) or under any law corresponding to that Act in force in any part of India;(*iii*) registered under section 25 of the Companies Act, 1956 (1 of 1956)(iv) a University established by law;(v) any other educational institution recognized by the Government or by any University established by law or affiliated to any University established by law;(*vi*) an institution wholly or partly financed by the Government or a local authority;(*vii*) an institution established with the object of controlling, supervising, regulating or encouraging games or sports and is approved for this purpose under section 12 (23); or(*viii*) a Regimental Fund or Non-Public Fund established by the armed forces of the Union for the welfare of past or present members of such forces or their departments].
4. Objects of the institution/fund and geographical area over which its activities are undertaken.
5. Names and addresses of trustees/office bearers of the institution or fund(*i*) If registered under section 12A(*a*) of the Income-tax Act, the registration number and date of registration.(*ii*) If notified under section 10 (23) or under section 10 (23C) of the Income-tax Act, the details thereof(*iii*) If responses to (*i*) & (*ii*) are negative, whether any application for the same has been filed? If yes, enclose a copy of the same.
7. (*a*) Period of last approval, if any. Please enclose a copy of the approval.(*b*) If any change in the aims and objects and the rules and regulations have been made since the last approval, the details thereof
8. Assessment particulars-(*a*) Ward/Circle where assessed and permanent account number/GIR number.(*b*) Is the income exempt under section 10 (22), 10 (22A), 10 (23), 10 (23AA), 10 (23C) or 11?(c) Whether any arrears of taxes are outstanding? If so give reasons.
9. Amount accumulated for objects mentioned ....in item (4) above.
10. (*i*) Details of modes in which funds are .... invested or deposited, showing the nature, value and income from the investment;(ii) Whether any funds have not been invested in the modes specified in section 11(5)?
11. (*i*) Is the institution/fund carrying on any business? If yes, give details.(*ii*) Is the business incidental to the attainment of its objects?
12. Details of nature, quantity and value of contributions (other than cash) and the manner in which such contributions have been utilized.
13. Details of shares, security or other property purchased by or on behalf of the trust from any interested person as specified in sub-section (3) of section 13.

14. Whether any part of the income or any property of the association was used or applied, in a manner which results directly or indirectly in conferring any benefit, amenity of perquisite (whether converted into money or not), on any interested person as specified in sub-section (3) of section 13? If so, details thereof.

I certify that information furnished above is true to the best of my knowledge and belief.

I undertake to communicate forthwith any alteration in the terms or in the rules governing the institution/fund made at any time hereafter.

Place.......................... Signature...........................

Date................... ....

Designation................

....

Address................................

....

Note: The application form (in triplicate) should be sent to the Commissioner of Income Tax having jurisdiction over the institution or fund along with the following documents:

(*i*) Copy of registration under section 12A or copy of notification issued under section 10(23) or section 10(23C).

(*ii*) Notes on activities of institution or fund since its inception or during the last three years, whichever is less.

(*iii*) Copies of accounts of the institution or fund since its inception during the last three years, whichever is less.

FORM NO. 49 A

Form of application for allotment of Permanent Account Number under section 139 A of the Income-tax Act, 1961

To

The Assessing Officer

....

....

Sir,

Whereas my/our total income/the total income of (name)................................ in respect of which I/we and/are assessable under the Income-tax Act, 1961, during the accounting year ending on (dd/mm/yyy)..................... exceeds rupees........ the maximum amount which is not chargeable to income tax;

Whereas my/our case does not fall under sub-section (1) of section 139, and I am/we are carrying on a business the total sales/turnover/gross receipts of which are or is likely to exceed fifty thousand rupees in the accounting year ending on (dd/mm/yyyy).....................

And where as no Permanent Account Number has been allotted to me/us:

Though earlier *PAN* had been allotted to me/us, no permanent account number under new series has been allotted;

I/we hereby request that a permanent account number/permanent account number under few series be allotted to me/us;

I/we give below the necessary particulars:-

1. Full Name (no initials please)

   Please tick as applicable: Shri Smt. Kumar M/s

   Last Name/Surname --------------------------------- First Name-----------------

   Middle Name---

2. Have you ever been by any other name?

   Please tick as applicable Yes No

   If yes, please give other name (no initials please)

   Please tick as applicable: Shri Smt. Kumar M/s

   Last Name/Surname --------------------------------- First Name-----------------

   Middle Name---

3. Address

   A. Residential Address

      Flat/Door/Block No.:..

      Name of Premises/Building/Village:...

      Road/Street/Lane/Post Office:...

      Area/Locality/Taluka/Sub-Division:..

      Town/City/District:...

      State/Union Territory:.............................. Pin.........................

B. Office Address

Flat/Door/Block No.:..

Name of Premises/Building/Village:..

Road/Street/Lane/Post Office:...

Area/Locality/Taluka/Sub-Division:..

Town/City/District:..

State/Union Territory:............................ Pin.........................

4. Address for Communication: Please Tick as applicable

A or B Tel. No. if any.......................

5. Status of the Application: Please Tick as applicable

(Only one box)

Individual	*Firm*	*Body of Individuals*
HUF	Association of Persons	Local Authority
Company	Association of persons (Trust)	Artificial Juridical Person

6. If an individual, pals give father's name (No initial please)

Last Name/Surname --------------------------------- First Name-----------------

Middle Name---

7. Sex (for individual applicant only)

Please Tick as applicable: Male Female:

8. Date of Birth/Incorporation/Agreement/Partnership or Trust Deed/Formation of Body of Individuals/Association of Persons...................................

9. Whether Citizen of India?

Please Tick as applicable Yes No

10. Registration number (in case of firms, companies, etc.)..................

11. Source(s) of Income: Please Tick as applicable

Salaries House Property Business or Profession

Capital Gains Income from other source(*s*)

12. Particulars of Business, if any

HEAD OFFICE

Name of Office:...

Flat/Door/Block No.:..

Name of Premises/Building/Village:..

Road/Street/Lane/Post Office:...

Area/Locality/Taluka/Sub-Division:..

Town/City/District:..

State/Union Territory:............................ Pin........................

Nature of Business.....................Tax Deduction..............

Account No. if any.................. Date of commencement (dd/mm/yyyy)............. No. of Branches.............

BRANCHES (if required, please add separate sheet, in the format given below, for each branch)

Name of Branch:...

Flat/Door/Block No.:...

Name of Premises/Building/Village:..

Road/Street/Lane/Post Office:...

Area/Locality/Taluka/Sub-Division:...

Town/City/District:..

State/Union Territory:............................ Pin........................

Nature of Business.....................Tax Deduction..............Account No. if any.................. Date of commencement (dd/mm/yyyy).............

13. If Firm/Hindu Undivided Family/Association of Persons/Body of Individuals/Company, the names, addresses, etc., of Partners/Members/Directors (for information about more persons, please add separate sheet(s) in the format given below.

DETAILS OF PARTNERS/MEMBERS/DIRECTORS

(*a*) Name of Partners/Members/Directors

(*b*) Full Name [(expand initials please)]

Please Tick as applicable: Shri Smt. Kumar M/s

Last Name/Surname ---------------------------------- First Name-----------------

Middle Name--

© Address

Flat/Door/Block No.:...

Name of Premises/Building/Village:..

Road/Street/Lane/Post Office:...

Area/Locality/Taluka/Sub-Division:...

Town/City/District:..

State/Union Territory:............................ Pin........................

14. Full Name, Address of the representative assess who is assessable under the Income-tax Act in respect of the person, whose particulars have been given in Columns 1 to 13 (Please see Instruction No. 14)

Full Name (No initials please)

Please Tick as applicable: Shri Smt. Kumar M/s

Last Name/Surname ---------------------------------- First Name----------------

Middle Name--

© Address

Flat/Door/Block No.:...

Name of Premises/Building/Village:..

Road/Street/Lane/Post Office:..

Area/Locality/Taluka/Sub-Division:..

Town/City/District:...

State/Union Territory:............................. Pin.........................

15. (*i*) Permanent Account Number, if any, allotted earlier...............

(*ii*) GIR No. if any, allotted earlier.......................

(*iii*) Ward/Circle/Range....................................

I/We,.............................., the applicant, do hereby declare that what is stated above is true to the best of my/our information and belief.

Verified today, the (dd/mm/yyyy)............ Signature of the Applicant

(Inside the white box

provided above

For Office Use

1. Permanent Account Number allotted..............................
2. Date of Allotment of Permanent Account Number (dd/mm/yyyy).............

Glossary of Terms

Activity: The action taken (training staff, preparing reports, etc.) to transform inputs (funds, training facilities, expert services) into outputs (trained staff, reports prepared, etc.).

Appraisal: The critical assessment of the relevance, feasibility and potential effectiveness of a project/programme prior to making a decision whether to undertake it.

Assumption: An external event or action which must take place, or a condition which must exist, if a project is to succeed, but over which project management has little or no control.

Beneficiaries: The direct (or intended) beneficiaries (target group) plus the indirect beneficiaries of a project.

Development (or Higher Level) Objective: The term characterizes a programming level beyond the immediate objective: it provides the reason for the project or programme and describes the desired end towards which the project efforts of the specialized agency, the financing agency and the beneficiary country or countries are being directed. (The equivalent term "higher level objective" is used outside the field of technical cooperation).

Effectiveness: The extent to which a project/programme is successful in achieving its objective(*s*).

Efficiency: The "productivity" of the implementation process-how economically inputs are converted into outputs and achievement of objective (*s*).

Evaluation: The process of Comparing (project/programme) objectives with results, employing methods which reduce dependence on subjective judgement, in order to assess the extent to which these objectives have been or are being achieved, and to analyze the reasons for any discrepancy. Such evaluation may be interim (of continuing projects), terminal (or terminating or completed projects or ex-post after the completion of the project or programme).

External Factor: Event, condition or decision which is necessary for project success, but which are largely or completely beyond the control of project management.

Follow-up: Actions taken or scheduled in order to utilize information gained or lessons learned from the monitoring or evaluation process.

Immediate Objective: The change which is to be created or accomplished by the project with a view toward correcting an identified problem; the effect which the project is expected to achieve, if completed successfully and on time.

Impact: The change produced usually at the development objective level-in a situation as a result of a project/programme which has been undertaken; for instance, the impact of the project on the target group.

Indicator: An explicit and objectively verifiable measure-either direct (proxy) of the achievement of an objective.

Inputs: Goods, funds, services, personnel and other resources provided with the expectation of undertaking specific activities, producing outputs and achieving objectives.

Linkage: The interrelationships between levels of a project design, *i.e.* between the means and ends. (Example: if inputs *A* are provided, then activities *B* can be undertaken; if activities *B* are undertaken, the outputs *C* can be produced; etc.).

Logical Framework Approach (LFA): Managerial tool which facilitates planning, execution and evaluation of a project. In this context, *LFA* also means;

- A format for presentation to donor, and partner authorities; project ideas. Pre-appraisal reports, project documents, progress reports, etc.
- A summary of the project in the form of a matrix that remains valid during project implementation but can be modified.
- A sequence of analytical tools which is used in an external/internal workshop situation.

Monitoring: Continuous or periodic Surveillance of the physical implementation process to ensure that input deliveries, work schedules, outputs and other required actions are proceeding according to plan.

Objective: The purpose and aim of a project/programme describing the desired state which is expected to be achieved within a given period and directed towards an identified target group or area.

Outputs: The specific products that can reasonably be expected to be produced by the product with the inputs provided and activities undertaken in order to achieve the stated objective.

Programme: A group of projects or services directed toward the attainment of specific (usually similar or related) objectives.

Project: A planned undertaking, a unit of management, designed to achieve certain specific objectives within a given budget and within a specified period of time.

Project Document Outline: A summary of project design which shows the key segments of a project and their inter-relationships as well as the expected consequences of completing each segment successfully.

Project Matrix: A summary of project design which identifies the key elements, external factors and expected consequences of completing the project successfully.

Project Manager/Management: The individual, group or office responsible for the supervision, day-to-day administration and implementation of a project or programme.

Relevance (Significance): The degree to which the rationale and objectives of a project/programme are, or remain, pertinent, significant and worthwhile in relation to the identified priority needs and concerns. (A project may be effective and efficient, yet not if it makes little or no contribution to meeting development objectives and priority needs.)

Sustainability: The extent to which the partner institutions will continue to pursue the objective after project assistance is over.

Target Group (Intended Beneficiaries): The specific group (underemployed, women, rural poor) for whose benefit the project or programme is undertaken; closely related to impact and relevance.

Work Plan: A management tool to organize the implementation of a project's activities, it involves the scheduling of the substantive administrative work required to transform inputs (resources) into outputs (results).

References

1. A Guide to M & E, *IFAD* Manual.
2. A Guide to Project Design, *ILO*, Geneva.
3. A Handbook of Monitoring & Evaluation, *UNDP*.
4. A New Appeal, Business India, January 1-28, 1998.
5. A. Phadke and A. Kale, Some Critical Issues in the Epidemology of Hepatitis-*B* in India, Indian Journal of Gastroenterology, Vol. 19 (Suppl.3)
6. A. Sen. Hepatitis-*B* Care : To Vaccine or Not, Rational Drug Bulletin, July 1, 1999.
7. Alnor Ebrahim, Accounting Myopia, Sage Publications.
8. Anant Phadke, Hepatitis-*B* A False Alarm, Times News Network.
9. Aparna Ravi, Combating Child Labour with Labels, Economic & Political Weekly, 2001.
10. Basic Managerial Skill for All, Prentice Hall Ltd., New Delhi.
11. Dag Larsen, Child Labour Impact Assessment, *NORRAD*, New Delhi.
12. Dr. Devendra Prasad Pandey, Strategic Management of *NGOs*, Aryanyak Prakashan, Allahabad.
13. Frances Kunreuther, Horward University, The Changing of Guard, Non-profit and Voluntary Sector Quarterly, September, 2003.
14. *GP* with *GPRS*, Business Today, February 1, 2004.
15. H. Deshpande, Study Injects Scepticism into Hepatitis-*B* Drive, Indian Express, September 11, 2000.
16. Handbook for *NGOs*, Nabhi Publications, Bhopal.
17. In Search of Middleman, Business India, January 10-23, 2000.
18. Inayatullah, Access to Distributive Justice for the Rural Poor, *ACDA*, 1976.
19. James Andreoni, A Abigail Payne, The American Economic Review, June 2003.
20. Janet Hilowitz, Labelling Child Labour Products: Preliminary Study, International Labour Organization, Geneva.
21. Linking Project Design, International Fund for Agriculture Development, Rome.
22. Making Charity Pay, Businessworld, May 23, 2004.
23. Monitoring & Evaluation Strategy, UNDP Manual.

24. Prof. Anil K. Gupta, "Why Don't We Learn" Seminar paper, IIM, Ahmedabad.
25. Prof. Udai Pareek, Education and Rural Development in Asia, Indian Institute of Management, Ahmedabad.
26. Propack, Catholic Relief Services, New Delhi.
27. R. Agrawal and S.R. Naik, Cost-efficacy Evaluation of Inclusion of Hepatitis-*B* Vaccine in Expanded Programme of Immunization, CBS Publishers, New Delhi.
28. Rajesh Tandon, *PRIA*, "Role of Voluntary Sector in the Current Context", Seminar paper, 1983.
29. Reach Out for a Cause, Business India, November 1-14, 1999.
30. Richard Freeman, What Role for Labour Standards in the Global Economy, Harward University.
31. Rugmark Foundation India, Rugmark: A Commitment to Social Welfare, Rugmark Foundation.
32. Ship-breaking Endangering India, Times News Network.
33. Times of India, New Delhi, 15.2.2005.
34. Vincent Austin, "Rural Industrial Development", Published by Cassell Ltd., London.
35. W. Haque, Towards a Theory of Rural Development, Development Digest, 1977.
36. William Foster & Jeffrey Bradach, Should Nonprofits Seek Profits, Harward Business Review, 2005.
37. William W. Clohesy, Fund Raising, University of Northern Iowa, Sage Publications.
38. Y. Madhavi, Hepatitis Vaccination, Economic & Political Weekly, 2003.